The Peripatetic Frame

The Peripatetic Frame

Images of Walking in Film

Thomas Deane Tucker

EDINBURGH
University Press

Edinburgh University Press is one of the leading university presses in the UK. We publish academic books and journals in our selected subject areas across the humanities and social sciences, combining cutting-edge scholarship with high editorial and production values to produce academic works of lasting importance. For more information visit our website: edinburghuniversitypress.com

© Thomas Deane Tucker, 2020, 2021

Edinburgh University Press Ltd
The Tun – Holyrood Road
12 (2f) Jackson's Entry
Edinburgh EH8 8PJ

First published in hardback by Edinburgh University Press 2020

Typeset in Monotype Ehrhardt by
Westchester Publishing Services

A CIP record for this book is available from the British Library

ISBN 978 1 4744 0929 2 (hardback)
ISBN 978 1 4744 8772 6 (paperback)
ISBN 978 1 4744 0930 8 (webready PDF)
ISBN 978 1 4744 0931 5 (epub)

The right of Thomas Deane Tucker to be identified as author of this work has been asserted in accordance with the Copyright, Designs and Patents Act 1988 and the Copyright and Related Rights Regulations 2003 (SI No. 2498).

Contents

List of Figures	vi
Acknowledgements	vii
Introduction: Framing Walking	1
1. First Steps	13
2. Tramping with Chaplin	30
3. The Pedestrian Camera	44
4. Gumshoes	64
5. Homing	81
6. Aimless Walks	98
Conclusion: Running Out of Frames	130
Bibliography	139
Filmography	149
Index	153

Figures

I.1	Boulevard du Temple	10
1.1	Roundhay Garden	20
3.1	Satantango	58
3.2	Werckmeister Harmonies	61
3.3	The Turin Horse	62
6.1	Breathless	108
6.2	Cléo	116
6.3	Umberto D.	123
6.4	Umberto D.	123
6.5	Umberto D.	127

Acknowledgements

This book would never have been written without the support of family, friends and colleagues. I want to first thank my wife Katy, whose patience reading countless drafts and encouraging words during many nights of trepidation were beyond measure. I owe a debt of gratitude to Tom Smith, who spent an inordinate amount of time and energy closely reading the final draft and offering sound advice. Thank you to Dean Jim Margetts, Provost Charles Snare and President Randy Rhine of Chadron State College for granting me a sabbatical leave to finish the project. To the people of Clifden, Ireland, I thank you for your endless hospitality in your wet and wild setting, especially in your pubs and cafés where I was always welcome to sit and write without ever feeling as if I had overstayed my welcome. I want to recognise my editor at Edinburgh University Press, Richard Strachan, for his understanding and patience in letting me extend deadlines I was unable to meet. Finally, I want to thank my three dogs, Pearl, Jasper and Allie for teaching me the real joys of going for a walk.

Introduction: Framing Walking

In November 1974, film-maker Werner Herzog learned that his mentor German film scholar Lotte Eisner had suffered a massive stroke in Paris and was at death's door. In a grand gesture worthy of any number of the enigmatic characters who populate his films, Herzog immediately set off on foot from Munich on a pilgrimage to Paris, intending to walk a 'million steps in rebellion against her death'. Burdened only with a new pair of boots, a jacket, compass and duffel bag, he somewhat mystically believed that Eisner would not die as long as he walked all the way to her doorstep. Herzog kept a journal of his trek, publishing it four years later as *Of Walking in Ice*.

Reading Herzog's *Of Walking in Ice* – organised in diary form around succinct chapters for each day walked and narrated in short bursts of dreamlike, hallucinatory passages in which he portrays himself in often gloomy surroundings – feels like watching a Herzog film screened in one's mind. Herzog recognises this himself, stating:

> When you travel on foot it isn't a matter of covering actual territory, rather a question of moving through your own inner landscapes. I wrote a diary of my walk to Lotte – the story of a journey on foot – which is like a road movie that never lingers on physical landscapes. (Cronin 2014: 281)

In her review of the book, Helen MacDonald called it a record of the 'wreckage of history and myth', a description that could easily apply to Herzog's entire cinematic oeuvre. With each documented step, Herzog jars the reader through an onslaught of ambulatory images and thoughts marching against the conventional beat of the 'rest of the world in rhyme' as he navigates blizzards, despair, stray dogs and wild forests in his ritual pilgrimage of hope. Cross-cutting between moods of gut-wrenching anguish and ecstatic delirium, Herzog's mental road movie leaps from harrowing scenes like this one:

> Wet, driving snow falls intensely in front, sometimes from the side as well, as I compulsively lean into it, the snow covering me immediately, like a fir tree, on the side

exposed to the wind. Oh, how I bless my cap. On old brown photos the last Navajos, crouching low on their horses, wrapped in blankets, covered in rugs, move through the snowstorm towards their doom: this image refuses to leave my mind and strengthens my resolve. The road is quickly buried in drifts of snow. (Herzog 2014: Kindle Locations 268–74)

then immediately to ones sublime and surreal:

I am a ski jumper, I support myself on the storm, bent forward, far, far, the spectators surrounding me a forest turned into a pillar of salt, a forest with its mouth open wide. I fly and fly and don't stop. Yes, they scream. Why doesn't he stop? I think, better keep on flying before they see that my legs are so brittle and stiff that they'll crumble like chalk when I land. Don't quit, don't look, fly on. (Herzog 2014: Kindle Locations 274–7)

The language, tone and style of the entries is quintessential Herzog. Anyone familiar with Herzog's jolting and often nihilistic off-screen narration delivered monotone in slightly German-accented English cannot help reading these passages without hearing this voice in their head.

Herzog did make it in time, leaving a remarkable personal account of the intrinsic links between walking and film-making.[1] In his interviews with Paul Cronin collected in *Werner Herzog, A Guide for the Perplexed: Conversations with Paul Cronin*, Herzog posits an almost epic vision of film-making in relation to walking. For instance, he hints that walking might actually be constitutive of the film-making process, offering this advice to aspiring film-makers, 'Writers and film-makers are all alone; there is usually no one to help you, so just get off your ass and start walking' (quoted in Cronin 2014: Kindle Locations 4724–5). And when asked about his ideal film school, he replies:

You would be allowed to submit an application only after having travelled, alone and on foot, let's say from Madrid to Kiev, a distance of nearly two thousand miles. While walking, write about your experiences, then give me your notebooks. I would immediately be able to tell who had really walked and who had not. You would learn more about film-making during your journey than if you spent five years at film school. (quoted in Cronin 2014: Kindle Locations 4182–6)

These are only two written texts in which Herzog way-marks for us the many intersections between the paths of walking and cinema (there are many more). The characters in his films are inveterate wanderers, meandering through the liminal spaces between civilisation and wilderness. Whether trekking through a Vietnamese jungle to avoid enemy capture or trying to haul a steamship over a mountain, their pedestrian speed is slow, sometimes up to the point of paralysis; yet, they are always in motion and usually on foot.

Then there is also Les Blank's 1979 short film titled *Werner Herzog Eats His Shoe* in which Herzog publicly pays a debt owed to Errol Morris after losing a bet with Morris that he would never have the guts to make a film on his own. Invoking Chaplin's performance in *Gold Rush* and assisted in the kitchen of Chez Panise restaurant by chef Alice Waters, Herzog boils his shoe for five hours in a soup stocked with garlic, onions, herbs and hot sauce and then literally eats it in front of an audience in Berkeley at a screening of Morris's first film *Gates of Heaven*. Near the beginning of the film, Blank shows Herzog getting off a plane followed by a short montage of him walking, with the camera focused in close-up on his shoes. Blank then cuts to Herzog riding in the back of a car where he looks into the camera and declares, 'I'm quite convinced that cooking is the only alternative to filmmaking. Maybe there's also another alternative, that's walking on foot.'

In the quote above, Herzog melds together three traits that make us human: image making, creating and controlling fire for cooking and warmth, and walking. It will be my argument throughout this book that all three coalesce in the cinema, both in its history as a modern technics and in its aesthetic practices. After all, the cinema depends on the camera to manipulate light to capture images (controlling fire), then to fix them on celluloid (image making) and finally to project them as moving images by advancing the celluloid through the projector (light again, walking, procession, marching). The peripatetic provides the soil (not the only, but primordial) from which each of these processes originates and, further, the use of the peripatetic in the image-narrative of cinema folds back, prompting an aesthetic experience that opens cinema as a human experience as well as the essential prompt of the creative act of cinema itself.

Walking, Writing, Thinking

Over the past decade or so, cultural theorists, historians and other scholars in the humanities have uncovered a rich cultural legacy imbued in the simple act of walking. A cursory look at recent publications on the subject of walking yields such titles as *The Art of Wandering: The Writer as Walker* (Merlin Coverley), *Wanderlust: A History of Walking* (Rebecca Solnit), *The Old Ways: A Journey on Foot* (Robert MacFarlane), *Walkscapes: Walking as an Aesthetic Practice* (Francesco Careri), *Tramp: Or the Art of Living a Poetic Life* (Tomas Espedal), *Ways of Walking: Ethnography and Practice on Foot* (Jo Lee Vergunst and Tim Ingold, eds), *The Lost Art of Walking: The History, Science, Philosophy, and Literature of Pedestrianism* (Geoff Nicholson), *The Vintage Book of Walking* (Duncan Minshull, ed.), and *Walking the Line* (Richard Long). To name just a few of the topics found in these and other contemporary texts about walking: walking as art, music and walking, labyrinths, public gardens, nature walks, technologies of walking, walking professions (detectives, police officers, prostitutes and mail carriers), walking in the Christian gospels or Buddhist texts, famous walkers, literary walks, psychogeography, the romantic movement (English and American), long distance footpaths, political and protest marches, the beat movement, tourism, death marches, pilgrimage, epic walks, itinerant preachers, and vagrancy or tramping.

As Merlin Coverley observes, the everyday performance of walking hardly seems to deserve such a role on the scholarly stage: 'For such a seemingly innocuous activity, and one which is commonly conducted with the participant largely oblivious to its operation, the act of walking has acquired a surprising degree of cultural significance' (Coverley 2012: 11). What then explains our current fascination with the history, philosophy and cultural significance of walking? Coverley's short answer is that walking deserves its role in the cultural spotlight not because the physical act of bipedal movement per se is culturally significant, but rather because of 'what such movement symbolises and where such movement leads' (Coverley 2012: 11).

What 'such movement symbolises' might be humanity itself. Drawing on the work of Francesco Careri, Coverley argues that an archaic division between the spaces of the walker as nomadic herder and the sedentary ones of the farmer can be traced through the Biblical story of Cain and Abel, circumscribing two different ways of being in the world – one mobile, playful and creative, the other stationary and laborious. Abel is the antediluvian equivalent of the romantic image of the nomadic pastoralist, meandering leisurely with his sheep from pasture to pasture, his mind free to wander as much as is his body, his path limned by his imagination as much as by his feet. Cain, on other hand, is place bound. He spends his days toiling with his back bent over the soil, like Millet's *Man with a Hoe*, treading on his dirt-clotted feet repetitively across the same patch of earth, performing a task that eschews thinking in favour of tiresome physical labour. Thus, the story of walking begins as an apologue for 'artistic creation, as well as the rejection of work' (quoted in Coverley: 2012, 20).[2]

As to where 'such movement leads' one might point to language, firstly to speech and conversation. Despite William Hazlitt's caution against engaging in conversation while trekking, walking and talking seem inseparable, whether through self-conversation or between individuals journeying together.[3] The path one creates in walking can therefore lead to sociability (and even to gossiping). Tim Ingold calls this movement *wayfaring*. Wayfaring integrates walking, thinking and storytelling as a way in which humans inscribe pathways in both the landscape and the imagination as our fundamental mode of being in the world, leaving traces to be followed and retraced by others in our wake. For some pre-modern cultures, walking as wayfaring is the 'very means by which stories are converted into knowledge' and this conversion means that knowledge and footprints are 'part and parcel of the same action' (Vergunst and Ingold 2008: 6).

Wayfaring is also integral to the act of writing. It embodies the shared rhythms between walking and writing and relates how their common metrics help to congeal a peripatetic writer's thoughts into a cohesive narrative necessary for storytelling. Coverley begins his book *The Art of Wandering: The Writer as Walker* with an epigraph from Geoff Nicholson's *The Lost Art of Walking*: '*Both walking and writing are simple, common activities. You put one foot in front of the other; you put one word in front of another*' (Coverley 2012: 11. Italics in the original). The perambulatory rhythms shared by the writer's hand moving across the enclosed terrain of the blank page and the walker on foot cutting across a landscape personifies the hand and the foot united in a journey of the mind and imagination. Writing, thinking and walking go hand in hand, so to speak. In this book, I will argue that we can substitute, or perhaps supplement, writing with the image, specifically the filmic image as an 'artistic creation', in our metronomic calculus of the shared rhythms of walking and thinking.

Walking and philosophical reverie have been connected since at least the peripatetic school which was founded by Aristotle in the fourth century BCE. Since then, walking has way-marked the mental landscapes of philosophers such as Rousseau, Kierkegaard, Bentham, Kant, Hegel and Heidegger with their own unique metaphysical ruminations. In *Wanderlust: A History of Walking* Rebecca Solnit asks us to consider the 'pelvis as a secret theatre where thinking and walking meet', noting that Thomas Hobbes had an inkhorn fashioned to the end of his walking stick so that he could record his ideas during his rambles (Solnit 2001: 42, 16). She also reports that in Central Europe the association between walking and philosophising was so strong that some cities named landmarks after it: 'The celebrated Philosophenweg in Heidelberg, where Hegel is said to have walked; the Philosophendamm in Königsberg, where Kant passed on his daily stroll (now replaced by a railway station); and the Philosopher's Way Kierkegaard mentions in Copenhagen' (Solnit 2001: 6).

But for the most part, when philosophers explore the role of tactility in relation to knowing and doing, they often privilege the hand as its incarnation.[4] Heidegger famously claimed that humans are world-forming and animals, particularly the great apes, are 'poor in the world'. What he means by 'poor in the world' is that animals lack certain human attributes in their physical being, specifically that of having hands, which translates into a lack of subsequent cognitive traits: 'Apes, too, have organs that can grasp, but they do not have hands. The hand is different from all grasping organs – claws, paws or fangs – different by an abyss of essence. Only a being who can speak, that is, think, can have hands and can be handy in achieving works of handicraft.' He further argues that man can think only because he speaks, and not the other way around. Everything we use our hands for is rooted in and at the service of thinking. Since he binds the human hand to thinking and thinking to the hand (thinking + hand = handicraft) and both to speaking ('the hand holds onto speaking') Heidegger concludes that thinking and speaking are 'crafts' our ape cousins cannot learn because they do not possess hands (Heidegger 1976).

In his response to Heidegger (*Geschlecht II*: Heidegger's Hand) Derrida finds this opposition between man and ape based on the hand itself rather poor, because it dogmatically rests on an aporia between grasping and giving, or taking and giving, a false dichotomy reducible to the following simplistic argument: 'Man's hand *gives and gives itself* . . . like thought . . . whereas the organ of the ape . . . can only *take hold of, grasp, lay hands on the thing*' (quoted in Sallis 1989: 175). Derrida argues that Heidegger's distinction between man and ape 'corresponds less to the opposition of being-able-to-give and being-able-to-take than to the opposition of *two ways* of being able to give and take' (Sallis 1989: 195). He also criticises Heidegger for not citing any zoological evidence or showing even any interest in zoological studies that apes might have 'hands' and therefore be bestowed with the gifts of language and thought. But perhaps just as poor is the lack of any subsequent discussion on a subject that should have logically followed: the foot. What about the role of the foot in thinking? Neither thinkers connect the hand to the foot, and therefore walking to speech and thought. While Heidegger was known as an inveterate walker who practised what we might call mindful meditation while hiking, he never really philosophised about either walking or the foot itself the way that he did hands.

The foot itself has largely been denigrated in Western philosophy. Bataille begins his essay 'The Big Toe' with this observation about how badly the foot has fared in philosophy, also using the great apes as his comparative model:

> The big toe is the most *human* part of the human body, in the sense that no other element of this body is as differentiated from the corresponding element of the anthropoid ape (chimpanzee, gorilla, orangutan or gibbon). This is due to the fact that the ape is tree dwelling, whereas man moves on the earth without clinging to branches, having himself become a tree, in other words raising himself straight up in the air like a tree, and all the more beautiful for the correctness of his erection. In addition, the function of the human foot consists in giving a firm foundation to the

erection of which man is so proud (the big toe, ceasing to grasp branches, is applied to the ground on the same plane as the other toes). But whatever the role played in the erection by his foot, man, who has a light head, in other words a head raised to the heavens and heavenly things, sees it as spit, on the pretext that he has this foot in the mud. (Bataille 1985: 20)

Because the foot is the most base, unelevated human organ, always mired in mud and prone to the most hideous and comically grotesque deformities such as corns and callouses, it has been the object of scorn and representative of our cadaverous ignobility which we try to shield from ourselves. And there is no more metonymically monstrous stand-in for the ignoble carnality of a human being than the bulbous big toe that sticks out at the end of a foot. But Bataille reminds us that the big toe can only stand in for man because it is the very organ that allows him to stand upright and elevated above the mud; without it, humans would not be able to properly balance themselves on two legs.

There have been a few other contemporary philosophers writing positively 'on foot'. In his 1931 essay 'The World of the Living Present and the Constitution of the Surrounding World External to the Organism', Edmund Husserl stresses the way in which walking kinaesthetically links up the lived body with the lived space through which it moves to bring home the fact that, as human beings, we are total organisms and not just a collection of organs. In the mundane act of walking, he argues, we affirm the distinction between our *lived* body which moves through space without locality and our physical body which is localisable in space. The foot is the part of the human body that is most associated with motion, since it is the appendage that touches the ground while we walk; it is the medium that plants the motion. The action of planting the foot engages the beginning of the muscular action needed to walk and the foot striking the organic ground while in motion is a fundamental aspect of the peripatetic humanness, which, in turn, is fundamental to active thought.

Perhaps the most poetic portrait of walking by a contemporary philosopher can be found in *A Philosophy of Walking* by Frédéric Gros, which begins with the sentence 'Walking is not a sport' (Gros 2015: 1). It is, rather, only child's play. Bipedal walking comes naturally to human beings. Perhaps it is even what essentially separates us from other species in the animal kingdom and best defines us as human. The moment the first homo sapiens stood up and took her first steps out of the forest and on to the African savannah, she ushered us into humanity. If the first mark of humanity is freedom, then walking upright is its first trace. It freed our arms to reach for fruit, pick up an infant, or to wield a weapon shaped with our own hands against an enemy. It freed our desires to roam, to make long journeys, whether to hunt migratory game through persistence or simply to satiate our curiosity to see what is in the next valley or around the next cove.

Gros describes three types of freedoms that can be realised through the purposeful act of walking, especially in long, slow, meditative walks. The first is *suspensive*. To go for a walk is to throw off the cares of everyday routine. Granted, in our daily walks, we may develop new routines – starting off at the same time each day, resting at intervals, tracing a familiar path – but these routines are now governed by *slowness* rather than hurriedness and speed: 'Walking frees us from our illusions about the essential' (Gros 2015: 4).

The second freedom is *transgressive*. While going for a walk rarely permits more than a temporary disconnection from our day-to-day routines, one always has the option to decide on a complete break with convention and walk right out of daily life altogether. Thus we have every type of peripatetic outcast, from the *gyrovagues* (wandering monks) to the perpetual pilgrim to those who renounce everything and answer the call of the wild to 'shout to assert [their] recovered animal presence' (Gros 2015: 7). If our identity is caught up in our social obligations, then 'the [transgressive] freedom of walking lies in not being anyone; for the walking body has no history, it is just an oddity in the stream of immemorial life' (Gros 2015: 7). Gros thinks of this freedom as the reconquest of the primitive animal each of us has forsaken to live in conventional society.

Lastly, the walker can choose the freedom of *renunciation*. This is the freedom of absolute detachment where one embarks on a 'life henceforth dedicated to travel in which endless walking, in one direction and another, illustrates the harmonisation of the nameless self with the omnipresent heart of the world' (Gros 2015: 9). This type of peripatetic freedom is both a privilege and a burden, a form of deprivation as well as excess, reserved for those who have time on their hands (retirees, pilgrims).

Images of Walking

The earliest depictions of the human form in prehistoric cave paintings show man upright and on foot chasing down much swifter four-legged prey. Almost all of these early pictographs depict man and animal as dynamic, living creatures in motion. Still lifes are rare. Our ancestral artists used every uneven surface of the cave walls – rock reliefs, bulging curves, stalagmites – to add depth and perspective to the two-dimensional subjects moving about, with the dramatic effect of making them seem to dance across the cave.[5] Some three hundred or so centuries later, the very first photograph to include a human being was taken in Paris by Louise Daguerre in 1838. The picture is of the Boulevard du Temple taken from a rooftop. On the bottom left, standing on the sidewalk with one foot resting on a box is a man having his shoe shined. Italian philosopher Giorgio Agamben (whose ideas I will discuss in more detail in Chapter 2) describes the photograph this way:

> The boulevard should be crowded with people and carriages, and yet, because the cameras of the period required an extremely long exposure time, absolutely nothing of this moving mass is visible. Nothing, that is, except a small black silhouette on the sidewalk in the lower left-hand corner of the photograph. A man stopped to have his shoes shined, and must have stood still for quite a while, with his leg slightly raised to place his foot on the shoe shiner's stool . . . The crowd of humans – indeed, all of humanity – is present, but it cannot be seen, because the judgement concerns a single person, a single life . . . While making the most banal and ordinary gesture, the gesture of having his shoes shined. In the supreme instant, man, each man, is given over forever to his smallest, most everyday gesture. And yet, thanks to the photographic lens, that gesture is now charged with the weight of an entire life. (Agamben 2007: 24)

The lonely image of the foot resting on the shoeshine box is visible only because the primitive photographic technology of the time has abandoned the motion swirling all around it to the unseen. Still, the image is pregnant with the possibilities of motion.

Within a few years, other photographers such as Nadar took their cameras directly into the Parisian streets and boulevards as mechanised *flâneurs*, whom Ann Friedberg calls 'armed walkers', ushering in the age of the 'mobilised virtual gaze' which culminated in the arrival of cinema (Friedberg 1994, 143). These early pioneers of photography were keen to capture the new speed and mobility of mid-nineteenth-century urban life, first heroised by Charles Baudelaire as hallmarks of modernity, finally revealing the secret of what happens during the 'fraction of a second when a person *steps out*' (Benjamin 1979: 248).

By the close of the century, photographic technology advanced to reduce exposure times to an instant, finally making it possible to arrest the fleeting and fugitive present of modernity in a *snapshot* of time. André Bazin compared these snapshots to the bodies of insects preserved in amber, noting how both the photograph and amber have the power to halt a life in a set moment of its natural duration, 'embalming time' in an instant:

> Hence the charm of family albums. Those grey or sepia shadows, phantomlike and almost indecipherable, are no longer traditional family portraits but rather the disturbing presence of lives halted at a set moment in their duration, freed from their destiny; not however by the prestige of art but by the power of an impassive mechanical process: for photography does not create eternity as art does, it embalms time, rescuing it simply from its own proper corruption. (Bazin 1968: 14)

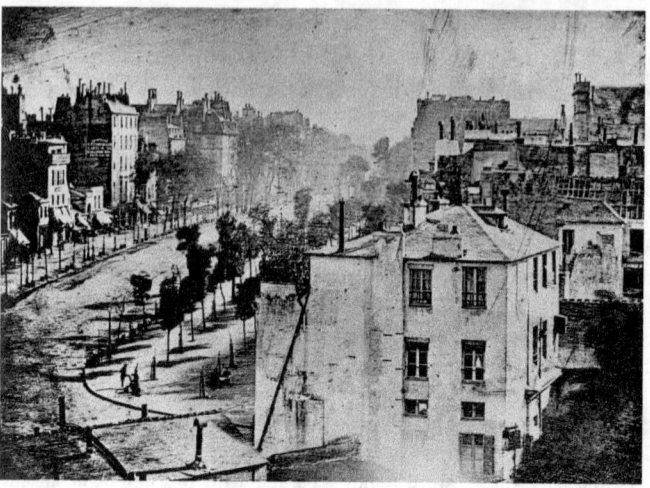

Figure I.1 Boulevard du Temple.

Time becomes a souvenir. Laura Mulvey notes that because the time embalmed in a snapshot is indexical – that is, it is a 'record of a fraction of time . . . [that] captures the presence of life stilled' – the snapshot is inscribed with a kind of death and instils in us an uncanny feeling of mourning for the persons in the photograph, even if they are still living (Mulvey 2006: 57). It was left to the cinema to resuscitate these instants – to resurrect an image of duration from its convalescence in the photographic – and make them ambulatory once again. Thus the snapshot becomes, as formulated by Deleuze, one of the determining conditions for cinema.

Plan of the Book

The very first moving picture to be shot with a single lensed camera on celluloid was made on 14 October 1888, by the inventor Louis Aimé Augustin Le Prince. Titled *Roundhay Garden Scene*, it was recorded at 12 fps, lasts only 2.11 seconds and depicts two men and two women walking around in a garden. In Chapter 1, I explore this film's roots in the photographic studies of motion by Muybridge and Marey, with special emphasis on their mutual interest in the bio-mechanics of human walking and why this is artistically and culturally relevant to cinema from its very beginning. I argue that walking is at the heart of the technological and narrative mobility inscribed in cinematic visibility.

In Chapter 2, I investigate the iconic on-screen walk of Charlie Chaplin's character 'The Tramp' and its cultural effect on early audiences.[7] Here, I write about walking as part of the mise-en-scène of a Chaplin film and how he as an actor and director uses his signature character's walk as a narrative device.

Chapter 3 is about the camera itself as a pedestrian. After tracking the use of dollies and the hand-held camera selectively throughout film history, I concentrate on discussing the Steadicam device – invented in 1975 by cameraman Garrett Brown and first used in a commercial film by cinematographer Haskell Wexler for *Bound for Glory* in 1976 – and the various ways it has been employed by innovative directors. I pay special attention to how the director Béla Tarr uses the Steadicam to create what I call a *participatory peripatetic point of view* resulting in a unique visual style coupled with distinctive narrative tendencies.

In Chapter 4 I examine walking in the genres of the detective noir film and the police procedural, paying particular attention to the films adapted from Raymond Chandler stories.

'Trying to get home' is probably the most common trope in narrative cinema. In Chapter 5, I will explore this trope in the wider context of human dwelling and its relationship to walking. Using this context as a backdrop, I work through a handful of films where walking is constitutive of a homeward narrative.

In Chapter 6, I use concepts derived from Baudelaire's (and Walter Benjamin's) theory of the urban *flâneur*, as well as ones from psychogeography, to examine representations of urban walks in film. I focus on a few films shot on the streets of Paris and Rome as indicative of *flâneurie* in cinema.

Notes

1. Eisner would live for another nine years, dying in 1983.
2. Careri makes a distinction between nomadism and roaming. The concept of roaming is reserved for Palaeolithic hunter-gatherers who 'erratically' pursued game across open terrain through persistence hunting. He defines nomadic journeys as those undertaken by pastoralists following the cyclical and regulated movements of livestock across a closed landscape. Nomadic journeys are possible only after Palaeolithic peoples began to settle on the land and abandoned persistence hunting. Abel's peripatetic pastoralist wanderings can be viewed as a liminal stage between the absolute mobility of roaming and the sedentariness of settling in a city or town and thus represents a rupture in human modes of walking (Careri 2002: 48). In *The Songlines*, Bruce Chatwin eloquently restates the same argument: 'Most nomads claim to "own" their

migration path (in Arabic *Il-Ra*), but in practice they only lay claim to grazing rights. Time and space are thus dissolved around each other: a month and a stretch of road are synonymous . . . a nomad's migration – unlike that of the hunter's – is not his own. It is, rather, a guided tour of animals whose distinctive sense of direction has been blunted by domestication' (Chatwin 1987 184).
3. In 'On Going a Journey', William Hazlitt writes, rather forcefully, about his objections to conversation while walking: 'I cannot see the wit of walking and talking at the same time. When I am in the country, I wish to vegetate like the country. I am not for criticising hedge-rows and black cattle. I go out of town in order to forget the town and all that is in it. There are those who for this purpose go to watering-places and carry the metropolis with them. I like more elbow-room and fewer incumbrances' (Hazlitt 1845: 343).
4. This is true of film directors too. Perhaps the director whose style makes best use of close-ups of hands is Robert Bresson, who deftly uses shots of hands as emblems of thoughts united to action.
5. The oldest known pictorial creations of upright man are found in the Chauvet Cave in Southern France. In 2008 Herzog was given rare access to film in the caves and the result is the 3D documentary *Cave of Forgotten Dreams* (2010). The film is narrated by Herzog and contains some of his more entertaining inner musings and observations, especially about representations of walking found in the cave. Here are two exemplary ones:

'In a forbidden recess of the cave, there's a footprint of an eight-year-old boy next to the footprint of a wolf. Did a hungry wolf stalk the boy? Or did they walk together as friends? Or were their tracks made thousands of years apart? We'll never know.'

'The artist painted this bison with eight legs, suggesting movement – almost a form of proto-cinema.'
7. There is a whole sociology of movement, especially of walking, that early pioneers of cinema like Chaplin produced. Joseph Amato observes that early movies:

> taught their viewers stereotypes – even created archetypes – of how the rich and poor, the snobbish and humble, the stylish and gauche moved. They gave examples of the upper classes shopping, strolling, getting in and out of carriages, pushing their fancy baby strollers, and having someone pick up and carry their luggage. At the same time, they showed, though much less, the lower classes trudging dusty roads, seeking work, or moving along the street in a crowded immigrant neighbourhood. Moreover, movies taught their audiences how to strut, slink, and glide – how to get in and out of a car (which the majority did not yet own), how to walk arm and arm, how to hop in and out of bed, how to window shop, or how to peruse a department store . . . movies provided a vast lexicon of walks, from that of the rushing messenger boy to that of the moseying and ambling cowboy, from those of the discouraged, beaten-down workers and quick-striding businessmen to that of the swaying and hip-rolling beauty queens. (Amato 2005: 211)

CHAPTER 1

First Steps

Aristotle seems to be the first philosopher to compare animal locomotion to mechanical movement. In his treatise 'On the Motion of Animals', he writes:

> The movements of animals may be compared with those of automatic puppets, which are set going on the occasion of a tiny movement; the levers are released, and strike the twisted strings against one another; or with the toy wagon. For the child mounts on it and moves it straight forward, and then again it is moved in a circle owing to its wheels being of unequal diameter (the smaller acts like a centre on the same principle as the cylinders). Animals have parts of a similar kind, their organs, the sinewy tendons to wit and the bones; the bones are like the wooden levers in the automaton, and the iron; the tendons are like the strings, for when these are tightened or leased movement begins. (Aristotle 2013: part 7)

Aristotle was limited to observation as his measuring tool, but subsequent scientists wanted to develop more accurate ways to measure animal locomotion, leading to the invention of an array of mechanical devices for recording human movement as a mechanical phenomenon. Of primary interest to anatomists was measuring the forces involved in walking, especially those inherent in the human gait to discover how forward momentum is produced. One of the first to create an experiment for measuring these was the Renaissance Italian physiologist Giovanni Borelli, a pioneer of iatromechanics and considered the father of biomechanics. Like Aristotle, Borelli's analogue for human motion was the machine. He imagined human bones as 'mechanical levers moved by muscles according to mathematical principles' and performed an experiment using a prismatic pivot to prove that the centre of a human body's mass indicates a 'lateral sway during gait' (quoted in Medved 2000: 6). In 1836, the German brothers Wilhelm and Eduard Weber published *Mechanics of Walking in Humans*, the first scientific study of the human gait. The Weber brothers anticipated photographer Eadweard Muybridge's later photographic studies of motion using optical instruments combined with time-measuring devices, including the chronograph, to isolate and mathematically model the specific positions of limbs and muscle groups during the phases of walking (Medved 2000: 6).

Muybridge's experiments to measure animal locomotion using photography to capture the successive movement of a galloping horse and other animals, including man, have been well documented. For the purpose of this study, a concise summary of Muybridge's work written by Vladimir Medved will suffice:

> Commissioned and financially supported by Leland Stanford . . . Muybridge started using photography to record horses running in Sacramento, California. It was partly a result of a wager. The matter to be settled was whether or not a horse left the ground completely at any point in time while running. The project took place from 1872 to 1877. Muybridge succeeded in developing a photographic emulsion capable of recording 1/1,000 (1/2,000 according to some sources) of a second. To measure the horse's stride, he used a series of cameras—12 and later 24. They were activated with delays, with the aid of a so-called 'rotating commutator mechanism for magnetic shutter release'. As a result, he obtained a time series of pictures of the moving animal on a wet glass plate. The analysis of these pictures gave the first real sequence of the animal's movements ('The Horse in Motion', 1882) . . . Muybridge's work offered a new 'kinematic scientific language'. (2000: 7–8)

While Muybridge's experiments are certainly important nascent steps in the stages of cinema's development, I would like to turn my attention to his contemporary, the French anatomist and physiologist Étienne-Jules Marey. Marey's invention of chronophotography brings us much closer to realising cinema as an art of moving pictures.

Étienne-Jules Marey

Unlike Muybridge, Étienne-Jules Marey was not originally a photographer but a physiologist who devoted almost all of his career to studying motion. He began his research into measuring movement using a method he termed 'chronography' (sometimes called the graphic method) in order to register the duration and sequence of a body in motion (time and space) that elude the naked eye. He was especially interested in recording time-measurements of human walking – 'the duration and sequence of the rise and fall of the foot' – developing several chronographic apparatuses such as pneumatic shoes and the odograph. These experiments eventually led him to invent the technique of *chronophotography* (time photography). Marey coined the term to describe the process of taking multiple successive images, sometimes layered on the same print to show overlapping and kinetic motion, and at other times across several frames in quick succession, in order to 'determine with exactitude the characters of a movement' (Marey 1972: 54).

His earliest chronophotographic motion studies were achieved with an ordinary camera taking multiple exposures on a fixed glass plate. He experimented with different photographic apparatuses and glass plate configurations, but found that these experiments achieved only limited results. For instance, Marey discovered that when he photographed the flight of an illuminated ball thrown in the air against a dark background with the lens shutter kept open for the duration of the ball's flight, the impression it left on the glass plate was that of a single, unbroken curved line which represented the ball's path. However, while this method provided a means to represent the overall trajectory of a body in motion, it did not register any impression of the form of the ball's movement nor its various positions at any particular moment along its path. In other words, it did not register time. But suppose, Marey writes:

> we repeat this experiment, but only admit light into the dark chamber [of the camera] in an intermittent fashion, and at regular intervals of time, an interrupted trajectory will be obtained [represented as a series of points on the glass plate] . . . This represents the successive positions assumed by the moving object at each moment when light is admitted. This is the chronographic trajectory. In this method the intervals of time separating two images are of constant and known duration. (Marey 1972: 54–5)

Marey pursued the instantaneous arrest and serial decomposition of movement through photography to illuminate what was invisible to the eye; he had no real scientific (nor aesthetic) interest in its recomposition beyond this goal. Yet Marey's chronophotography can lay claim to being a closer progenitor to cinematography than Muybridge's freeze-frame stills. He discovered a means beyond the single exposure photograph to capture simultaneously the various intervals of a moving body's trajectory across space juxtaposed together to create a synthesis of movement in space over a length of time. Whereas Muybridge's intervals were achieved artificially by interrupting the horse's gate at various points (through the horse's legs tripping the camera wires), Marey's breaks were produced by manipulating the photographic apparatus itself, namely the shutter, to inscribe the fissures between instants of movement as images. The object's motion itself was left untouched.

In 1883 Marey used funds awarded by the French government to set up a centre for motion studies where he applied his chronophotographic method to analysing human locomotion, especially walking. By 1892 he had perfected the chronophotographic technique by adapting his chronophotographic apparatus to use rolls of celluloid film instead of glass plates and had worked out the ideal combination of shutter speed and duration of exposure to achieve the results he wanted.

What is striking is how Marey's mechanistic conception of animal locomotion led him to create a machine which measured that movement using the same mechanical principles as that which he was measuring. As François Albéra notes, Marey pairs the animal machine (a living being) 'whose locomotion is distinct and successive' as an object of analytical study with its non-living analogue, the cinema machine (an illusion-producing machine) whose movements produce '[distinct and] successive images' of the animal machine in motion to construct a 'conception of the living being and a model to capture reproducible movements' (Albéra 2010: 61). So already with Marey we have what Agamben calls the 'transcendental conditions' for cinema, namely *repetition* and *stoppage* (Gustafsson 2015; 145).[1]

Marey teamed up with his former student, French anthropologist Félix Regnault, to study and compare the gait of West Africans to French soldiers in the interest of helping the French state in 'restoring the muscles of the ordinary citizen and soldier' which he believed had become nervous and weakened due to the overstimulations of modern urban life (Braun 2009). He used chronophotography to film Africans walking and shared his research with the Académie des sciences with the aim of convincing the French military that their rigid marching gait could be much improved by adopting the Africans' *marche en flexion* gait, which consisted of artificially bending the knees while stepping with the foot lower to the ground. Regnault argued that the *march de flexion* was the natural gait of both prehistoric man and Africans, and was less fatiguing and therefore superior to both the French military gait and the artificial walk of the cosmopolitan upper classes. Marey even filmed French Commandant de Raoul demonstrating the superiority of the *march de flexion*.

The key to these demonstrations was chronophotography as an educator of the French body in peripatetic motion. In his preface to Regnault and de Raoul's 1898 book *Comment on marche: Des divers modes de progression, de la supériorité de mode en flexion*, Marey writes about his confidence in chronophotography as a new tool for improving the French national body:

> [Chronophotography] will educate us. It will show us to imitate the walk of the primitive, will return us to a more natural gait, health, and the conservation of energy. It will provide our army with a walk that will give it an unquestioned superiority. (quoted in Braun 2009)

By my count, Marey and Regnault (along with Regnault's assistant Charles Comte) shot at least twenty-three chronographic studies of Africans performing the *march de flexion* at the 1895 *Exposition ethnographique de l'afrique occidentale* which was held at the Champ de Mars in Paris. Some of these were shot on location at the exposition while others were filmed at Marey's laboratory, the *Station Physiologique*, and ranged in subject from single semi-nude male figures to groups of African children in traditional dress. At least two showed a woman walking with an infant child on her back and two others showed a woman walking across the screen carrying a loaded basket on her head. Except for one of Regnault sitting on a palanquin ported away from the camera by four barefoot African men, all the chronophotographs show the subject walking in profile. These 'films' are very short in length, usually consisting of between twenty and thirty frames. With few exceptions, the subject was shot walking across a raised platform, which was ruled in black paint on the side facing the camera to measure distance, against a white sheet as a backdrop with a chronometer in the frame to measure time. With this setup Marey and Regnault were able to capture the 'visible expression of a continuous passage of time over equidistant and known intervals within a single tracing' to measure the duration of his African subject's gait (Braun 2009).

Fatimah Tobing Rony has argued that Marey and Regnault's *marche de reflexion* chronophotographs are rooted in the turn of the century colonial obsession with 'evolutionary typologies' to document, categorise and classify non-Western colonised peoples as the 'Ethnographical Other' against the normative 'Historical Same' embodied by their French colonisers (Rony 1996). The idea of the primitive is essential to Marey's studies. In the face of views that saw non-whites as inferior, Marey follows the standard investigation of the 'stages of man' (we can think of the charts that show the passage of man as a movement from hunched-over to an upright stance). His research is certainly guided by evolutionary impulses that suffuse with the supposition of the colonial, scientific racist world he occupied. The very fact of using African peoples in a controlled experiment has obvious connotations of colonisation. However, for Marey, the search for and recovery of the elementary nature of the peripatetic impulse in humanity, especially the gait that best exemplified the emergence of the upright human stripped to its essence, was the goal. Marey provides an example of how the supposed uncontested othering embedded in the colonial project was indeed subject to a host of understandings and goals that, even though it did not displace the overall framework of colonial assumptions, perhaps allowed for other understandings.

Louis Aimé Augustin Le Prince

Although chronophotography is a precursor to cinematography, the two are aesthetically distinct forms which 'give rise to incompatible yet intertwined ideas about the truth of images and the understanding of time and motion' (Campany 2008: 22). Many scholars cite the Lumière brothers' Cinématograph as the first cinematographic camera capable of decomposing movement and recomposing it through projection. However, there is mounting evidence that the true lineage of cinema belongs to French inventor Louis Aimé Augustin Le Prince, who created a single-lens film camera and projection system with which he shot and publicly screened two films in 1888 seven years before the Lumière brothers.

Born 1841 in Metz, France, Le Prince spent his youth playing and loitering in the studio of photographic pioneer Jacques Daguerre, who was a friend of his father. He even sat for a daguerreotype portrait by the inventor himself. After initially studying art in Paris, he went on to study photography and chemistry at the University of Leipzig, two subjects in which he developed an interest during his time with Daguerre. After University he was invited by his classmate and friend John Whitley to move to Leeds, UK to join Whitley's brass foundry. Le Prince married Whitley's sister and together they established the Leeds Technical School of Arts where they perfected a process for fixing tinted colour photographs onto ceramic and metal surfaces. In 1881 he moved to New York City as an agent of Whitley Partners representing its American interests. While there, in 1885, he also worked as a painter and designer for French panoramist Theodore Poilpot, who was in New York creating his first moving panoramas for American audiences. The subject of these panoramas was American Civil War battles, and Le Prince played a key role in building one titled *Monitor and Merrimack Engagement*, which re-enacted a famous battle between two iron clad ships. But despite the scale and dynamism of this panoramic composition, Le Prince experienced the limitations of these static, still-life painted figures for creating the illusion of movement in all but a rudimentary way. For the illusion of movement to be truly realised, he recognised that photography must replace painting in panoramic works. His biographer Christopher Rawlence writes:

> When Le Prince set out late in 1884 along the arduous moving-picture trail, he was inspired not so much by a need to expand the possibilities of photography but by a desire to improve on the illusionistic powers of the panorama. Three tributaries of Western image-making were joined in his mind ... his experience as a painter, his panorama work, and his knowledge of photography. To this he brought his experience as an engineer and his knowledge of optics ... Le Prince's goal, in his own

words, was to create a photographic equivalent of a 'moving panorama in colour'. (Rawlence 1990: 145)

With this goal in mind, he devoured every news article and scientific proceeding he could find announcing an array of new pre-cinematic photographic technologies that were on the cusp of producing 'moving' pictures. This led to his first photographic experiments and, in 1886, while in America, he created and patented – in both the US and UK – a sixteen-lens camera which utilised two rolls of Eastman Kodak gelatine and paper film. The two rolls of film alternately advanced past two banks of eight lenses each, which, when developed as transparencies, were projected by the camera in reverse fashion for exhibition:

> The pictures were recorded alternately on each roll. The eight lenses facing the first roll were released in rapid succession, and then the remaining eight on the other side followed suit while the first roll was being moved on ready for a successive set. The lenses were operated by a complex system of double shutters released by electro magnets connected to a battery and a rotary switch. Two additional lenses served as view-finders, one for each roll of film. (Howells 2006: 187)

While technically his first apparatus did 'reproduce' motion from a series of captured images, each of the sixteen lenses photographed a subject from a different angle, resulting in unstable and jumpy movement when projected.[2] The design was overly complicated and the entire apparatus cumbersome to operate. This led him to hire a cabinet maker and mechanic to help construct a more refined but simplified apparatus known as the 'Le Prince Single-lens Cine Camera' (which doubled as a projector) that shares remarkable technical similarities both in construction and operation with modern motion picture cameras. According to Richard Howells, the camera operated using '$2\frac{3}{8}$ inch-wide un-perforated film which was wound past the lens via a pair of spools'. The film was held fast for exposure by a flat, brass plate, and the exposure controlled by way of a circular slotted brass shutter 'which revolves behind the lens in the same way as a modern shutter' (2006: 187).

He first used this camera to shoot *Roundhay Garden Scene* on (or about) 14 October 1888, in the garden of Joseph Whitley's house in suburban Leeds (Roundhay Cottage) depicting Le Prince's son Adolphe and mother-in-law Sarah Whitley along with Joseph Whitley and Harriet Hartley walking around the garden and laughing. The original film itself is extremely short, consisting of twenty frames shot at 12fps on 60mm film stock with a running time of just 2.11 seconds. Since *Roundhay Garden Scene* was shot on celluloid (Eastman's gelatine-based paper-backed stripping film) with a

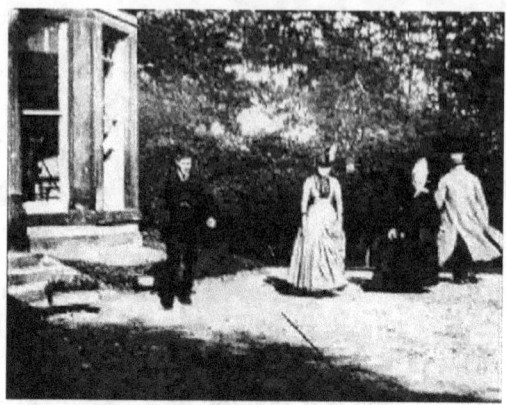

Figure 1.1 Roundhay Garden.

single-lensed camera, it is widely recognised as the first true 'motion picture' and thus the earliest cinematic work. According to many film historians (though not without contention), this makes Le Prince the real father of cinema, despite scholarly attribution to the Lumière brothers and Thomas Edison's later litigious patrimonial claims.[3]

Though he never showed *Roundhay* in public, Le Prince did screen it privately in the Whitley factory for a small group of friends, family and collaborators. For a Victorian audience in 1888, watching the banal episode of four people walking in circles around a suburban garden must have been overshadowed by the sheer novelty of seeing these images thrown up on a screen moving at a smooth and natural rate. Le Prince repeated this feat in his second (and last) film *Traffic Crossing Leeds Bridge* shot with the same camera. Shot from a third-floor window in the Hick Brothers building above and to the right of Leeds Bridge, this brief film (like *Roundhay* it comprises a mere twenty frames) shows both horse drawn vehicles and pedestrians moving along the bridge. All the pedestrians, except one man who is crossing the street, are strolling down the pavements on either side of the bridge. On the right side of the bridge, a smartly dressed man has his arm around the shoulder of a young boy as they amble together. Two women walk just behind them in the same direction. They pass another man who has stopped to peer over the bridge (perhaps smoking a pipe) while two others approach, one of whom wipes his nose on his sleeve as he marches briskly along wielding a walking stick in his other hand. The pedestrians on the other side of the bridge are obscured by the horse drawn traffic, but one can make out both men and women sauntering down the pavement.

One gets the sense that none of the subjects know they are being photographed. To a contemporary eye, the scene has the look of modern CCTV footage, and leaves one to imagine a storyline for each pedestrian, especially for the man and his young companion or the one hurriedly crossing the street through the traffic. The same could be said of the realism later found in the Lumières' first film reels: *Workers Leaving the Lumière Factory* (*Sortie des usines Lumière*), *Arrival of a Train* (*L'Arrivée d'un train*) and *Lyon, Place Bellacour*.

Cinematic Movement

Tom Gunning argues that the new aesthetics of modernism 'saw motion as a force in itself, a plasmatic energy that creates forms rather than simply moves them about' (Gunning 2006: 27–8). In his writings on time and movement, French philosopher Henri Bergson was one of the first to articulate a theory which embraced this idea of movement as force. Bergson argued that, contrary to the classical concept of movement, *real* movement in our everyday world is distinct from the space (as a series of points) a moving subject covers and is therefore *actually* indivisible (and even, in some ways, invisible). Space itself is divisible, but real movement through it can neither be arrested nor reconstituted in space and time except as an illusion of the mind. Gilles Deleuze summarises Bergson's argument this way:

> You cannot reconstitute movement with positions in space or instants in time [*coupes*]. You can only achieve this reconstitution by adding to the positions, or to the instants, the abstract idea of succession, of a time which is mechanical, homogeneous, universal and copied from space, identical for all movements. And thus you miss the movement in two ways. On the one hand, you can bring the two instants or two positions together to infinity; but movement will always occur in the interval between the two, in other words behind your back [this is one of Zeno's paradoxes]. On the other hand, however much you divide and subdivide time, movement will always occur in concrete duration [*durée*]; thus each movement will have its own qualitative duration. Hence we oppose two irreducible formulas: 'real movement → concrete duration', and 'immobile sections + abstract time'. (Deleuze 1986: 1)

Writing at the dawn of cinema, Bergson wanted to bridge the divide between matter and memory, between images of movement and real movement. All attempts up until the emergence of the cinema to reproduce and present an image of real movement created only false and artificial movement (using one of the two formulas noted by Deleuze). But what about the cinema as a new medium for moving images? Given that the cinema is constituted by individual, instantaneous snapshots spliced together consecutively and made to move invisibly within a mechanical apparatus that then projects these images on a screen to create an illusion of successive movement, is it not the very model of false and artificial images of movement? This is what Bergson thought, even naming this reproduction of universal and archaic illusion of movement 'cinematographic'. But Deleuze comes to the opposite conclusion. Cinema does not reconstitute false or artificial images of movement; it gives us an entirely new image he calls the 'movement-image' which operates beyond the conditions of natural perception: 'In short, cinema does not give us an image to which movement is added, it immediately gives us a movement-image' (Deleuze 1986: 2). Cinema introduces a new relationship between movement (action) and time that was not visible in Marey and Muybridge's motion studies: time is now subordinate to movement. D. N. Rodowick sums up the movement-image this way:

> Even in these early motion studies, the management of time is a central problem for the so-called scientific perception and analysis of movement. Action cannot be clearly represented without reducing the interval of exposure to a fraction of a second; the action itself must be carefully 'timed' in relation to the relay of cameras to assure that movement is recorded as successive and contiguous segments. Thus time is subordinated to movement and represented only indirectly through the agency of movement in two ways. First it is reduced to a constant (in Muybridge's case, 1/100th of a second), repeated as equidistantly spaced intervals. Second, it is restricted to a line of action; it flows only through rationally segmented, contiguous movements. Time serves here as the measure of space and movement; it can only be 'seen' through the intermediaries of space and movement. These two principles were necessary, of course, for the perfection of cinematographic technology. Yet the cinema [Le Prince's invention] added what pioneers such as Marey and Muybridge neither desired nor imagined: it automated movement by projecting these images at a fixed rate. (Rodowick 1997: 9)

For the first time in history we have an image which moves within itself: not just a false image of movement, but a real *moving* image. It is worth noting Agamben's observation that true art aims not 'to construct the image of the body, but a body for the image' (Agamben 2011: 66). But until the cinema, this body was cadaverous, and a cadaver, as Maurice Blanchot reminds us, 'is its own image. It no longer entertains any relation with this world, where it still appears, except that of an image' (Blanchot 1989: 258). The new body constructed for the image by cinema is animate and alive. Vivian Sobchack argues that this is the very feature that separates the *photographic* from the *cinematic*:

> ... the cinematic has something more to do with life, with the accumulation – not the loss – of experience. Cinematic technology *animates* the photographic and reconstitutes

its visibility and verisimilitude in a difference not of degree but of kind. The *moving picture* is a visible representation not of an activity finished or past, but of activity coming-into-being. (2000: 74)

Beginning with the advent of photography, artists working with other visual media had to contend with a medium that privileges the moment, expanding and freezing it into a static 'now'. But photography still had no way of representing the serial nature of the moment in its mobility. The first artists to respond to the challenge and limitations of photography were the Cubists. One potential response of Cubism to photography would have been to somehow create an aesthetic of the moment that aspired to the 'imaginary stasis of the photograph' (Charney 1998: 35). But Cubism reached beyond this and responded with an attempt to find a 'representational form that would stitch movements into moments', seeking a representational possibility that would neither 'isolate itself to one discrete moment' nor 'imagine that one moment could encompass more than one moment' (Charney 1998: 35–6). The Cubist movement succeeded in its task of undermining the validity of the fixed present moment, opening up the parameters of the static canvas to a new form of expressing the distended moment. But the goal of Cubist painting to displace the present moment was ultimately limited by the closed, fixed nature of the canvas, and they were never able to fully set the moment free to wander in the vagaries of perception and reception. The aspiration to surpass these limitations would be answered by the cinema.

Sergei Eisenstein

What is unique about cinematic time? The short answer is that the filmic image is never really in the present; nor is it fully 'present' to the spectator. There is no *now* in film. The arrival of the cinematic image imbued the sphere of representation with the potential overcoming of the desire for presence:

> By putting peak moments into motion, film techniques forged the impossibility of presence into a new form of spectatorial participation. Editing created a collage of fragments that could not help but render the viewer's experience as discontinuous. This discontinuity opened gaps and spaces throughout the action, nagging echoes of discontinuity that haunt film's premise of continuity. (Charney 1998: 86)

Cinema's aptitude for presenting the mobile sensation of the fragmentary moment is elaborated in Eisenstein's theory of montage and his complex view of spectatorship (Charney 1998: 128). Beginning with the notion that the single shot forms the building block of cinema – the shot is a 'montage cell' – Eisenstein formulated a theory to account for the way in which the 'cinema impels these shot-cells into movement' (Charney 1998: 131). Cinema is created only when these singular montage cells are stimulated and galvanised into dynamic motion. In his earliest writings, Eisenstein drew inspiration for the basis of cinematic dynamics from reading Japanese haiku poetry and the Japanese alphabet (much like Pound and the Imagists). He discovered that Japanese ideograms function through the collision of two ideas, or what he called 'attractions'. As one attraction collides with the other in the ideogram, the change produces an entirely new signification that is more than a sum of their combination:

> The point is that the copulation (perhaps we had better say, the combination) of two hieroglyphs of the simplest series is to be regarded not as their sum, but as their product, i.e., as a value of another dimension, another degree; each separately corresponds to an *object*, to a fact, but their combination corresponds to a *concept*. (Eisenstein 1969a: 29–30)

Montage, he discovered, functions in the same way:

> But this is montage! Yes. It is exactly what we do in the cinema, combining shots that are *depictive*, single in meaning, neutral in content – into *intellectual* contexts and series . . . By what then is montage characterised and, consequently, its cell – the shot? By collision. By the conflict of two pieces in opposition to one another. (Eisenstein 1969a: 30, 37)

Eisenstein's collision of shots generates meaning by engaging the spectator's senses to apprehend the attraction of each shot. The collision of shots enhances their differences, stimulating the spectator's mind to join these attractions into a higher unity created through difference and momentarily producing a 'unified' psychological effect. It is the violent, aggressive interaction of each shot, as an effect of difference, which creates meaning (Eisenstein 1969a: 53).

In his later writings, Eisenstein began to view the relationship between spectator and filmic form as an 'organic-machine'. This metaphor allowed him to investigate the effects of film spectatorship as a combination of collision and cooperation between the montage cells (Andrew 1976: 67). However, this analogy still implies that there exists a relay station or an 'aesthetic transformer' between the content of the individual shots and the meaning which results from their combination. 'The meaning is not in the image,' Bazin writes, 'it is in the shadow of the image projected by montage onto the field of consciousness of the spectator' (Bazin 1968: 26).

In general, Eisenstein was interested in exploring how montage *affects* the spectator. His theory of montage is a way of working out the dynamics of how the spectator creates the filmic image by splicing together all the relationships between the attractions, which gives the spectator not a 'completed image', but the 'experience of completing an image' (Andrew 1976: 73). Eisenstein's theory of montage emphasises the radically momentary nature of the temporal process of this experience. To illustrate this, he uses the analogy of the 'overtone' from music.

Through this musical analogy, Eisenstein suggests that filmmakers should avoid simply joining montage fragments along a dominant line and instead strive to orchestrate a vibrating 'whole' which will create a final impression in the viewer of a 'unity through synthesis' (Andrew 1976: 60). Each sequence of a film should be guided by an interconnected montage, or 'polyphonic montage', where each shot is linked to another through the composition of a 'simultaneous advance of a multiple series of lines, each maintaining an independent compositional course and each contributing to the total compositional course of the sequence' (Eisenstein 1969b: 75; Charney 1998: 133). As these lines progress forward, they create relations among themselves analogous to the vertical structure of an orchestral score. Each part of an orchestral score is developed horizontally, but it is the vertical line interwoven with the horizontal structure that gives the musical piece a temporal measure which maintains the forward progression of the entire piece. Like the orchestral score, Eisenstein theorises that as the lines of a montage film move forward, they 'produce meaning only through their dialogue with one another, their systemic relationships', which occur along a vertical axis (quoted in Charney 1998: 134).

Eisenstein's argument illustrates a deconstructive model of cinema by exploiting the ways in which the cinema deploys its 'momentary nature as a structure' with which the spectator will manufacture 'shifting and interrelating "centres"' to form 'momentary clusters of meaning that anchor the film as it moves continually forward' (Charney 1998: 135). Thus cinematic time is constructed through intermittence.

Dziga Vertov

One of the first filmmakers to realise a fully bio-mechanical vision of the cinema was Dziga Vertov. Vertov theorised as an ideal the merging of a mechanical eye with the human eye through the gaze of the camera in what he called the *kinopravda* principle. *Kinopravda*, which means 'film-truth', is the photographic process of capturing 'life unawares', or recording 'life-as-it-is'. In this principle, the camera's speed and ability to see more than the human eye makes it superior in perceiving the true structure of reality in flux, overcoming the limitations of the human optical sensory apparatus which is unable to perceive all the invisible phases of movement. The camera is an ideal eye that perfectly embodies what Nietzsche calls 'the optical habit of seeking' truth (Nietzsche 1968: 185). Kino-truth is a vision of cinematography as a new sensational tool for human perception, one that can enunciate reality, not just as it appears, but as it truly is, by permanently affixing the segments of movement in images that can be scrutinised. Vertov saw the entire cinematic apparatus as a superb bionic prosthetic for our body and senses. The cine-machine takes on a living perception, transforming itself from an eye to an all-perceiving 'I', and in the process creates what Vertov calls the 'autonomous cine-thing' that expresses real life in all of its change and mobility. The cine-thing is a new visual structure that penetrates into the hidden reality of the external world, a witness to the speediness of life-facts. The cinema functions as a panoramic mirror 'freed from the frame of time and space' capable of representing 'in a new way a world unknown to you' (Vertov 1984 18). Deeply immersed in Marxist theory and dedicated to the cause of the Russian revolution (as was Eisenstein), Vertov conceived of the cine-thing almost solely in terms of the dynamism of dialectical materialism. Annette Michelson argues that, for Vertov:

> The systematic development of the specificity of cinematic processes – slow, accelerated, and reversed motion, of split-screen, and of superimposition, those disjunctions, tensions and movements specific to cinema – were indeed to be harnessed in the service of revelation: but that revelation was a reading, a communist decoding of the world as social text, inseparable from the identification of class structure and class interests. (Vertov 1984: xlv–xlvi)

Vertov supplemented *kinopravda* with another principle he called *kinoglaz* or 'film-eye'. *Kinoglaz* is the method of assembling the visual structure of reality captured by the camera through montage. Since the cinematic frame is not static like the still photograph, the cine-thing must be constructed by associating bits and pieces of recorded reality. Life is constantly in motion, and must have a kinetic method for revealing it. Though the roots of cinematography can be found in photographic realism, the real essence of the cinema lies in 'the art of organising the necessary movements of objects in space', both within the frame and in the movement between the frames (Vertov 1984: 8). The cine-thing is constructed by an association of individual film frames through montage in a kinaesthetic organisation of a cinema of facts and, as such, is not just a sum of recorded facts but 'the product of a higher mathematics of facts' (Vertov 1984: 84).

Vertov's *Man with the Movie Camera* (1927) is the film in which he fully exploits the dialectical movement between kino-truth and kino-eye. The movie documents both a day in the life of ordinary people in Moscow and the cameraman as an integral and mobile worker capturing it all on film. It also celebrates the camera by revealing the camera at work as the roving kino-eye. *Man with the Movie Camera* exploits the constructivist practice of 'baring its own devices' by constantly revealing the presence of the peripatetic cameraman and his camera as well as self-referencing the process of editing the film. The camera enunciates itself as an 'outside' that is 'inside', consciously moving through the city as the unblinking eye of truth.

Yuri Tsivian goes so far as to declare that *Man with the Movie Camera* realises the power of cinema 'not to show, but to think – that is, to disclose the invisible connections between things' (2006: 99). Walter Benjamin goes even further, linking the power of cinema beyond conscious thinking to a new form of probing analysis, even citing walking as an exemplary case:

> Evidently a different nature speaks to the camera than opens to the naked eye – if only because an unconsciously penetrated space is substituted for a space consciously explored by man. Even if one has a general knowledge of the way people walk, one knows nothing of a person's posture during the fractional second of a stride . . . Here the camera intervenes with the resources of its lowerings and liftings, its interruptions and isolations . . . The camera introduces us to unconscious optics as does psychoanalysis to unconscious impulses. (Benjamin et al. 1968: 236–7)

As a medium inscribed in the primacy of vision, the cinema would seem to exemplify ocular-centrism and the film image instituted by immediacy and presence. There are, however, many reasons to object to these claims. We have already discussed montage as a constitutive element of the filmic image, but the mechanisms of montage in the cinema which conspire to displace presence – concentrated in the relationship between the filmmaking process and the spectator – are not limited to the 'shot' or image. This is an argument alluded to by film theorist Jean-Louis Baudry. Arguing that the film camera is one in a long line of optical instruments since the Renaissance that has produced a new mode of representation in which the 'subject' becomes the centre of meaning, Baudry writes about the ideological effects produced and concealed by the technical operations of the camera. Important for our discussion is the montage structure which provides the framework for the camera's process of producing images: 'Central in the process of production of the film, the camera – an assembly of optical and mechanical instrumentation – carries out a certain mode of inscription carried out by marking, by the recording of differences . . . between the frames' (Rosen 1986: 288). The camera takes 'instants of time' or slices of reality that are selected, elaborated, and worked upon, and registers them as a succession of images through mechanical instrumentation. But the succession of images inscribed by the camera can only be animated through the operation of a projector which 'restores continuity of movement and the temporal dimension to the sequence of static images' (Rosen 1986: 290). What Baudry finds problematic is the relation between the illusion of continuity provided by projection and the discontinuous elements inscribed by the camera. The meaning effects produced by this relation depend neither exclusively on the content of the image, nor on the process of projecting the illusion of continuity. Rather, they are produced in the intervals between their interrelated elements and systemic relations:

> Couldn't we thus say that cinema reconstructs and forms the mechanical model . . . of a system of writing . . . constituted by a material base and countersystem . . . which uses the system while also concealing it? . . . The projection mechanism allows the differential elements (the discontinuity inscribed by the camera) to be suppressed, bringing only the relation into play. The individual images as such disappear so that movement and continuity can appear. But movement and continuity are the visible expression (one might even say, the projection) of their relations, derived from the tiny discontinuities between the images. (Rosen 1986: 291)

The differences and discontinuities between the separate frames inscribed by the camera are essential for the creation of the illusion of movement and continuous passage of time in the cinema. Movement and continuity are thus only the visible expression of their relations of difference (Rosen 1986: 291). But for Baudry, the dilemma is expressed in the one condition under which these differences can produce this passage; that is, they must be effaced as differences. Baudry believes that this dilemma is finally resolved by the spectator, who is liberated by the transformation of discontinuity into continuous movement because his subjectivity is 'positioned' through a similar process of negation and denial of difference: 'With continuity restored, both meaning and consciousness are restored' (Rosen 1986: 291).

In the end, cinematic movement aligns with one of the many vectors of modernity. It is produced by an inherently fragmented apparatus, addressed to a divided and fractured spectatorial subject, sent as an already broken text, and transmitted through a mechanism which enunciates that text's heterogeneity. Yet, in its visual and audibly vagrant intermittencies, one can find an analogue to that most humble of movements, that is, walking.

Notes

1. In 'Notes on Gesture' Agamben situates what he considers an important founding gesture of cinema in Gilles de Tourette's experiment to graph the human step in 1885:

   > A roll of white wallpaper around seven or eight meters long and fifty centimetres wide is rolled to the floor and split in half lengthwise with a pencilled line. In the experiment the soles of the subject's feet are then sprinkled with powdered iron sesquioxide which gives them a nice rust-red colour. The footprints left by the patient walking along the guiding line enable the gait to be measured with perfect precision. (Agamben 1993: 135)

   Agamben compares this experiment to Muybridge's earlier photographic studies. De Tourette's method is an example of chronography (a graphic method), and illustrates the widespread scientific interest in studying human locomotion using chronography as an experimental tool. However, Marey's chronographic studies of walking predate de Tourette's experiment, and, as we have shown, by 1883 Marey had already abandoned chronography after inventing the much more precise method of chronophotography.
2. The last surviving film shot with this camera is *Man Walking Around a Corner*. Only sixteen frames long, it shows a man turning a corner in front of a factory building. Because the frames lurch around so much, it is difficult to make out much detail when watching the film, making for a frenetic viewing experience. However, I find it notable that the first two examples of cinema take as their subject peripatetic motion.
3. For a thorough summary of the complicated history of Le Prince and Edison's patent war, see Howells, Richard (2006), 'Louis Le Prince: The Body of Evidence', *Screen* 47, no. 2, 20 June 2006, pp. 179–200.

CHAPTER 2

Tramping with Chaplin

> *Those Charlie Chaplin feet,*
> *Those funny Chaplin feet,*
> *When he comes down the street*
> *He starts to slip, trip,*
> *And tumble 'round the block.*
> Chorus of *Those Charlie*
> *Chaplin Feet* by Edgar Leslie

A dusty country road winds its way around the bottom of a steep, grassy hill. In the middle of the lane, a down and out looking man clumsily, yet gaily, walks towards the camera. In one hand he carries a small bindle and in the other a flimsy bamboo walking stick. His clothes are loose and ill-fitted, especially his baggy trousers. Our gaze is drawn to his feet, which are fitted with shoes that are absurdly large, the thin leather of the toe caps bent upwards. These shoes cause him to walk with an uncomfortable looking splay-footed gait, knees bent outwards. Only the heels of his shoes touch the ground with each step. As he gets closer to the camera he stops to remove something from a hole in the sole of his right shoe. A car comes up from behind and almost hits him as it passes, kicking up a cloud of dust. He falls over backwards and loses his bowler hat. Just when he picks it up, another car speeding from the other direction barely misses him, causing him to spin around and fall backwards again with hat, bindle and cane still in hand. As he gets up, he puts his hat back on, pulling a clothes brush out of his coat pocket. After cupping his mouth with his hand and muttering something to no one in particular, he begins regally brushing the dirt off of his old and battered clothes as if they were brand new. Bending over with his bum to the camera, he reaches between his legs to brush the back of his pants, revealing two holes in the back of his coat, then pulls the back of his baggy pants to the front like wing flaps to give each side a good dusting off. After wiping his brow, he glances inside the waistband of his pants, checks his bindle, shrugs his shoulder and merrily walks undefeated towards the camera and out of frame. Thus we are introduced for the first time to Charlie Chaplin's fully fledged character of 'The Tramp' in the opening scene of his 1915 Essanay film *The Tramp*. That same year *Motion Picture Magazine* gave high praise to Chaplin's new creation, declaring:

> While he was walking down the road, there was dejection in every movement. But the light-heartedness of the nomad again gained the ascendancy. Chaplin shook himself, gave a characteristic flirt of his coat, and wandered jauntily out of the picture. And the audience smiled, with tears in its eyes. (McQuirk 1915: 89)

The modern word 'tramp' derives from the middle English verb *trampen* which means 'to walk heavily'. It was not until the late seventeenth century that it took the pejorative form of a noun signifying a vagabond, vagrant or a homeless transient and was lumped together with other undesirable types of vagrants such as chronic alcoholics, peddlers, habitual criminals and lunatics. In an essay tracing the figure of the tramp throughout American literature, Christine Photinos shows that by the turn of the twentieth century the image of the tramp, and tramping, slowly shifted from that of a congenitally lazy social deviant (often an immigrant) to a heroic figuration of a new form of American masculinity that eschewed bourgeoisie domesticity as effeminate (Photinos 2008). Dubbed the 'gentleman of the road', the tramp distinguished himself from the common hobo mainly by two traits: preferring to beg for his daily wants rather than seeking work and travelling on foot rather than riding the rails (although the vastness of the North American continent made hopping trains a necessity for the American tramp beating his way between large cities and towns). Self-acclaimed Welsh *super-tramp* and poet W. H. Davies writes affectionately of a tramp named Brun with whom he tramped for a time in America:

> Brum was a genuine beggar, who did not make flashes in the dark, having one day plenty and nothing on the next day. What he required he proceeded to beg, every morning making an inventory of his wants. Rather than wash a good handkerchief he would beg an old one that was clean, and he would without compunction discard a good shirt altogether rather than sew a button on – thus keeping up the dignity of his profession to the extreme . . . Begging was to him a fine art, indeed, and a delight of which he never seemed to tire. (Davies 2015: 36)

The tramp became an icon of the masculine outsider, who sets off alone to reassert his manhood in wandering and adventure-seeking, like the cowboy heroes of the previous century (though without their work ethic). After 1910, leftist literary radicals such as John Dos Passos began to portray the tramp not just as a man fleeing the 'strictures of domesticity' but also as 'a kind of industrial hero for whom wandering represented a successful escape from the indignities of the industrial factory' (Photinos 2008: 4).

Chaplin's iconic character followed this same evolution, beginning life in 1914 at Keystone Studios as a negative stereotype of the tramp more commonly found in the nineteenth century. A semi-employed and more often than not married rake, the early character Chaplin called 'the little man' was an unsympathetic persona verging on villainy. Chaplin refined his on-screen persona through a series of Keystone one-reelers until landing at Essanay Studios in 1915, where the final version of the tramp emerged fully forged in the 1915 film *The Tramp* as the sympathetic hero of the everyman, familiar to us today. Chaplin described the essence of the Tramp's character as 'shabby gentility'. Though Chaplin himself grew up in crippling poverty in London slums – even spending eighteen months of his childhood in a boarding school for orphans and the destitute – his character exudes the dress and mannerisms of a middle-class gentleman who has fallen on hard times and is forced to go out onto the road.[1] Robert Warshow elaborates on the Tramp's attempts to maintain this gentility as a rootless (though not aimless) outcast in the midst of bourgeoisie culture:

> Chaplin's Tramp, taken in his most direct significance, represented the good-hearted and personally cultivated individual in a heartless and vulgar society. The society was concerned only with the pursuit of profit, and often not even with that so much as with the mere preservation of the ugly and impersonal machinery by which profit was gained; the Tramp was concerned with the practice of personal relations and social graces. Most of all the Tramp was like an aristocrat fallen on hard times, for what he attempted in all his behaviour was to maintain certain standards of refinement and humanity, to keep life dignified and make it emotionally and aesthetically satisfying. (Warshow 2002: 177)

The ill-fitted and absurd costume worn by the Tramp – ridiculously baggy trousers, a bamboo walking stick, a tight cutaway waistcoat and oversized boots – seems to be concocted by Chaplin not only to epitomise the Tramp's sideways slide into trampdom, but also to facilitate and motivate his awkward and comedic style of walking. In fact, the Tramp's splay-foot walk, what Bazin called his duck-like waddle, was largely the effect of Chaplin, whose own shoe size was a minuscule five, donning size fourteen brogans. According to Chaplin, his choice of shoes was a deliberate decision to complete his character:

> I debated a long time about the shoes. My feet are small and I thought perhaps they might be funnier in tight shoes, under the baggy trousers. At last, however, I decided on the long, flat, floppy shoes, which would trip me up unexpectedly. (Chaplin 2005: 169)

For the most part, the Tramp is a city dweller. His domain is the street and crowded immigrant neighbourhoods. Henri Lefebvre defines the modern city as '*production of society on the ground*', inscribed with the rhythms and patterns of the social order as a whole (Kofman and Lebas 1996: 108; italics in the original). It is a site of conflicting and contested desires, but also a centre of organised decision-making concentrated on regulating these desires resulting in the '*exploitation* of the whole society' (Kofman and Lebas 1996: 108; italics in the original). This decision-making filtered individual desires into the rhythm of a social order based on timeliness, production, schedules and work. But this contestation of desires means that the city can also be a site of individual resistance to the social order. One form of resistance is the everyday practice of walking.

Walking and Resistance

In Chaplin's case, this possibility of resistance is made even more evident if we adopt Michel de Certeau's 'rhetoric' of walking in the city as a way to make legible the Tramp's subversive disordering of the power structures embedded by urban planners as he moves about the cityscape. In his essay 'Walking in the City', De Certeau describes pedestrians as 'ordinary practitioners of the city' and argues that walking is a primary modality of everyday life in the city. He presents a semiotic analysis juxtaposing an ideal city ('concept-city') as planned by official urban bureaucrats and managers with the 'real' one inhabited at street level by urban dwellers. Modern city planners have created urban spaces as a rational matrix purposefully organised to suppress any physical, mental or socio-political urban practices that opposes its regulatory forms and structure. These forms take the shape of rigid geometrical patterns dreamt up by urban space planners as imagined from atop a skyscraper, a sort of panoptic simulacrum of the real city 'down below', where the movements of people can be regulated, especially as they move through officially sanctioned spaces as seen from above. This panoramic city exists only as a projection of these space planners, a fiction that makes the 'complexity of the city readable' from above while at the same time immobilising '[the city's] opaque mobility in a transparent text' and whose possibility is conditioned on an 'oblivion and a misunderstanding of practices' (de Certeau 2011: 92). In contrast, the inhabitants of the real city escape the 'imaginary totalisations produced by the eye' of the cartographers and urban planners through ordinary, everyday practices such as walking:

> The ordinary practitioners of the city live 'down below', below the thresholds at which visibility begins. They walk – an elementary form of this experience of the city; they

are walkers, *Wandersmänner*, whose bodies follow the thicks and thins of the urban 'text' they write without being able to read it. These practitioners make use of spaces that cannot be seen . . . A *migrational*, or metaphorical, city thus slips into the clear text of the planned and readable city. (de Certeau 2011: 93)

While it is possible to retrace the path of a walker on a city map, the individuated, singular moments of 'passing by' such places as a shop window, restaurant, city park and other passers-by that constitutes the act of walking in the city escapes the totalising effects of mapping. Such everyday pedestrian passer-by encounters erase themselves, as they happen, from the geographical system designed to contain them. It is not city maps that give shape to urban spaces; it is rather the infinitely 'intertwined paths' of walkers as an 'innumerable collection of singularities' way marking the urban landscape with their own invisible signatures as their moving bodies articulate the shape and syntax of a walk (de Certeau 2011: 97). Walking is more than just a spatial activity; it is a gesture of spatialising itself that perpetually reworks the meaning of city streets and pavements. There is a psychodynamics of 'place' at work in this gesture in which the cartography of walking as a practice is remapped as a subversive, prohibitive activity which disrupts the design of urban space. Thus, the city as metropolis bears little resemblance to the city as panoply.

The Tramp is the disruptor par excellence of the panoptic city. As a director, Chaplin likes to shoot the Tramp from street level. Whether he is ambling aimlessly down a pavement or being chased by a policeman around city blocks, we almost always view the Tramp in full frame. Garbed in this outlandish footwear, Chaplin's feet can carry his performance from the real to the surreal, effortlessly slipping from one to another. He can go instantly from a casual stroll to a gravity defying flat-out run when chased, skidding around corners 'in geometrically intricate patterns, like a 90-degree angle balanced on one leg' before executing his escape with a pivot on the heel (Bean 2011: 243). Oscillating between motility and immobility, the Tramp zigzags from one instant to another, hopping, halting, kicking and swerving in fits of staccato rhythms.

The Tramp's jerky perambulations and mechanical gait mirrors the automatism at the heart of modern city life, a form of innervation that is an emblem of alienation at the same time as a protest against it. The hiccups and hesitations in his quirky gait makes Chaplin appear to be in a perpetual state of discontinuity, not only with gravity but also with his own immediate surroundings and necessities (Wall-Romana 2015: 170). This discontinuity, as Benjamin observes, mirrors the dialectical structure of film's technological dimension itself, where 'discontinuous images replace one another in a continuous sequence' (Benjamin et al. 2002b: 94). It is this doubling of gestures of discontinuity in both the production and consumption of moving images that accounts for Chaplin's comic success. Chaplin reconstructs movement in sequence with a film's innervations that unsettles the false unity of panoptic life. This is perhaps one of the reasons audiences of all classes, gender and social status begin laughing so hard as soon as Chaplin begins to move on the screen, 'dissolving the unified integrity of civilised spectators into a mass of uncontrollable bodies' (Wild 2015: 254). People laugh, nervously, because Chaplin's abnormal ambulation directly confronts them with the absurd, staccato nature of modern life they recognise in their own experiences:

> Chaplin's way of moving [Gestus] is not really that of an actor. He could not have made an impact on the stage. His unique significance lies in the fact that, in his work, the human being is integrated into the image by way of his gestures – that is, his bodily and mental posture. The innovation of Chaplin's gestures is that he dissects the expressive movements of human beings into a series of minute innervations. Each single movement he makes is composed of a succession of staccato bits of movement. (Benjamin et al. 2002b: 94)

In the passage above, Benjamin hints at his own unique use of Freud's concept of *innervation*. Freud developed a rich theory of innervation that connects to Benjamin's use of the term and has special relevance for the nature of the cinematic apparatus.

Innervations

In 1895 Freud, who began his medical career as a neurologist, and his mentor Joseph Breuer published a book titled *Studies in Hysteria* based on the case of one of Breuer's patients named Anna O. It is in this text that Freud first laid out his psychodynamic theory to explain mental processes that he would later fully develop into the psychoanalytical method of therapy we know today. An important principle of Freud's psychodynamic theory is that our feelings and behaviour as adults are rooted in our childhood experiences, often traumatic ones, which we have repressed. But the central tenet of his by now well-known theory is that much of mental life – including thoughts, feelings and motives – is unconscious, which means that people can behave in ways or develop symptoms that are inexplicable to themselves. Thus, in his early paraneurological writings Freud seized on the concept of innervation. He defined innervation as 'an energy transfer from the psychic to the somatic' where repressed psychic energy is discharged into the nervous system resulting in a hidden cause of unwanted and uncontrolled bodily compulsions. The process of innervation usually works unidirectionally to convert energy from the nervous system outwards to the muscles, but Freud postulated that it can work in the opposite direction (Frymer et al. 2011: 83).

In *Interpretation of Dreams*, Freud compares the psychical apparatus to an optical instrument with various lenses:

> All our psychical activity starts from stimuli [whether internal or external] and ends in innervations. Accordingly, we shall ascribe a sensory and a motor end to the apparatus. At the sensory end there lies a system which receives perceptions; at the motor end there lies another, which opens the gateway to motor activity. Psychical processes advance in general from the perceptual end to the motor end. (quoted in Hansen 2012: 136)

Elsewhere Freud connects it particularly to ocular perception, arguing that the most common instances of innervation are of images and the movement of images.

Freud's postulations about innervation led him to ascribe the complex working of our psychical apparatus to the operation of two distinct systems, the perception-consciousness system where perceptions are recorded without retaining any permanent traces and the mnemonic one where our perceiving consciousness stores our enduring perceptions. Freud found an analogical key to how the two systems worked in combination in a child's toy marketed as the Wunderblock or 'Mystic Writing Pad'. Freud viewed the Mystic Writing Pad, like the psychical apparatus itself, as yet another kind of optical machine. It is composed of a block of wax overlaid with a sheet of paper consisting of two layers; the top layer is a transparent sheet of celluloid, and the bottom layer is made up of a thin translucent sheet of wax paper. Both sheets are firmly secured to the wax and one another at their top edge, the bottom edges resting loosely without being fastened to the block of wax. The operator of the machine uses a pointed stylus to 'record' (scratch) on the celluloid covering sheet, pressing the wax paper onto the block of wax, leaving deep impressions (images) in the wax, but leaving no visible marks on the surface of the celluloid. The layer of celluloid serves as a protective layer over the wax paper, which otherwise would tear from the violence of the stylus. The advantage of this double system of image making is that if one wishes to destroy what has been recorded, they need only lift the double covering from the surface of the wax block and it is cleanly erased and ready for the next fresh impression.

Freud likens the protective nature of the celluloid covering to the model of the perceptual apparatus of our mind that consists of two layers, the top layer functioning as an external protective shield over the surface of memory against the direct and immediate impression of perceptual stimuli. This top perceptual layer receives the perceptual stimuli, yet retains no traces of the violent impression of the stimuli, which are only left underneath in the layer of memory. So memory receives traces of perception that never appeared on the top protective layer which directly received the original impressions. Thus, there is never a pure or wholly defined image of perception; conscious perception is always delayed through the device of memory and we only gain access to the stimuli of perception through the detour of memory. Hence, the Mystic Writing Pad might be called a cinematic apparatus (which in turn might be described as an innervation machine), projecting subjectivity as a flickering of arrested images erased as soon as they appear followed by a repetition of the entire process.

Like Freud, Benjamin's concept of modernity is neurological and rooted in shock (Buck-Morss 1992: 16). By the time he began writing on the cinema in the 1920s, the physiology of film spectatorship was already well studied and documented. The idea of the cinema as an apparatus of both distractions and attractions that delivers visual and psycho-motor shocks to the sensorium of spectators was a recurrent theme in scholarly articles and newspaper film criticism alike. Jean Epstein's assertion in 1921 that '[film] is nothing but a relay between the source of nervous energy and the audience' was a typical claim for the era.[2] But Benjamin is one of the first thinkers to write about cinema as a total apparatus of shocks and jolts, one which operates reciprocally on both sides of the screen. He directly connects his discussion of film and innervation to new understandings of human consciousness and places Chaplin at the centre of its expression.

Benjamin views cinema as an innervation machine which promises to 'make the vast technical apparatus of our time an object of human innervation' (quoted in Hansen 2012: 132). Thus cinema is a new optical unconscious, possessing the 'ability of the apparatus and particular photographic techniques to register aspects of material reality that are invisible to the unarmed human eye' – and, conversely, an opening up of a 'new region of consciousness' (Richter 2002: 66). As Mariam Hansen argues, Benjamin's application of the psychodynamic concept of innervations to cinema, and particularly to Chaplin's machine-like way of moving and walking through space, hinges on the 'chance to engage the senses differently . . . in the epochal reconfiguration of body- and image-space', a space in which Benjamin 'observes a [new] mode of reception, corresponding to this new image world, that combines sensational affect with reflexivity and, conversely, reflexivity with sensory immediacy' (Richter 2002: 64–5). Furthermore,

Benjamin likens Chaplin himself to the embodiment of this new reciprocating innervational machine: 'Whether it is his walk, the way he handles his cane, or the way he raises his hat – always the same jerky sequence of tiny movements applies the law of the cinematic image sequence to human motorial functions' (Benjamin et al. 2002b: 94).

Chaplin's innervational modes of movement might also be described as *unnerving*, straining the nerves of spectators and on-screen characters (including the Tramp) alike as they become physically unstrung (the audience through laughter and the characters through frustration). His repetitive and rhythmic movements serve to randomly 'shock' people he passes on the street and even some objects that suddenly appear in his way. In *The Pawnshop*, he examines an alarm clock as if it were a medical patient, eventually dissecting it using a can opener as a scalpel. He dines on his own shoes in *The Gold Rush*, then playfully turns two dinner rolls into dancing feet at the end of his forks. When Big Jim in his hunger hallucinates the Tramp turning into a chicken, Chaplin in his chicken costume walks like the Tramp and not a chicken.

Jean Epstein commented on what he called Chaplin's *photogenic neurasthenia*, observing that 'Chaplin has created the overwrought hero . . . [whose] entire performance consists of reflexes of a nervous, tired person' (quoted in McParland 2014: 99). Thus, in his kinesis he treats his own body as an object, one that becomes unnerved by a reciprocal shock from an object he tries to control. In *The Rink* the Tramp is a hapless waiter who tries to mix a cocktail in a cocktail shaker, only to find the shaker immobile between his hands as the rest of his body shakes and shudders as if he were using a jackhammer. He might unexpectedly kick open a swinging saloon door only to have it kick him back. Sometimes his repetitive movements unnerve him so much that he 'forms instant habits', his body going on autopilot, such as the feather dusting scene in *The Pawnshop* where he gets so habituated in his work routine he ends up dusting an electric fan which 'shred[s] the duster into a blizzard of swirling feathers' (Kamin 2008: 61).

But the Tramp's shocks are most unnerving to other characters whom he gleefully treats as kinetic objects. Dan Kamin has noted key instances of what he calls Chaplin's 'body-as-thing' idea in gags such as when 'fallen bodies are trod over as if they're carpets', a man's injured foot, wrapped in an absurdly large and bulky bandage, is 'stepped and sat upon, caught in a revolving door, and kicked' repeatedly by Charlie. Another example is when rear ends are 'gently moved aside then put back as Charlie passes' as he does repeatedly in *The Rink* (Kamin 2008: 61). But no other gesture embodies the body-as-thing idea better than the Tramp's signature backward kick. Bazin dissects it this way:

> It is with a simple and yet sublime gesture that Charlie expresses his supreme detachment from that biographical and social world in which we are plunged and which, for us, is a cause for regret and uneasiness, namely that remarkable backward kick which he em-ploys to dispose alike of a banana peel, the head of Goliath and, more ideally still, of every bothersome thought. It is significant that Charlie never kicks straight ahead. Even when he kicks his partners in the pants he manages to do it while looking the other way. A cobbler would explain that this was because of the points of his outsize shoes. However, perhaps I may be allowed to ignore this piece of superficial realism and to see in the style and frequent and very personal use of this backward kick the reflection of a very vital approach to things. (Bazin 1968: 149–50)

It is important to note that Chaplin's 'vital approach to things' means that in the Tramp's world, objects do not behave according to their utilitarian purpose and this includes his own body as an object in the world. Thus Bazin and others find in gestures such as the backward kick a nuanced reflection of the Tramp's refusal to be attached to the conventions of the past while at the same time disrupting any utilitarian hopes for an ideal future where things built for man by man, including society, serve him according to their original built-in purposes. Since 'things' do not behave for Charlie as they would normally; he is therefore free to constantly improvise with whatever object is at hand – or foot – to overcome any situation that is not going his way, even turning an object's malfunction to his own advantage. His outsized shoes can thus function as improvisational props (things in the world) to be deployed when necessary while at the same time pointing to their own malfunction as the cradle for his need to improvise in the first place (his vital approach to things). Thus his duck-waddle walk is one physical signifier among many of his ability to work out an almost care-free improvisational solution to any problem. The comic effect of the gag works so well because the audience can easily imagine another perhaps more rational solution to the problem – to simply exchange his gargantuan shoes for a smaller size.

Subjectility, Projectiles and *Modern Times*

I see in Chaplin's screen kinesis, especially his walk, an almost perfect example of an actor using his body as a *subjectile*, a concept most fully fleshed out by Derrida in his book *The Secret of Antonin Artaud*. A term originally belonging to art, the dictionary definition of subjectile is a 'substrate, material, or support upon which a painting or engraving is created'. The term can also be used to denote the underlying and often unnoticed support for any type of image or text. Derrida goes further, finding in the *subjectile* a site where the age-old cleaving between subject and object is once again put into play:

> Both a substance and a subject . . . Between the beneath and the above, it is at once a support and a surface . . . everything distinct from form, as well as meaning and representation . . . Is not a subject, still less the subjective, nor is it the object either . . . (Derrida and Thévenin 1998)

It is also a useful concept for describing what lies beneath the valence of an actor's performance on screen (as the screen itself is a subjectile), those 'interior constants that are the true constituents of [a] character' (Bazin 1968: 144). There are affinities between a subjectile and a projectile and for the remainder of this chapter I will explore these as they coalesce in perhaps Chaplin's most famous performance as the Tramp in *Modern Times*, a film which also marks the last screen appearance of Charlie's little Tramp.

We take it for granted, perhaps, that a film actor's performance is projected to us *on* the screen and not the actor *through* the screen. Stanley Cavell claims this 'projected visibility' accounts for our 'sublime comprehensibility of Chaplin's natural choreography' (Cavell 1979: 36). But with Chaplin I would go further and argue that sometimes the force of his screen performance is projected *at* us. This is the case of the Tramp in *Modern Times*. The film has already been the subject of multiple analyses citing it as a biting, stylised satire of Fordism. It pokes serious fun at the perilous rise of industrial automation and the corresponding nightmare of a standardised way of life regulated by the tyranny of the machine ruling over workers performing monotonous, repetitive tasks on assembly lines to the point where they become a collection of overwrought, dehumanised automatons. Scholars and audiences alike recognise the film's opening act as a humorous but not over exaggerated critique of Taylor's human efficiency studies in which he used photography to atomise the gestures of factory workers in order to synchronise their movements with the hands of a clock. While taking a similar tack, my analysis will focus on just one scene where the Tramp gets caught up in the unbridled mechanisation of life in the streets while simply walking. It takes place after the more famous factory assembly line scene, when, after being caught up in the gears of a conveyor belt then forced to test a mechanical feeding device, he suffers a nervous breakdown and is carted off to a mental hospital.

The scene opens as the Tramp is walking out the door and down the steps of the hospital from which he has just been released after being 'cured' of his nervous breakdown suffered in the factory. Yet perhaps he is not fully cured. Before the Tramp reaches the bottom of the stairs, we see a short montage of dissolving shots of automation scenes framed in canted angles – a pair of hands operating a pneumatic wrench, two fire engines whizzing by, street cars, buses, cars and crowds of pedestrians crossing busy streets – then a dissolve to a full shot of the Tramp walking into the frame on a pavement from the right side of the screen. He is walking aimlessly – a true tramp and dejected vagabond on the verge of loitering. His dejection is captured in Paul Virilio's observation that the individual 'will always be in a state of resistance, whether accelerating as he is going down, or slowing down as he is climbing up, whereas when one walks on a horizontal plane weight is nil (or equal)' (Virilio 2001: 51). The frame is dominated by a brick building with a large 'Closed' sign across its double doors. His body as subjectile is in a state of surrender as he walks past the closed up factory, yet he seems to be gearing up in his movements for some oncoming struggle. Just to the left of the doors is another sign hanging on the brick wall that reads in all capitals 'PRIVATE KEEP OUT'. As he is passing in front of the 'Closed' sign, the Tramp trips over his own left foot and gives a backward glance over his shoulder (a slightly less defiant form of the backward kick) as he walks on, then turns his head to throw a fleeting look at the private property sign before reaching a street intersection. As he waits on the corner to cross the street, a construction truck passes in front of him and he takes notice of a red warning flag hanging precariously on a board of oversized lumber sticking out from the truck's tailgate. We next see a shot from inside the truck bed of the board and flag hanging over the street as the truck is moving away from the Tramp. We catch glimpses of the feet of pedestrians crossing the street behind the truck when, finally, the flag falls off the board into the middle of the street. As it hits the pavement, the Tramp comes into view again running into the intersection to retrieve the flag. It is here where the Tramp's inertia as he walks passes from – or through – the subjectile to the projectile: 'The subjectile, a screen or support for representation, must be traversed by the projectile. We have to pass beneath the one that is already beneath' (Derrida and Thévenin 1998: 77). He picks up the flag and begins to wave it towards the camera, receding into the backdrop of a harbour at the end of the street as the truck and camera move further away. Chaplin then cuts to a medium shot of the Tramp in centre frame shouting and waving the red flag to signal the truck driver to stop. The driver fails to notice him, but, unbeknownst to the Tramp, a crowd of unemployed protesters carrying signs agitating for solidarity and shouting communist slogans are coming around the corner, marching up behind him as he innocently keeps waving the red flag. Just as the marchers reach him, the Tramp, still ignorant of their presence, begins marching himself towards the truck, still wielding the red flag and shouting. Suddenly, the camera rises slightly up to a low bird's eye view as the Tramp and the protesters behind him stop, a look of fear sweeping across their faces, until we see mounted riot policemen enter from the front of the frame and begin to beat and break up the mob. Like in the factory, the Tramp is again caught up in the cogs of the capitalist machine. And just as before, his disruption of this machine leads to an eruption of chaos. During the melee, the Tramp somehow ends up in a manhole, and when he emerges holding the flag above his head as a gesture of surrender he is mistaken for the leader of the communist protest and promptly arrested and thrown into jail, proof once more to the Tramp and the marchers that the inert body passing through the projectile 'must not resist too much. If it does, it has to be *mistreated*, violently attacked' (Derrida and Thévenin 1998: 76–7).

Once again the Tramp *casts* himself into a situation where, in his attempt to use a tool in the social function for which it was designed, he is betrayed by that very object through society's misconstruction of its purpose. But it is not just the function of the red flag that social forces misconstrue; it is also the Tramp's perambulating body that sets the framework for the social misunderstanding.

From the moment he trips over his own feet his body acts compulsively – moving from inertia to propulsion to expulsion within a matter of seconds. Here Chaplin's subjectility is the support for a *misrepresentation*. It is only when we see the Tramp in a medium shot that he begins to 'resist too much', but without his even knowing it. The crowd behind him *propels* him as if he is the leader of a resistance. The little Tramp as subjectile becomes an inverse projectile whose inertia in the face of – or back to – the forward propulsion of the mob leads him from behind into a state of unknowing resistance to what is in front of him – namely the construction truck. The truck too is another subjectile perforated by the number of unemployed who would rather have a job as the truck driver than be out of work and on the street. The Tramp is flagging down the entire capitalist system to stop and look behind it at the thousands of unemployed beating the pavement looking for work. His own inertia in walking is nil, yet somehow it becomes a march for justice, a form of horizontal resistance. Yet the Tramp is part of the collective protest only accidentally. He is only walking and never really marching. The city laid out on a grid pattern makes it that much easier for the police to break up the march. The city street and sidewalk themselves offer no resistance to the social forces of industrialised capitalism; that is a job for the Tramp and his fellow walkers.

Notes

1. In a speech he gave to the Academy of Sciences Hall in San Francisco in 1902, Jack London observed that:

    The tramp does not usually come from the slums. His place of birth is ordinarily a bit above, and sometimes a very great bit above. A confessed failure, he yet refuses to accept the punishment, and swerves aside from the slum to vagabondage. The average beast in the social pit is either too much of a beast, or too much of a slave to the bourgeois ethics and ideals of his masters, to manifest this flicker of rebellion. (London 2012: 46)

2. For a detailed study of how ubiquitous these ideas were, see Rae Beth Gordon (2001), 'From Charcot to Charlot: Unconscious Imitation and Spectatorship in French Cabaret and Early Cinema', Critical Inquiry, 27 (3), 515–49.

CHAPTER 3

The Pedestrian Camera

You walk out of the theatre and drift along in one unbroken flow. Turning is panning. Moving is tracking. Seeing is shooting. Time is duration. Being is drifting is recording is dreaming. Steady. Steady. You're a camera.

Eric Hynes 'Center of Gravity'

Our legs and neck didn't wait for the cinema to invent the tracking shot and the pan.
André Bazin, *Orson Welles: A Critical View*

Open just about any textbook on film-making, turn to the chapter on cinematography, thumb over to the section on camera movement and you will learn that there are two functions of camera movements: motivated and unmotivated. Motivated camera movements are easy to spot. A character walks across a road, and the camera follows them. The camera simply tracks the action across the screen by means of dollies, various hand-held techniques, or pans. Unmotivated shots are a bit more difficult to discern, because they occur when the camera chases the action more intimately. The character reaches the other side of the road and suddenly stops to look at her watch. The camera rushes in to a close-up of the watch face. Sometimes the camera will move unmotivated in such a way that it imposes upon the story itself. Tracking back from the watch to a long shot, the camera trails the character as they resume walking. They turn left and walk out of frame as the camera loses them and tilts up to the sky to reveal a jet contrail. This then amounts to two different points of view from the moving camera's perspective: observer and participant.

In the preceding chapters we explored the most basic form of movement in film – subject and object movements in front of the camera and within the projected image. That is, mobility within the frame. The aim of this chapter is to foreground the mobility of the frame itself, how a camera, itself in motion, captures the motion of subjects and objects it films. I will follow David Bordwell and Kristin Thompson's suggestion in *Film Art: An*

Introduction that we define mobile framing to mean 'that, within the image, the framing of the object changes. The mobile frame thus produces changes of camera angle, level, height, or distance during the shot' (Bordwell and Thompson 2004: 266). A specific type of mobile framing is generated by camera movement, (as opposed to other ways of producing mobile framing, such as through zooms or CGI), which will be the focus of this chapter.

Since the invention in the last decade of the nineteenth century of the tripod and a mounted rotating head, film-makers have taken advantage of the possibilities of moving the camera through various types of deliberate pans and tilts. By the 1910s, more ambitious film-makers experimented with other ways of mobilising the camera, such as lashing it to the side of a moving train or car, even mounting it in the cockpit of an airplane. Later, tracking shots became possible with the invention of the dolly, a moving platform fastened on wheels or miniature train tracks mounted with a camera and seat for the operator. When pushed, the entire camera platform was free to glide smoothly around a film set, moving in and out, following alongside or around a moving subject or object. As lighter, more mobile friendly hand-held cameras became available, film-makers had a truly unchained instrument at their disposal, multiplying the possibilities of camera movement for operators who were now able to follow the action into the tightest spaces and move at a quicker pace. The inability to keep a hand-held shot absolutely smooth and free from shakiness led to the invention of the Steadicam, which finally allowed the camera to move about like a human body to create what I will call a *participatory peripatetic point of view*. By this I mean a filmic event focusing on someone perambulating, an event where we feel as if we are walking with the shot, our mind, body and vision all actively intertwined in the same way as the subject's when we actually walk.

Since camera pans and tilts are usually achieved by moving the camera around the rotating head mounts of a stationary tripod (equivalent to someone turning her head or looking up) as opposed to a fully mobilised camera, I will limit my exploration to dolly and Steadicam shots, especially where these shots allow the camera to become a pedestrian filming its subject at a walking pace.

Dolly Shots

The first phase of camera mobility in cinema seems to have peaked around 1916. The Edison Company's 1912 short *The Passer-by*, directed by Oscar Apfel, is usually credited as the first film to use a dolly shot. The shot moves in on the central character standing behind a desk in a stock brokerage and is motivated by the character's realisation that he just lost all of his money.

The first feature film to use dolly shots extensively is the 1914 Italian film *Cabiria*. By the early 1920s, most directors stopped experimenting with mobile framing and returned to the convention of shooting static shots with a fixed camera. However, on the rare occasion where we find camera movement in films of this period it is commonly a type of dolly shot called a parallel tracking shot, usually employed, as the term suggests, to track alongside an actor walking across the action-space at a fixed distance from the camera (Salt 1992: 157).

While working at Decla Studios, German director F. W. Murnau yearned to create a camera which 'has at last been dematerialised' so that it can glide freely across any space and at any speed. Only after the creation of such a camera would it be truly possible to make a film that captured the 'fluid architecture of bodies with blood in their veins moving through mobile space . . . a symphony made up of the harmonies of bodies and the rhythm of space; the *play of pure movement*' (quoted in Eisner 1973: 84). Anticipating by a generation Austruc's notion of *camera-stylo* (camera pen), Murnau's camera would glide through space just as smoothly as a pen across paper, and just as the pen absents itself at the end of every stroke and the reader apperceives through the hyletic data of squiggly lines of ink on the page to perceive words, sentences and ideas, so too must the moving camera disappear behind the moving image it creates.

Murnau realised this dream just as the silent era was coming to a close with his first Hollywood feature *Sunrise* (1927). In *Sunrise* he pioneered a new type of camera movement that revolutionised the way dolly shots were produced and made mobile framing conventional again. Granted an extravagant budget by 20th Century Fox, Murnau spent lavishly on building sets to accommodate very elaborate and complex tracking shots. Murnau experimented with various dollies to create innovative point of view (abbreviated from here on as POV) shots, allowing the camera, perhaps for the first time, to take the place of the film's characters and anchor the spectator within their gaze. For the most famous of these shots, a long tracking POV shot of the male lead walking through a marsh, a special elevated dolly platform was built that allowed the camera to move back and forth across the platform along with the movement of the entire dolly apparatus (Schrader 2015: 59). The shot is almost a minute and a half in length, following a nameless character ('The Man') as he treads a serpentine path through the misty glade. The shot begins with the man in the right side of the frame, the camera trailing him from behind, then tracking him on his right moving forward through the mist before he turns to his left to cross a creek. The camera dollies leftwards with the man passing under tree branches, then through a bush and then across a fence as he steps over it. He turns again and walks towards us and the camera tracks to the left away from him until he is out of frame, then dollies in to reveal a woman standing on the edge of a pond spinning a flower in her hand and then touching up her lipstick. The shot ends with the man walking back into the frame from the left to passionately embrace and kiss the woman. Murnau then cuts to the man's wife at home weeping over a child.

Dorsality

I view the movement within this shot – of both the camera and character – as a marker of what David Wills calls the 'dorsal turn' (Wills 2008: 1). Wills coins the word *dorsality* to refer, at least partially, to 'operations of reversal or reversibility as a fact of technology' (Wills 2008: 9). I find this concept of dorsality to be a rich analogue to peripatetic camera movements.

Most anthropologists view the slow turn in our evolution from quadrupeds to bipeds as hinging on the corresponding developments of our brains into a much larger organ (especially the frontal lobe) and the improvement of manual dexterity gained with the acquirement of opposable thumbs and the anatomical changes to our spine, neck and pelvis (Ingold 2004: 316). These developments in turn promoted the unique accoutrements of language and tool-making. Man becomes the inventor of technology. At the centre of this evolutionary narrative is the claim that man's uprightness, combined with the frontality of his visual stance (predators such as humans usually have forward facing eyes, whereas the eyes on most prey animals are located on the sides of their heads) allowed him to reason towards a foreseeable and knowable future, a trait claimed to be uniquely human. To rephrase Bruce Chatwin: 'The foot makes the man' (Chatwin 1987: 237).

Wills argues that we should rethink this relationship between human beings, nature and technology. This rethinking requires a reversal of the standard narrative about man's uprightness, a turning away from the notion that man is an animal who creates technology to one refocusing on the technology of the human itself. This shift requires a *return* to a view of ourselves as technological beings, a view that already lies behind, as it were, our accepted ideology of man as a forward thinking animal whose being is beyond technology. Wills names this dorsal turn back towards our original technicity *dorsality* and aligns it specifically with walking:

> Technology as mechanicity is located – not for the first time but in a particularly explicit way, that is to say, as fundamental relation to the earth as exteriority – in the step. In walking, one, the human, any given biped, is with each step correcting its bearing, limping from one foot to the other, realigning its centre of gravity, compensating

> for the disequilibrium of each movement, as it were turning one way then the other in order to advance. The particular importance of the privilege I am giving to the turn resides, therefore, in its sense of a departure that is also a detour, a deviation, a divergence into difference. We will imagine the human turning as it walks, deviating from its forward path in order, precisely, to move forward, advancing necessarily askew. To repeat: the turn is the deviation from itself by means of which the human, in being or 'moving' simply human, is understood to become technological. And such a turn begins as soon as there is understood to be any human. The human is, from the point of view of this turn, understood to become technological as soon as it becomes human, to be always already turning that way. (Wills 2008: 4)

Dorsality names a turn away from our previous animal-being as anthropoids and a return to an acknowledgement of the technological origin of the human being. Wills' original insight is to locate this technicity in the *back* of the human anatomy, in the spine as the nerve centre and support for the skull and brain, which is precognitive and before vision:

> It is in the human back as the spinal – or can we already say dorsal? – turn or adjustment, the primary or primal vertebral articulation that frees the hands to pick up stones and fashion tools, that redistributes the weight of the head and jaw to allow the brain to develop and the tongue to speak. (Wills 2008: 9)

The dorsal backbone in Murnau's shot is the moving dolly. It allows the shot to crystallise around a mixture of elements found in traditional mobile POV shots – ones that focus on the actor's face – with those of the kind Brandon Colvin calls 'displaced point of view' shots, that is, following shots where the moving camera's viewing position shifts to the back of a character's head (Colvin 2017: 194). The term 'point of view' has a double meaning, both activated in POV shots: it means seeing something from a particular vantage point, that is, from the standpoint of the subject who sees; and, it indicates a focal point in the field of view of a subject in the act of seeing (Schrift 2014: 23). Oscillating between proximity and distance between the camera and the man, Murnau's POV shot has the effect of fostering an uncanny alignment between spectator and character who share the same focal and vantage points and an overlapping sense of vision and subjectivity. All POV shots can seem uncanny, because they essentially give the spectator access to someone else's gaze, to see the world through someone else's eyes as an autonomous cognitive process. But mobile POV shots strike us more uncannily because, unlike conventional film editing techniques such as the eye line match POV which fracture our gaze, they are pre-reflective or precognitive. That is, as we move through a space we discover its parameters and depths at the same time as the roving camera does; we have virtually no way of anticipating in what direction we will be going, when we will turn, stop, lurch forward or backwards, nor even what we will see as the camera walks around exploring the screened space. Through its constant reframing and refusal to assert beforehand any psychological motivation for the character's pedestrian movements, Murnau's POV shot imposes a kind of non-cognitive spectatorial discipline on us, so that we align ourselves with the *form* rather than the content of 'The Man's' actions; that is, his walking. As the man darts back and forth towards and away from the camera, we cannot be sure if he is dodging us as unwanted pursuers or inviting us along as he in turn pursues his lover to her hiding place, a goal we cannot know about until the end of the shot. We can only attribute a psychological or emotional motivation to his numerous detours and deviations from this forward momentum towards his lover's embrace later on in the narrative by way of a backward glance. As it turns out, this peripatetic POV shot prefigures and registers his hesitations of infidelity, his turning back to, or on the way back towards, the wife he is neglecting, the one he is planning to drown so he can marry his mistress. Even the mist in the shot contributes to this feeling of hesitation as it billows out from behind us, parting as the camera glides unhurriedly through the marsh in pursuit of the man. Dudley Andrews writes compellingly about how this shot implicates the spectator in the couple's infidelities, even behind *their* backs:

> Later, the man, back to us, wanders toward the marsh and the camera, full of our desire, initiates one of the most complex and thrilling movements in all of cinema. It crosses the fence at its own spot, turns on the man who in his stupor passes by it and makes for the vamp. But the camera finds its own, more direct path, pushing past bushes until she is revealed in the moonlight. When the man re-enters screen left we are doubly startled, having forgotten that we had abandoned him. Indeed, we are perhaps ashamed to have reached the vamp before him in our driving impatience. (Andrew 1984: 35–6)

And we cannot forget that a film is also projected from behind our backs. We are always somehow behind the camera just as we are always in front of the projector – and we never actually see this technology. In fact, we might even argue that the entire cinematic apparatus – that is, the totality of cinema's mechanisms, including lenses, photochemical processing, projectors, splicers, digital coding and lighting, along with its commodity factors such as capital, advertisements, trailers and audience surveys; in short, what Foucault named a *dispositif* – is a dorsal event that happens behind us, while we are not looking. As mentioned already, a film, although made up of solitary photographic stills, must mobilise these fragments to present the illusion of movement: that is, to present the work. The individual frame is mobilised precisely at the point of its borders with the other frame only in so far as it erases the borders between them. The meaning effects of the image contained within each shot are guaranteed only through the mobilisation of that which borders it – which are other frames – along with the effacement of the entire process of framing from one shot to the next. This means that the borders between each individual shot remain, because they must remain, invisible when viewing a film in order for the work to be seen. The frames erase themselves to disappear completely outside (or is it inside?) the film. The individual film frame itself becomes the absolute border of visibility: 'The moment of negation or lack of sight that permits vision to take place', hiding itself at the same time that it makes it possible for us to see it (Brunette and Wills 2014: 104). We should note here the important technical nature of the entire process. The celluloid border of the film frame is created in conjunction with the dual actions of the camera shutter and the projector lamp, creating a 'temporal overlap between the time the image remains in front of the lamp and the time it remains imprinted on the retina'. And, as Bruce Kawin points out, due to the rapid opening and closing of the projector's shutter 'for about half the time we are watching a movie, the screen is totally dark' (Brunette and Wills 2014: 104).

Just as it helps to constitute the human by facilitating our upright bipedal way of moving, dorsality is a constituent part of the accentuation and coherency of filmic motion. I would like to now turn to a discussion of the most formidable dorsal instrument that the cinematic apparatus has at its disposal: the Steadicam.

Steadicam Shots

Dorsality as a feature of the peripatetic camera became much more pronounced with the invention of the Steadicam by Garrett Brown in 1975. With Brown's invention, directors finally had an instrument that made it possible to make a film centring on a pedestrian character and to give spectators what I have called a *participatory peripatetic point of view*. If a camera on a dolly or hand-held shot is like inhabiting someone else's gaze and mind, a Steadicam shot is like inhabiting that someone else's body too, like walking with another's limbs.

Brown's invention consists of a vest worn by an operator with an articulating stabiliser support arm attached. At the other end of the arm is a telescoping post that supports the camera mounting platform, centred over a free floating gimbal, and a monitor. The entire system is designed as a peripatetic camera apparatus to replace hand-held shots, its ingenious structure engineered to achieve optimal camera stability and balance by isolating the camera from the shocks and jerks caused by a cameraman's body as they walk (a feat our brain normally performs when we are walking). The way the Steadicam works requires the operator to walk dorsally, keeping their weight mostly on one foot and correcting their posture at the pelvis when the camera rig needs to be rebalanced at its centre of gravity and brought back to its optimal position on the operator's body.

As a cinematographic tool, the Steadicam can contribute in multiple ways to the principal forms of a film's narrative dynamics – from creating stylistic flourishes and effects that enhance a film's plot to playing the role of an actual narrator as 'a gaze among many gazes' actively engaged as a participant in the construction of the story (Ferrara 2001: 75). It can perform all of the camera moves of tripod-mounted or dolly cameras (pans, tilts, rolls, tracking), but is most adept at creating shots that require long takes and where dolly tracks cannot be set up, such as when a character is moving over rough ground or through crowded spaces. It also allows the cameraman to move in front of, behind, or even circle around an actor walking in just about any kind of space without interruption. Or, it can just wander aimlessly (Ferrara 2001: 16–23).

After experimenting with the Steadicam shooting commercials and perfecting his dexterity with the device, Brown was hired as a cameraman by cinematographer Haskell Wexler to shoot a few scenes for Hal Ashby's Woody Guthrie biopic *Bound for Glory* (1976). The first Steadicam shot to appear in a feature film begins with David Carradine, playing Guthrie, stepping off the bed of a truck then tails him as he walks through a squalid migrant worker camp, weaves with him through the crowd before ending with Carradine walking back towards the camera in conversation with a migrant. The peripatetic shot resonated with the vagabond nature of Guthrie portrayed in the film. After its premiere in Ashby's film, the Steadicam quickly became the main creative tool in the hands of directors who grew into virtuosos of the mobile long take such as Stanley Kubrick, André Tarkovsky, Béla Tarr, Terence Malick and Martin Scorsese.

The Steadicam emerged ready to hand (or rather, foot) with dorsality; it is the dorsal prosthetic in *step with* and engineered for *stepping with* the human gait par excellence. Because it is actually mounted on a human body, it quite literally turns the cameraman into a walking dolly. It can create peripatetic following shots that are steps ahead of dolly based dorsal shots. Lotte Eisner reports that in one review of *Sunrise* a sympathetic critic praised Murnau as a modern-day centaur, a new mechanical organism in which he and the camera morphed together into a single cinematic body.

The critic spoke too soon; the real cinematic centaur is the Steadicam operator:

> Wearing the Steadicam, the operator becomes something 'more', a new entity, united and separate; the Steadicam comes to resemble the mind's creativity, the fusion of what you see with your eyes and a viewfinder and what you imagine will be its best technical realisation. (Ferrara 2001: 63)

The rig can be mounted in front of, behind, or on the side of the operator (Ferrara 2001: 101). The Steadicam operator is the ultimate imbrication of the human and technology, a hybrid technics of muscle and mechanics unique to the cinema. Below is how Eric Hynes sums this up (italics are mine):

> Steadicam shots are uncanny. They mimic how we move and see, and furthermore they seem to anticipate how we expect to be able to move and see, but can't – they're like elusively remembered dreams, native and foreign at the same time. They do come from a body: a person is carrying the machine that's making these images, at human height, usually at human speed, moving and *turning* and observing. The imagery has a fluidity undisturbed by the normal clumsiness of a body holding an unwieldy machine. This is akin to how our bodies and eyes operate, except the technique doesn't settle for approximating how we move through the world; it makes improvements, surpassing our capabilities with a *precognitive* fluidity of movement. We're not quite looking along with the shot, but rather scrambling just slightly *behind* with a sense of impossible clarity, an otherworldly poise and motivation with which to encounter a chaotic, noisy, unchoreographed world. Steadicam shots are *like tails to our tailbone*, things beyond us that seem of us. They're both *alien and familiar*. (Hynes 2016: 29)

Notice the dorsal language in Hyne's description of Steadicam shots. Their movements are precognitive and 'anticipate how we expect to be able to move and see, but can't'. Their velocity comes from a body 'moving and turning and observing' from 'human height' and measured at 'human speed'. Our point of view is always 'scrambling just slightly behind' and they are both 'alien and familiar' and appear to us 'like tails to our tailbone'.

Hyne's language illustrates the ways Steadicam shots fluctuate between opening and closing our field of vision and helps to explain why they make us feel a bodily engagement with a filmic world that is so mysteriously close to our lived world and conventional modes of embodied perception. For instance, we never see all sides of a three-dimensional object at once, but we still know from lived experience that when we view an object frontally for the first time it has a backside, and this unseen, or yet to be seen, fact exists as a concrete presence in our overall field of vision. Because the

Steadicam, its operator, the actor-character and the spectator are all part of a collective field of vision, there will always be mutually acknowledged absences in the shared perceptual field. Phenomenologically, these blind spots nonetheless remain as invisible yet indeterminate presences which thicken, rather than diminish, the visual sphere. The incompleteness of vision combined with a sinuous and uninterrupted human-like movement through space that the Steadicam presents accentuates the tensions between knowing and unknowing, interiority and exteriority, clarity and ambiguity that already exist in mobile POV shots. Merleau-Ponty called this visual perceptual process *indeterminate vision* – because what is seen is dependent on what cannot be seen – even using the language of dorsality to describe these indeterminacies as positive phenomena: '. . . what is behind my back is not without some element of visual presence' (Merleau-Ponty 1962: 6). Steadicam shots are the cinematic equivalent of real-life instances of indeterminate vision, especially when used as a tool to narrate an exchange of gazes between the viewer and a character. They perform a kind of phenomenological reduction of the on-screen visual field, reminding us of how much our sense perceptions are rooted in the invariances of precognitive experience. Thus, Steadicam shots are modes of embodied perception that situate the viewer in a space where there are innumerable yet indeterminate points of view anchored by a fluid and equally indeterminate pedestrian point of orientation.

By some estimates the Steadicam has been used in over eighty percent of feature films made since its invention. Over the years, directors have developed various conventions for deploying the Steadicam as a principal tool for narrative construction that takes full advantage of its functions as a peripatetic device. For example, the American director Richard Linklater has almost perfected the use of the Steadicam as a peripatetic dialogic tool to narrate the back and forth nature of conversation in films such as *Slacker* and his *Before* trilogy.

Other virtuoso examples of notoriety can be found in *The Shining*, *The Sheltering Sky*, *Coup de tourchon*, *Boogie Nights*, *Marathon Man*, *Full Metal Jacket*, *Goodfellas*, *Rocky* and *Dunkirk*. I would be remiss not to mention the Steadicam's tour de force performance in Andrei Sokurov's *Russian Ark* (2002), a film consisting of a single peripatetic Steadicam shot ninety minutes long, that follows a nineteenth-century aristocrat as he guides us on a walking tour of the entire Hermitage Museum. But for the remainder of this chapter I will focus my analysis on Hungarian film-maker Béla Tarr's distinctive use of the Steadicam. Tarr has shown how, in the hands of a dexterous director, the Steadicam can craft *participatory peripatetic points of view* to construct instances of indeterminate vision adding narrative and stylistic depth to a film.[1]

Béla Tarr – Everyday Body Without Event

Born in Pécs in 1955, the largely self-taught director Béla Tarr has created an oeuvre over the last three decades that has secured his reputation as one of European art cinema's most exciting film-makers. His unorthodox working methods, recurrent themes and character types, and the visual qualities of his narrative style combined with his grappling with the problems of filmic rhythm and time have all contributed to his status as an auteur.

András Bálint Kovács has noted several consistent characteristics of Tarr's working methods and style as he has matured as a director. These include his concentration on actors and locations at the expense of the scripted narrative (he prefers amateur actors for their expressive faces and almost never shoots on a studio set, even claiming that locations have faces too); composing and recording the film's music before shooting begins then playing the music while actually filming; downplaying the role of editing; and, improvising camera movement and blocking. Most importantly for this study is his stylistic use of extreme long takes as individual sequences with their own narrative flow and internal tensions, especially when he combines this with camera movement. Like Tarkovsky, Tarr envisions cinematic time in terms of rhythm of movement within the frame as opposed to that of individual shots assembled into specific sequences that progress linearly in time. For the most part, his use of long takes is a consequence of his camera movements rather than the other way around. Stylistically, Kovács divides Tarr's work into two periods: the films he made before *Almanac of Fall* (1984) in which his films exhibited the influences of *cinéma vérité* on his documentary-fiction style and those he completed afterwards that combined the visual techniques of neo-realism with features of lyrical and poetic cinema. In the first period one can locate a variety of camera movements in Tarr's films, but most of these are employed to add narrative texture and not necessarily for their stylistic functions. Tarr only begins to isolate camera movements from their narrative functions in favour of stylistic ones with *Almanac of Fall* (Kovács 2013: 15–18, 42–5). It is this second period that interests us, since it is here that Tarr began to craft his films with extreme long takes composed of complicated tracking shots choreographed to follow his character's peripatetic movements with the Steadicam. Although in interviews Tarr has said that he prefers dollies, for many of the tracking shots in these later films dolly tracks were impractical so he relied heavily on the Steadicam which, as

I will argue, led to his expertise in creating *participatory peripatetic points of view*.

Tarr's peripatetic Steadicam shots, for the most part, are devoid of dialogue. Rarely do his characters converse as they walk together along a road or footpath. The focal point of the shot is mostly on a character's gait in relation to their body's position in the frame. Tarr's Steadicam shots are, to cite Deleuze, images of thought, captured in his phrase, 'Give me a body then.' Deleuze continues, asserting that it is 'through the body ... that cinema forms its alliance with the spirit, with thought' and that to give a body to cinema is 'first to mount the camera on an everyday body' (Deleuze 1995: 189). How can we make sense of this passage by Deleuze? We know what the camera mounted on a body is – the Steadicam. But then this leaves us with three important questions: 1) What does Deleuze mean when he claims that it is through the body that cinematic images think?; 2) What is the everyday body?; and 3) How can we conceive of this in relation to the peripatetic Steadicam?

Let us answer them in order and start with the first question. Deleuze conceptualises thinking primarily as an automatic and autonomous process generated at the molecular level before it becomes anchored in consciousness. The body is not just a mere intermediary of thought, but its source. Thinking begins physiologically in the material body of the brain as bursts of precognitive molecular automatisms that create 'images of thought' prior to what we normally call 'thinking'. These images of thought are like nomadic bits of data roaming around our brain circuitry, constantly moving and changing as they confront one another as well as other molecular systems wholly unlike themselves: the unthought. Thus, Deleuze speaks about the image of the 'unthought in thought' to show how thinking is linked to something outside of thought itself which only then combines into 'concepts'. But Deleuze envisions even the formation of the concept to be a process and result of the auto-movement of thought that occurs outside the subject. For Deleuze the human brain is an automatic thought machine that produces the subject itself as a type of moving image. Deleuze discovered that the cinema too was an automatic thought machine and that its mechanisms for producing images of thought corresponded neatly to the automatic system of thought production in the human brain: '*Automatic movement* gives rise to a *spiritual automaton* in us, which reacts in turn on movement' (Deleuze 1995: 156). Movement is inherent and immediately given in the cinematic image; that is, we do not have to think or imagine anything to make it move, since it is endowed with motion itself. Cinematic movement is independent of a moving body; it is not attached to a body, as say a dancer's movements are anchored in their body and the spectator is not required to move parts of their body (not even their eyes, like when reading a book). The cinema image's movement is also independent of a mind (subject and spectator), since it occupies the place of the subject whose mind can only respond to the moving image as opposed to causing it to move.

Intrigued by this revelation, Deleuze wrote two books on film – which move somewhat opaquely from philosophy to cinema and from cinema to philosophy – exploring these correlations between the image of thought and the cinematic image as a form of thought. One might pithily summarise the arguments of these works with the following quote from an interview with Deleuze published in 1986 in *Cahiers du cinéma*: 'Cinema not only puts movement in the image, it also puts movement in the mind . . . The brain is the screen' (Flaxman 2000: 366). So, in cinema, image and thought continuously change places, transfiguring from images of thought to cinematic thought images and back again. Cinema provides bodies (images, characters, spectators) for thinking.

Let us now try to answer the second question. What then, is the everyday? And what is an everyday body? The everyday is first of all the 'ordinary' in our lives. It is how we exist and behave at work, leisure and in our private lives. The everyday is the average, tedious, banal side of our existence which seems insignificant and amounts to the commonplace. Blanchot describes the essence of the everyday this way:

> Whatever its other aspects, the everyday has this essential trait: it allows no hold. It escapes. It belongs to insignificance; the insignificant being what is without truth, without reality, and without secret, but also perhaps the site of all possible signification. The everyday escapes. In this consists its strangeness – the familiar showing itself (but already dispersing) in the guise of the astonishing . . . the everyday is what we never see for a first time but can only see again, having always already seen it by an illusion that is constitutive of the everyday. (Blanchot 1993: 240)

The everyday exists in the fact that 'nothing happens' and is the 'always already there' in the ontological sense. The everyday body, then, is the body of unthinking routine (and what can be more routine bodily than walking?). It is the human, physical abode of the *noneventful*, existing temporally not in the present, but always moving from the past to the future postured between tiredness and waiting (Deleuze 1995: 189). If we try to apply to the everyday the traditional definition of an event, that is, something singular that occurs in a specific time and place and is imbued with presence, then the everyday and the everyday body is without event. Therein lies the incongruity of the everyday. Therefore, no *image* of an event is able to reproduce the everyday body. Furthermore, no event in itself is ever presentable.

Following Badiou, we can say that every event is localised, meaning it is always tied to a situation, yet it can consist of multiple sites (spatially and temporally):

> If there exists an event, *its belonging to the situation of its site is undecidable from the standpoint of the situation itself* . . . [firstly] the event belongs to the situation. From the standpoint of the situation, being presented, it *is*. Its characteristics, however, are quite special. First of all, note that the event is a *singular* multiple (in the situation to which we suppose it belongs). If it was actually normal, and could thus be represented, the event would be a *part* of the situation. Yet this is impossible, because elements of its site belong to it, and such elements – the site being on the edge of the void – are not, themselves, presented . . . *To declare that an event belongs to the situation comes down to saying that it is conceptually distinguished from its site by the interposition of itself between the void and itself* . . . [secondly] the event does *not* belong to the situation. The result: 'nothing has taken place except the place.' For the event, apart from itself, solely presents the elements of its site, which are not presented in the situation. (Badiou 2007: 181–2)

Badiou calls this singular-multiple doubling in an event the *evental site*, asserting that the 'event is a one-multiple made up of, on the one hand, all the multiples which belong to its site and, on the other hand, the event itself' (Badiou 2007: 179). This brings us to our last question. The undecidability between an event and its situation is precisely the state of affairs we find with the cinematic *shot*. If we say that the shot is cinema's primary evental site, then the event *of* the shot and the event *in* the shot, while inhabiting at least two different sites (and many more, if we take into account multiple screenings), are commingled and impossible to untangle situationally. But does this mean that these two events are different yet also identical? No. It is true that photographic shots are always artefactual, as Stanley Cavell has convincingly shown, and therefore their significance is often grounded in the actuality (past or present) of the objects they portray and their own ontological status as objects in the world (materially or digitally). And this is certainly true of mobile long takes as well. But, as I will argue, the significance of Tarr's long, mobile long takes with a Steadicam as *participatory peripatetic point of view shots* lies in their each being sites of an *everyday body without event*.

Let us begin with *Satantango* (1994), a film just under seven hours long and composed almost entirely of long takes. According to the Cinemetrics database, the film consists of a total of 171 shots with an average shot length of 145 seconds. The longest take lasts just over ten minutes, just below the eleven-minute capacity of a standard roll of 35 mm film, a limitation Tarr has described as a 'form of censorship' (Cinemetrics – Movie, n.d.). Many of these shots are mobile long takes that ambulate along with peripatetic characters, some from behind and some from in front (Cinemetrics – Movie, n.d.).

Take for example the sequence titled 'Rise from the Dead'. It opens with a two-minute long Steadicam following shot of two men walking side by side down the middle of a dismal street in an equally bleak Eastern European town. The pavement is wet from rain and both men wear almost identical black raincoats. The two walk at an even pace, the camera following at varying strides behind them, consistently keeping their full bodies in the frame to focus on the rhythm of their gait. Windswept litter – paper, leaves, empty tin cans, discarded cardboard boxes – gusts up from behind the camera like a ground blizzard, blowing down the street around their feet and swirling over the pavements. The two do not speak and except for the sound of wind blowing, the scene is silent. The angle, height and movement of the camera is roughly the same as a third pedestrian following from behind who sometimes has to hurry to catch up before hesitating to overtake the two men, then slowing down to let them gain a bit of distance again. They seem oblivious to the detritus billowing all around them, even when scraps of paper strike their heels and ankles. Finally, at the middle of a cross section of two streets the camera stops following the two men but continues to hold them in the same frame as they keep walking several more paces away from it.

The framing and camera movement is typical of what I have already described as a peripatetic dorsal shot. It shares some common characteristics of Murnau's tracking shot in *Sunrise* I discussed earlier, yet there is

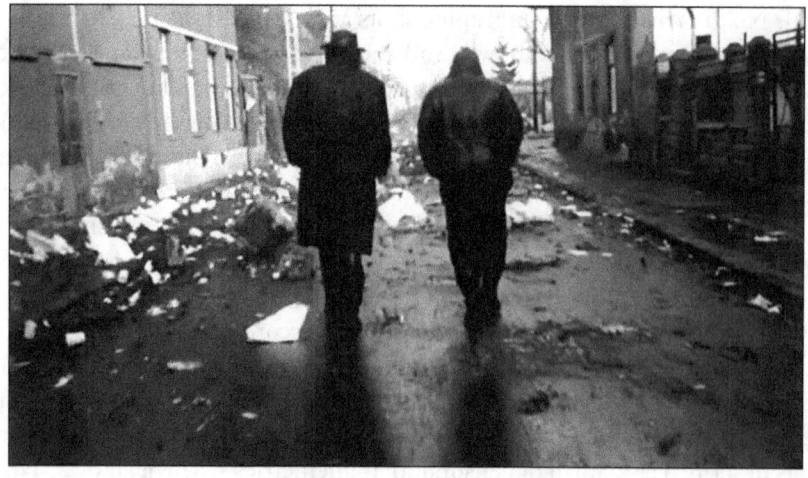

Figure 3.1 Satantango.

one glaring difference: in *Sunrise*, it is the character who wavers in his movement, whereas in Tarr's shot it is the camera (Steadicam) that hesitates while the characters' movements remain resolute. Dorsally, the trash blowing through the frame reminds us of the mist in Murnau's shot, yet it functions narratively completely differently. Whereas the mist in *Sunrise* served as a motif for an uncertain, hazy and hesitant future, the detritus in Tarr's shot is a motif of ruin, destruction and decay emblematic of how much the past still pollutes both the present (without presence) and the future. What we follow and participate in through the Steadicam is the decelerated decomposition of history as it lurches forward at a pedestrian pace.

The two sites of the shot event – the event in the shot and the event of the shot – crystallise around the artefactual situation of plot time flowing at the same rate as screen time, both of which are situated temporally in the past. The prolongation of the shot subjects the spectator and protagonist to the same pressure of time in its distended duration, showing the porousness between the ambulatory camera and the characters walking. As we share with the two characters a direct perception of time passing, we begin to think through the image we see on the screen in order to find narrative meaning in the shot. We have time to both scrutinise the image and our thinking about the image. We breathe with the shot. We may become bored or even anxious as we wait for the shot to cut. This is an example of what Deleuze has called a *crystal-image*. Deleuze developed a taxonomy of new signs in the cinema – inspired largely by Bergson's writings on the relationships between perception, memory and duration – which initiate the constitution of the direct time-image. One of these is the *crystal-image*. The crystal-image is a direct image of time configured as the 'uniting of an actual image and a virtual image to the point where they can no longer be distinguished'. So, like the evental site of the shot, the crystal-image has two definite sides in an indivisible unity: the actual and the virtual image. The actual image is a real image of a 'present which passes' while the virtual image is an imaginary image of a 'past which is preserved'. I equate the *actual* image with the *event in* Tarr's shot, since this is the one we experience through multiple sites of viewing and the *virtual* image with the *event of* the shot since it is an artefact of people and objects from a distinct time and place.

Like the two sides of the evental site of the shot, the distinction between these two images is often indiscernible. In Tarr's peripatetic Steadicam shot, the *event of the shot* decomposes alongside the *event in the shot* so that the evental site of the time-image crystallises into showing us simultaneously a '*present of the future, a present of the present, and the present of the past*' all rolled up inside a single image-without-event (Deleuze 1995: 100). As we follow without interruption both behind and within the gaze of the Steadicam mounted on a peripatetic body, the time-image thinks for us, transfiguring us as spectators into everyday bodies without event.

Tarr repeats this stylistic excess of the everyday in various long takes in *Werckmeister Harmonies* and *The Turin Horse*. Let's take the opening three shots of *Werckmeister Harmonies* (a film 145 minutes long consisting of only 39 shots). The first is just over ten minutes long. It begins with a close-up of a coal burning stove in a dilapidated bar in a small Hungarian town. We see the bartender extinguish the fire with a pint of beer then announce to a handful of drunks that it is closing time. One patron utters 'just wait a bit for Valuska to show us' and then drunkenly walks towards the camera to greet Valuska as he walks into the bar. He then coaxes Valuska to show the remaining customers how to act out the movements of the solar system, saying, 'Valuska. Come on. Show us.' Valuska clears the floor of tables and chairs, gathers the collection of unsteady patrons all together, then soberly helps them to rotate around one another like planets circling the sun. Just as he is demonstrating the waning of a solar eclipse, the bartender finally throws them all out. The shot ends with Valuska as the last to leave. The long take of the shot pulls all participants (including the viewer) into a *participatory peripatetic point of view*.

Tarr then cuts to a long, peripatetic Steadicam shot of Valuska walking alone from the bar down the middle of a deserted, snow covered street. As the camera pulls Valuska along, the long cadence of the shot is highlighted by the camera's outpacing him until he is little more than a dark shadow barely lit from behind in the distance.

In the next shot we see Valuska arriving at his uncle's house at the end of his long walk from the bar. For the next six and a half minutes, we follow him as he walks into the house, takes off his coat and silently helps his uncle to undress and change into pyjamas, then puts him to bed. He then lights the water heater in the bathroom before straightening and cleaning up the dining room and kitchen. When he finishes these mundane chores, he puts his coat back on and leaves.

Together, these three shots present us with a time-image of the everyday in its uneventful essence where the mundane activities of life coincide with the material demands of living. The solar system dance orchestrated by Valuska seems to be a nightly closing routine for the bar regulars. Valuska walks in the street knowing there will be no cars at such a late hour of the night because it is his routine. He habitually goes about his chores in caring for his uncle. What we witness in the everydayness contained in these mobile images is what Deleuze calls an 'optical drama' as opposed to

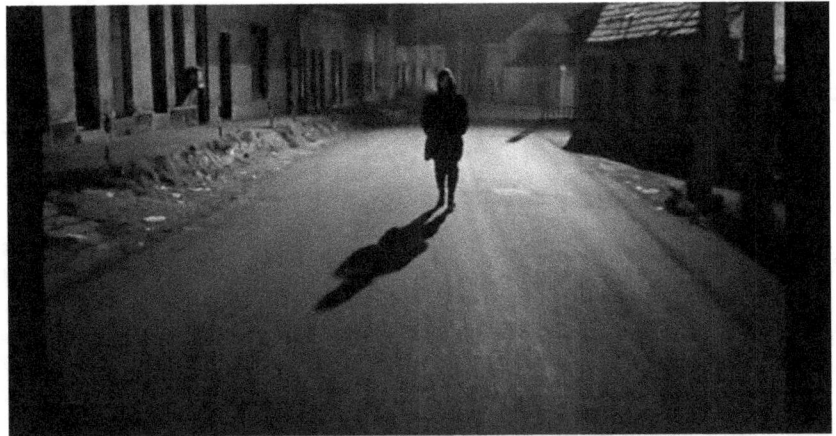

Figure 3.2 Werckmeister Harmonies.

a traditional one. The long cadences of each shot propel us into thought and therein lies the drama, a drama of style over narrative.

We find a bleaker example in a seven-minute shot in *The Turin Horse*. For the entire seven minutes, we see the daughter engaged in the singular act of getting out of bed, dressing and walking outside to fetch water from a well. All is peaceful and quiet in the house as she routinely dresses. Stepping into the doorway, she is briefly framed from behind, echoing the posture of John Wayne in the final shot of *The Searchers*. But when we follow her out the door, we are greeted by a flat, desolate, howling landscape and immediately bombarded by dirt, grit and dead leaves blowing from every direction (debris of dead nature as opposed to the industrial detritus we saw in the example from *Satantango*). She is dressed in the same drab, earthy colours as the windswept, treeless plain where she lives. She carries a bucket. When she reaches the well, she lifts the wooden lid, draws the water, replaces the lid and then walks back to the house. The shot ends as she re-enters through the door.

The Steadicam shot is dorsal, silent, singular. The angle is low and her whole body is always kept in the frame. The action consists of nothing more than routine activities; a direct time-image of the everyday body without event. Tarr's provocative scene sets up the doorway as a supposed break between interiority and engagement with the outside (exteriority). While the dorsality of the shot coheres with the motion of walking beyond the mechanics of filmic production and accentuates the routinisation of walking, it also evokes an evental site, flattening the doorway into a passage/node of subjectivity and exteriority that doubles back again, commingling

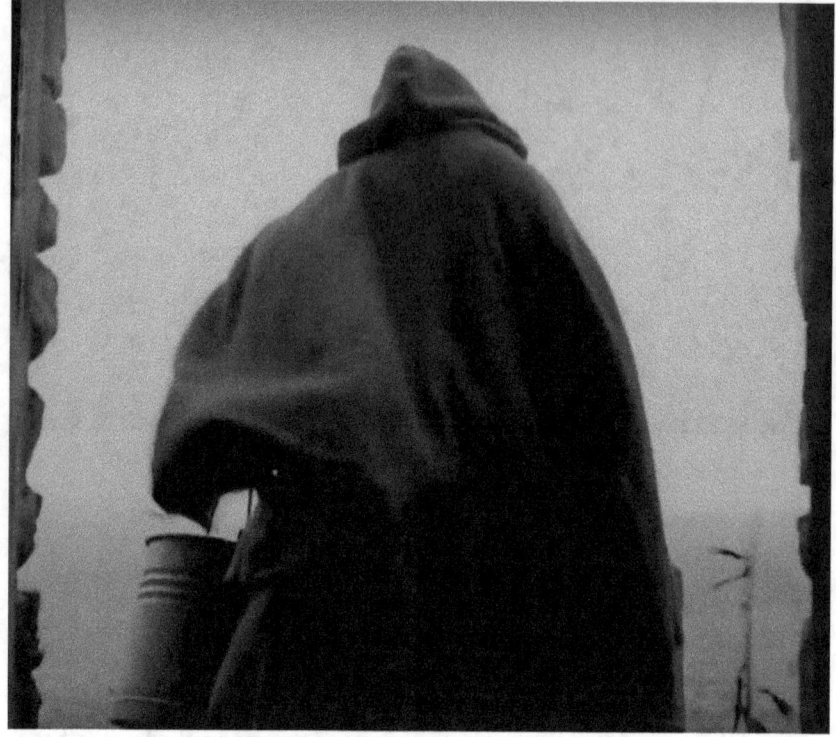

Figure 3.3 The Turin Horse.

the shot and the event. The production of such routine, primordial walking events empowered by the Steadicam and related dorsality flattens not only human subjectivity and the exterior aesthetic, but also meshes the event, the capturing of the event and the viewing of that capture into a whole. Tarr's stylistic use of the Steadicam demonstrates the fluidity of a form that collapses the anticipation of an event into the filtering of the event, while also melding thought and unthought together to create a style of ontological awareness that outstrips narrative.

Notes

1. One other film-maker worth mentioning is Gus Van Zandt, whose quartet of walking films – *Gerry* (2002), *Elephant* (2003), *Last Days* (2005) and *Paranoid Park* (2007) – owe a great debt to Tarr's Steadicam work. One of the most illuminating analyses of walking in these films is the article 'The Vestibular in Film: Orientation and Balance in Gus Van Zandt's Cinema of Walking' by Luis Rocha Antunes. Antunes defines the vestibular in relation to film along three

axises: phenomenology, physiology and cinema specificity. Phenomenologically, the vestibular is about how we bodily orient ourselves guided by what Merleau-Ponty called the 'thread of the world', which gives bodily movement both meaning and direction, as implied in the French word sense (quoted in Antunes 2012: 523). Physiologically, the vestibular system refers to the sensory apparatus of the inner ear which is involved in balance and spatial orientation for coordinating movement and detecting the position and motion of the head. As far as cinema specificity goes, it is best to cite the full Hugo Münsterberg quote from the article:

> We want to keep the interest in the plastic world and want to be aware of the depth in which the persons move, but our direct object of perception must be without the depth. That idea of space which forces on us most strongly the idea of heaviness, solidity and substantiality must be replaced by the light flitting immateriality. (quoted in Antunes 2012: 523)

Taken together, the three lines of thought about the vestibular in film add up to give film viewers 'access to a multisensory experience . . . and [creates] new ontology of the senses' (Antunes 2012: 524). Antunes uses Van Zandt's four films as a case study, analysing the vestibular in each film through the lenses of time, the camera, character identity, and loss of balance and orientation. His article illuminates the ways in which Van Zandt deftly uses the camera to explore the 'cinematic aspect of walking' and how this exploration is enhanced by scenes 'edited with long walk scenes that establish multiple points of view', allowing the spectator to experience the full durational force of 'what it means to walk, what it feels like to walk, and the potential for a cinematic representation of walking' (Antunes 2012: 531).

Yet, for such a lucid argument about the vestibular camera and how it embodies walking in these films, it is odd that Antunes never refers to the Steadicam in this article. The vestibular might be another interesting concept for illuminating Tarr's Steadicam work, but such an analysis is beyond the limited space of this book.

CHAPTER 4

Gumshoes

Some place over there I had left my car and started walking, burying my head in the collar of my raincoat, with the night pulled in around me like a blanket.
Mickey Spillane – *One Lonely Night*

A spy? No, a private detective. Surveillance. Investigations. Encounters. Disguises. Blackmail. Pursuit. Anonymous letters. Love letters.
François Truffaut – *Stolen Kisses*

'Come, Watson, come!' he cried. 'The game is afoot.'
Arthur Conan Doyle – *The Adventure of the Abbey Grange*

If you were to ask a random stranger on the street how Sherlock Holmes earned his livelihood, you are more likely than not to hear the correct reply, 'private detective'. If you asked that same person to describe Holmes, they would probably say something like, 'Tall and gaunt; wears a tweed frock coat, a deerstalker hat, smokes a pipe, and carries a walking stick.'

Arthur Conan Doyle's detective Sherlock Holmes is the late Victorian offspring of Edgar Allan Poe's creation C. August Dupin, the first detective in the modern literary sense to appear in fiction.[1] Holmes has proven to be a much more popular fictional character than Dupin and holds the honour of being the most prolific and popular screen character in film history, with over 70 actors portraying him in an estimated 200 films. The first film to feature Holmes was a one reel short produced in 1900 by the American Mutual and Bioscope Company titled *Sherlock Holmes Baffled*. The most recent is Bill Condon's 2015 feature film *Mr. Holmes* with Ian McKellan starring in the title role.

The strangest characterisation of Holmes on film is probably George C. Scott's performance in *They Might Be Giants* (1971). Scott plays Justin Playfair, an eccentric New York millionaire who suffers a nervous breakdown after his wife's death and retreats into a paranoid delusion that he is Sherlock Holmes. While under observation in a psychiatric hospital, he is treated by a psychoanalyst who just happens to have the name Dr. Mildred Watson. She soon becomes fascinated by his fantasy of being Holmes, especially since, like Doyle's Sherlock Holmes, he possesses an uncanny facility for adductive reasoning. Dr. Watson follows Playfair, who is garbed in Holmes's iconic deerstalker hat and tweed cape, as he rushes around Manhattan on foot in his quest to find the elusive criminal mastermind Moriarty. Watson becomes increasingly intrigued by her patient, especially as his methods and the enigmatic clues he follows around the city become more and more intelligible to her. One of his investigative methods is stalking, a stealthy, peripatetic form of analysis which he claims helps him infiltrate the secretive world of criminals. He tries to teach Watson this stalking method, but it turns out to consist of nothing more than walking in a zig zag pattern down the sidewalk in plain view of other pedestrians.

Both Dupin and Holmes are the sort of peripatetic investigator referred to metonymically in later hard-boiled fiction parlance as a *gumshoe*. According to *The Oxford English Dictionary* the word's first use is found in Alfred Henry Lewis's 1906 *Confessions of a Detective* to characterise both a sneaky criminal and the detective in stealthy pursuit: 'One of Red Bob's gang had crept upon me, gumshoe fashion, and dealt me a blow with a sandbag.'; [detective] 'Cull, you're d'gum-shoe guy I was waiting 'fer, see!'

London only began constructing flat pavements and streets for foot passengers in the early eighteenth century. Walking on pavement was a novel experience for most London pedestrians and they quickly developed new codes of pedestrian etiquette and practical habits for walking, including choosing practical footwear. The novelty of ambling on pavement is captured by John Gay in his satirical poem *Trivia: Or, the Art of Walking the Streets of London* from 1716 in which he recommends to the walker, 'Let firm, wellhammer'd Soles protect thy Feet.' Humorous as it sounds, his advice was pretty much on the mark for the next century (quoted in Ingold 2004: 326).

The first London detective squad was founded by novelist and magistrate Henry Fielding in 1749 and became known as the Bow Street Runners. They were formed while pavement was still being laid and, as their name implies, operated largely on foot. While pavers were hard at work, Fielding's peripatetic detectives were at the mercy of street surfaces which fluctuated between new clean, smooth, flat pavement and hard, uneven, dirty, broken cobblestones. Additionally, they were hobbled in their street detective work by having to walk or run in Gay's recommended hard soled footwear.

But by the end of the nineteenth century, most of London was paved. At the same time, new gum-soled shoes were invented. Police officers and detectives quickly discovered the advantages of wearing this new footwear, which were fairly easy on the feet when walking a beat or hoofing it down an alley. Just as importantly, the rubber soles were quieter on pavement than the outmoded leather hammered ones, which often squeaked, letting a policeman sneak up stealthily on a suspect (or vice versa).[2] The gumshoe designated a peripatetic style that arose from the practical nature of detective work as the modern, paved city took form. Thus, by the middle of the twentieth century, the label *gumshoe*, used as either a noun or verb, replaced 'flatfoot' as slang for a police detective in the popular imagination.

Most, if not all, of the great detectives in modern fiction can be described as gumshoes. That is, they spend a lot of time walking. When not lingering in the corridors of Scotland Yard, Inspector Lestrade can often be found stalking behind the footsteps of the bloodhound-like Sherlock Holmes through the streets of London, always trying to play catch up. Sam Spade traipses up and down the hilly streets and sidewalks of San Francisco, as does Frank Hastings. The detectives of Ed McBain's 87th precinct pound the pavement in the fictional city of Isola, a barely disguised version of New York. As for New York City gumshoes, there are too many to mention. Maigret's crime solving ideas come to him while he is either walking the boulevards of Paris or drinking at an outdoor café (his creator, Georges Simenon, claimed that all his best stories about Maigret came when he was walking). Even private eyes like Mike Hammer and Philip Marlowe operating in car crazy and less than pedestrian friendly Los Angeles often step out of their automobiles and beat the streets.

Holmes himself combines cerebral methods with physical motility, running around a crime scene, sometimes even crawling, looking for a clue. Holmes famously honed his forensic skills of detection by embracing and mastering the burgeoning sciences of fingerprint and handwriting analyses, even well before real police forces accepted their use in solving crime. But James O'Brien reminds us of how important forensic foot print analysis was to Holmes's crime solving success:

> Fully 29 of the 60 stories include footprint evidence. The Boscombe Valley Mystery is solved almost entirely by footprint analysis. Holmes analyses footprints on quite a variety of surfaces: clay soil, snow, carpet, dust, mud, blood, ashes and even a curtain. Yet another one of Sherlock Holmes's monographs is on the topic ('The tracing of footsteps, with some remarks upon the uses of Plaster of Paris as a preserver of impresses'). (See O'Brien 2013a: quote from https://blog.oup.com/2013/09/six-methods-forensic-detection-sherlock-holmes/)

Torn from the pages of true crime fiction and hard-boiled detective novels, the gumshoe became a stock character in two interrelated film genres that emerged from the Hollywood studio system after World War II: the detective film noir and police procedural. For the rest of this chapter, I will explore the figure of the gumshoe in each genre, using a handful of films that revolve around a peripatetic detective hero.

Film Noir

Stylistically, the police procedural and detective noir are offspring of the film style known as *film noir* which flourished between the early 1940s and the beginning of the 1950s in Hollywood. The coinage of the term derives from a popular series of French translations of American hard-boiled detective fiction called *romain noir* (dark novel) which gave rise to the term *film noir*, which means dark film (Sklar 2002: 278).

There has long been a debate in film studies about whether or not film noir can be classified as a genre. But the concept of genre itself is problematic. Since the 1960s, film theorists have argued about how to define genre beyond using it as a tool for cataloguing films according to a generic system of classification. For instance, should we call the three main categories of film recognised by film historians – narrative, documentary and avant-garde – genres? Or are they types of film, each with their own genres and subgenres? What are the differences between a film genre and film movement? None of these questions have an easy answer. This is because the umbrella of genre theory covers much more than the codes and conventions we might use to type films. It also covers ways in which a film is produced and marketed (technological and ideological considerations), film industry and audience expectations, historical and cultural contexts (periodisation), and complex forms of cross-media intertextuality or intermediality. Moreover, none of these categories are static. It is therefore difficult to permanently harness any film to a single genre, even when its seems on the surface to be an obvious fit.

It is in this context that Paul Schrader argued in his 1972 essay 'Notes of Film Noir' that film noir is not a genre. He preferred to categorise film noir as a specific period of film history and film movement coloured by a certain tone or mood of disillusionment mixed with a hardened realism manifested by the American public just after World War II. In what follows, I too will treat film noir as a movement and period of film history and not as a genre. But I will locate some of its distinctive stylistic and narrative features as seminal to the police procedural and the detective noir film. For the purpose of my investigation, I will take for granted that each is recognised by most film scholars as two distinct genres of the film noir style and movement.

My argument is foregrounded by Rick Altman's useful theory in which he proposes a dualistic semantic/syntactical approach to the question of genre that diachronically accounts for historical periodisation while resolving most of the problems I mentioned above. Semantic genre categorisations, he argues, use 'a list of common traits, attitudes, characters, shots, locations, sets', found across a spectrum of individual films and thus stresses a genre's 'building blocks themselves'. Syntactic approaches, on the other hand, 'privilege the structures into which they [a genre's building blocks] are arranged' (Altman 1984: 10). Thus, I will show that, while the detective noir and police procedural genres may appear to be semantically different, they share many of the same syntactical patterns.

Following Schrader and others, we can isolate a few conventions of film noir as a visual style that appears in almost all detective noir films and to a more limited degree in police procedurals. First, there is the lighting. Indoor and outdoor scenes, even in daytime, are lit as if it were night. Influenced by German Expressionism, the nocturnal tone of film noir is created using low key, high contrast lighting that produces extreme silhouettes and long, dark shadows. Both actors and setting are given the same lighting considerations in claustrophobic framings. Shadows are cast across an actor's face to partially envisage or entirely conceal their feelings. Light enters rooms from oblong and oblique angles choreographed to splinter the screen. Shafts of streetlight spill through the slits of partially opened venetian blinds, coiling around cigarette smoke, giving the impression that the 'windows were cut out with a pen knife' (Schrader 1996: 57). These splinters of oblique light undermine and diminish a given character's agency so that they find it hard to 'speak authoritatively from a space that is being continuously cut into ribbons of light' (Schrader 1996: 57). Characters might only be half lit, their bodies split in two by light and shadow to intensify the sense of tension and claustrophobia. Or, a shadow might be thrown across their entire body, as when an actor is 'hidden [as a shadow] in the realistic tableau of the city at night' to create a pessimistic, fatalistic mood. Sometimes the only light in a scene comes from the glow of a lit cigarette dangling from someone's lips or from a bare bulb hanging from the ceiling.

Secondly, there are the characters. Film noir is populated by characters driven by selfishness, cruelty and greed who are willing to lie, cheat, steal and murder to achieve their ends. The main antagonists are borderline sociopaths who are fatalistic and ultimately doomed to failure in their criminal careers. Then there is the convention of the *femme fatale*, a young, beautiful, worldly, sexually charged woman who is a mortal danger to the men who cross her path and other women alike. Her alluring sexuality arouses in the male protagonist an obsessive desire that leads him 'away from certainty and order into a world of lawlessness and guilt' (Sklar 2002: 279).

Thirdly, there are the narrative conventions. The world in film noir is broken and bleak, and the plot devices mirror this theme of fragmentation. Film noir persistently relies on the devices of flashbacks and voice-over narration, primarily from the male protagonist's point of view. Flashbacks in particular are used as a device to rupture the linear narrative, explicitly expressing the sense of post-war contingency and moral confusion. Sometimes the plot is complicated by competing diegetic narratives stemming from different characters, again often delivered through the devices of flashback and voice-overs.

Lastly, there is the setting. The mise-en-scène of film noir is crime-ridden post-war cities in decline, where bleak alleys and darkened streets signify the isolation and alienation of citizens who are 'observed scurrying furtively beneath the street lights and along the alleyways and wet streets' or found 'sitting alone in a darkened room, fearful and lonely' (Mayer and McDonnell 2007: 47). Film noir cities are gritty, nocturnal, neon lit urban jungles on the verge of abandonment, geographies of alienation and estrangement from their opposite landscape, the emerging suburbs. Darkness seems to be perpetual. Even when it is daylight, the action is staged in a barely lit dingy office or in the back room of a dark seedy bar or greasy diner. The streets are often empty and soaked in rain. Schrader argues that film noir 'has an almost Freudian attachment to water . . . Docks and piers are second only to alleyways as the most popular rendezvous points' (Schrader 1996: 57). But even when glistening after fresh rain, streets and sidewalks still look grimy.

Nicholas Christopher argues that the key to understanding the city as portrayed in noir films is found in the concept of the 'labyrinth'. The setting is most often a capital city undergirded by a hidden labyrinthine world of crime and corruption. It is through this urban labyrinth that the hero must roam on foot.

The linguistic origins of the word 'labyrinth' are somewhat murky, lost in their own etymological labyrinth of time and history. Yet, we can at least link the word to the Minoan word *labrys*, which means 'double-headed axe'. Since at least the Greek myth of Daedalus, who designed and built an elaborate labyrinth of meandering halls to imprison the ferocious Minotaur that he himself could barely navigate, the word has been used to describe any maze-like structure. The most paradigmatic labyrinth is perhaps the one built as part of the temple and pyramid compound in Hawara during the 12th Egyptian dynasty. The Greek historian Herodotus claimed to have visited it, describing his amazement as he walked through the 'passages through the houses and the varied windings of the paths across the courts' before the excitement of passing 'from the courts into chambers, and from the chambers into colonnades, and from the colonnades into fresh houses, and again from these into courts unseen before' (Herodotus, Wilkinson, Rawlins and Rawlins: 1859: 195).

Christopher notes three levels in which the concept of the labyrinth as the underbelly of a city operates in noir films. First, there is the level of external spaces in the city, its physical maze of 'streets, sidewalks, automobile tunnels, underpasses, docks and piers' (Christopher 2010: 39). Packed into this maze and rising above it are a myriad of warrens consisting of 'office buildings, apartment houses, department stores, and tenements . . . casinos, nightclubs, cafés, and bars . . . train and bus terminals' (Christopher 2010: 39). These are closed, imprisoning spaces where movement is restricted and which can become traps for those who enter them. Second, there is the labyrinth of plot twists and the 'inscrutable enmeshments of time, space, and chance' in which the characters interact and intersect in the urban maze (Christopher 2010: 39). Lastly, there is the labyrinth of the protagonist's mental and physiological inner workings mirrored by the tangled web of the city's inner machinations. Mentally, the hero's internal labyrinth of motives, confusion, and flaws is reflected in the city's underworld of organised crime, its corrupt political system, ethnic tensions and class conflicts within which he becomes entangled. His physiological stresses are mirrored in the city's subterranean labyrinthine infrastructure of sewers, gas pipes and water mains, which he must often literally penetrate, walking blindly through a dark and dank alien world about which he knows little. But for the criminal, these subterranean spaces are familiar places where they can disappear and seek shelter from their pursuers.

Brian McDonnell cites a scene in *Johnny Eager* (1941) in which all three levels of Christopher's noir labyrinth are put into play. In the scene, we follow Johnny, a cab driver played by Robert Taylor, as he enters an unmarked door in a building at a dog racing track:

> Johnny walks confidently through several front offices and through a number of ordinary doors in a new office building at a dog racetrack, then moves through a big steel door that leads to a luxury apartment, where he changes into very expensive clothes. The audience now realises that this secret back area is the hub of his criminal empire and learns a strong lesson about the typical deceptiveness of surface appearances in this genre. (Mayer and McDonnell 2007: 52)

Johnny's transformation from ordinary cabbie to underworld crime lord is revealed peripatetically as he leaves behind the two-dimensional city above and enters the intricate labyrinth of the criminal underworld. By the end of his walk, he stops pantomiming the one-dimensional persona of an honest, hard-working taxi driver to reveal his own complex labyrinthine character that coalesces with his hidden, underworld lair.

Along with setting, narrative, character types, and lighting, we can add camera movement to our list of film noir stylistic conventions. Most often, the camera is positioned on a static tripod and shots are framed within extreme angles, such as low, dutch, mirrored or cantilevered. Lighting and camera placement is privileged over camera movement to create noir's chiaroscuro and claustrophobic world. When a mobile camera is used, it will most likely be an outdoor crane shot. There are very few dolly shots in noir films.

One notable exception, however, are the intricate series of tracking shots that opens *D.O.A.* (1949), directed by Rudolf Maté. Beneath the opening credits, the film begins with a shot of the top of Los Angeles City Hall at night, then tilts down to street level as Frank Bigelow, his back to us, walks from the left into the frame and starts to cross the street towards the building. Maté dissolves to a tracking shot from behind Bigelow as he walks purposefully down a long, straight corridor, following him until he enters the police department. Bigelow is framed in the middle of the symmetrical space of the corridor just below ceiling level, the camera maintaining a consistent walking pace behind him. He reaches the end of the hallway, where a policeman engaged in conversation with another man points down another corridor to Bigelow's left. Bigelow, his back still to the camera, turns and starts walking down the left-hand corridor. After another dissolve, the camera continues to track behind Bigelow until he comes to a door on the right, near the very end of the corridor, that reads 'Homicide Division'. After he opens the door, the camera cuts to the inside of the homicide squad room as Bigelow walks up to a desk, asks to see the man in charge, and is ushered into another room. When the police captain asks if he can help him, Bigelow says, 'I want to report a murder,' then sits down heavily in a chair. He and the captain then have the following rapid-fire exchange:

> CAPTAIN: Sit down. Where was this murder committed?
> BIGELOW: San Francisco last night.
> CAPTAIN: Who was murdered?

The camera cuts to a close-up of Bigelow's face, the first time we see him frontally. After a long pause, Bigelow finally utters the laconic words, 'I was.' For the rest of the film, Bigelow narrates, in flashback, his story about being poisoned by a slow, deadly toxin that takes 24 hours to kill him. Throughout the flashback we follow him as he hurries to solve the mystery of his own murder. The opening shot which tracks Bigelow from behind mirrors the flashback device at the heart of the plot, propelling the mystery of his poisoning dorsally from the past to its resolution in the present.

We find a different yet equally iconic type of noir walking in Louis Malle's thriller *Elevator to the Gallows* (1958). Based on the French pulp fiction novel by Noël Calef, this noir film, in a nod to *Double Indemnity*, is about an adulterous affair that leads to murder. Florence Carala (Jeanne Moreau) is married to arms dealer Simon (Jean Wall) but is having an affair with his employee Julien Tavernier (Maurice Ronet). Together, they hatch a plan to murder Simon and make it look like suicide.

The plan seems simple enough. Julien will climb into Simon's office using a grappling iron, shoot him and stage it to look like a suicide. Julien's well designed plan depends on precision timing and the tactical skills he learned as a former paratrooper. But a chain of ill-fated events follows after he makes the mistake of leaving the grappling iron dangling from Simon's balcony and rushes to retrieve it. Returning to the office building, Julien enters the elevator just as a security guard cuts the power for the weekend, leaving Julien stranded between floors and cut off from Florence. Florence is left alone to roam the rain drenched streets of Paris at night searching for Julien, oblivious to his precarious entrapment in the dark elevator.

Florence prowls the city streets perched on the edge of madness, muttering out loud to herself. At one point, she steps incautiously into traffic, oblivious to the sound of screeching cars braking to avoid running her over. In true noir fashion, her peripatetic body is illuminated by the rain soaked pavements reflecting the street lamps in tandem with the light from the windows of cafés pulsating with her gait as she is propelled by the rhythm of Miles Davis's cool jazz soundtrack.

Detective Noir

The detective noir genre has all of the same stylistic bare bones of film noir but fleshes them out with some semantic and syntactical narrative elements. The stories are adapted from American hard-boiled pulp fiction, with all of the fast-paced, wise cracking dialogue from their primary source kept in the script. The plots are labyrinthine and complicated, shuffling back and forth between realism and flashback. Like their film noir cousins, detective noir films are set in large metropolises populated by the same kind of ruthless criminals clawing their way up through a seedy underworld. But the illicit underworld of detective noir is much more rampant and dangerous than the ones found in standard noir fare. Raymond Chandler sums up this underworld as one in which:

> gangsters can rule nations and almost rule cities, in which hotels and apartment houses and celebrated restaurants are owned by men who made their money out of brothels, in which a screen star can be the fingerman for a mob, and the nice man down the hall is a boss of the numbers racket; a world where a judge with a cellar full of bootleg liquor can send a man to jail for having a pint in his pocket, where the mayor of your town may have condoned murder as an instrument of moneymaking, where no man can walk down a dark street in safety because law and order are things we talk about but refrain from practising; a world where you may witness a hold-up in broad daylight and see who did it, but you will fade quickly back into the crowd rather than tell anyone, because the hold-up men may have friends with long guns, or the police may not like your testimony. (Chandler 1944: 59)

Much of the action in hard-boiled detective noir is motivated by walking. When it comes to the demand for action, Chandler's advice to hard-boiled screen writers is that, when in doubt, have a man walk through a door holding a gun. In contrast to Chaplin's comically rebellious peripatetic uses of city streets and sidewalks, the private detective's peripatetic actions are fraught with danger. Walking, so essential as lived experience in urban life, now becomes a walk of survival, stripped of all the niceties of the civilised etiquette of the pavement.

The private eye is a figure who can operate seamlessly in both the underworld and the world of law and order, yet is essentially a person of integrity and honour. He is street wise and often cool and cocky, whether dealing with a rich, high society client or a gun-toting sociopathic killer. He has a flair for repartee, using colourful vocabulary as a weapon. He almost always carries a gun himself, and is undaunted at the prospect of using violence when his verbal judo skills fail. He has an ambivalent relationship with the police and the law in general, sometimes because he was once a policeman who lost his badge for some indiscretion or other. He works alone, but sometimes relies on his beautiful and sexy secretary, whose looks and demeanour bump up against the traits of a femme fatale. He drinks too much, is always strapped for cash, and is sometimes immured by something in his past which is alluded to in hazy, partially constructed flashbacks. But most importantly, he is a gumshoe who is 'able to move with comfort across and between the layers and spheres of the city' (Farish 2005: 98). He walks the streets unburdened by social constraints or urban sidewalk etiquette, confident in his abilities to slip into the shadow of an alleyway or unlit vestibule and then reappear again undetected. As a solitary peripatetic anti-hero, the private eye is the embodiment of the modern, alienated urban subject released into, yet liberated by, the menacing gloom of America's broken post-war urban-scapes.

Philip Marlowe

The quintessential hard-boiled detective is Philip Marlowe, the Los Angeles gumshoe created in 1939 by Raymond Chandler. Beginning with *The Big Sleep*, Chandler immortalised Marlowe as he 'walked the mean streets' of Los Angeles in a series of seven novels – all of them adapted for the screen (a few more than once, for a total of ten films). Marlowe's biography is typical of the classic hard-boiled private eye. A hard bitten, never married bachelor, he used to be employed by the Los Angeles District Attorney as an investigator before he was fired for insubordination. He now works as a private detective alone out of a small office downtown. Because of his previous work as a policeman, he is no stranger to the Los Angeles underworld. Though never hesitant to curry favours or solicit information from friends he still has in the D.A.'s office, he is excruciatingly honest and hates corruption. His main haunts are the bars, diners, and hotel lobbies in downtown Los Angles, whose streets in the late 1940s were much more pedestrian friendly than they are today. His cases often require him to step off the beaten path of safe, well-policed pavements to venture down dark back alleys and streets into the seedy underworld of illicit gambling, pornography, and blackmail.

Marlowe walks a lot more in the novels than portrayed in the films. For instance, in *The Big Sleep*, Marlowe stakes out a bookstore owned by a man named Geiger that he suspects is a front for peddling pornography. As he sits in a chair pretending to be a customer waiting to see Geiger, Marlowe watches a man come into the store with a wrapped parcel in his arms. He hands the parcel to a woman behind a desk who then presses a buzzer to open a door secreted in the panelling which closes behind the customer as soon as he walks through into a back room. After a few minutes he emerges from the room carrying another wrapped parcel and exits the store. Marlowe decides to tail him on foot. Here is Chandler's description of the scene:

> He left as he had come, walking on the balls of his feet, breathing with his mouth open, giving me a sharp side glance as he passed. I got to my feet, tipped my hat to the blonde and went out after him. He walked west, swinging his cane in a small tight arc just above his right shoe. He was easy to follow. His coat was cut from a rather loud piece of horse robe with shoulders so wide that his neck stuck up out of it like a celery stalk and his head wobbled on it as he walked. We went a block and a half. At the Highland Avenue traffic signal I pulled up beside him and let him see me. He gave me a casual, then a suddenly sharpened side glance, and quickly turned away.

> We crossed Highland with the green light and made another block. He stretched his long legs and had twenty yards on me at the corner. He turned right. A hundred feet up the hill he stopped and hooked his cane over his arm and fumbled a leather cigarette case out of an inner pocket. He put a cigarette in his mouth, dropped his match, looked back when he picked it up, saw me watching him from the corner, and straightened up as if somebody had booted him from behind. He almost raised dust going up the block, walking with long gawky strides and jabbing his cane into the sidewalk. He turned left again. He had at least half a block on me when I reached the place where he had turned. He had me wheezing. This was a narrow tree-lined street with a retaining wall on one side and three bungalow courts on the other. He was gone. (Chandler 1998: 25–6)

Eyeing Marlowe from behind a cypress tree where he is trying to hide, the man panics and pitches the parcel into the branches of another tree. Then he lights a cigarette, and casually saunters back towards Marlowe, swinging his cane and whistling, passing him as they both pretend not to notice one another. After he is out of sight, Marlowe retrieves the parcel and walks on.

In his 1946 film adaptation starring Humphrey Bogart as Marlowe, Howard Hawkes keeps the scene in the bookstore but ditches Marlowe's subsequent gumshoe work of tailing his man. The scene does make the cut in Michael Winner's 1978 adaptation with veteran noir actor Robert Mitchum cast in the role of Marlowe. But Winner moves the setting from the gritty streets of 1940s Los Angeles to 1970s London and shoots the film in colour, sacrificing the American noir period milieu for a more faithful portrayal of drugs, homosexuality, and explicit pornography found in the novel that Hawkes had to censor from his film version because of the Hays code. The upshot of the reset to London is that Marlowe is able to stalk the streets on foot much more easily than in Los Angeles, since London is a city built for walking.

Marlowe is propelled into another peripatetic moment in *Farewell, My Lovely* when he is forced to trudge up 280 steps to keep an appointment made with a man named Lindsey Marriott who lives on the fictional Cabrillo Street. Marriott advises Marlowe that Cabrillo Street is hard to find by car, since it is located in a hilly neighbourhood where the streets are laid out in a serpentine pattern, and suggests that he walk to up to his house by taking a staircase adjacent to a pavement café. Chandler narrates Marlowe's walk this way:

> Above the beach the highway ran under a wide concrete arch which was in fact a pedestrian bridge. From the inner end of this a flight of concrete steps with a thick galvanized handrail on one side ran straight as a ruler up the side of the mountain. Beyond the arch the sidewalk café my client had spoken of, was bright and cheerful

inside . . . I walked back through the arch and started up the steps. It was a nice walk if you liked grunting. There were two hundred and eighty steps up to Cabrillo Street. (Chandler 1992: 46–7)

This walking scene is missing in all three film adaptations of Chandler's novel: *The Falcon Takes Over* (1942), *Murder, My Sweet* (1944), and *Farewell, My Lovely* (1975). The adaptation that shows the most fidelity to the gumshoe work highlighted in the novel is *Murder, My Sweet*, directed by Edward Dmytryk with Dick Powell playing Marlowe. But even here, Dmytryk eschews images of Marlowe walking for evocations of him doing so in Powell's narration. For instance, in the opening scene Marlowe is being interrogated at the police station as a suspect in several murders. When the police captain asks him about his alibi for the night of the first murder, Marlowe tells him he was at his office. Incredulous, the captain snaps back, 'What were you doing at the office that late?' Marlowe then begins to narrate his story in a flashback. As the camera pans out the window, the neon lights of the city below at night comes into view. Over this shot we hear Marlowe say, 'I'd been out peeking under old Sunday sections for a barber named Dominick whose wife wanted him back. I just found out all over how big this city is – my feet hurt.' The camera then dissolves to a series of shots of the city at street level before finally dissolving to a shot looking through a window in a brick office building from outside. Marlowe is framed in the bottom half of the window facing the camera and sitting with his feet up on the sill making a phone call. In the upper part of the window the name of Marlowe's detective agency is etched in gold letters. As the camera dollies in closer towards Marlowe, the light from a neon sign across the street flickers across the window as Marlowe's office pulsates between light and shadow. The camera then cuts to a close-up of Marlowe lighting a cigarette as his voice over says, 'There's something about the dead silence of an office building at night. Not quite real. The traffic down below is something that didn't have anything to do with me.'

The Police Procedural

The police procedural film shares many of the stylistic features of detective noir. They differ, however, in their plots and types of character. Like detective noir films, they are rooted in mystery novels, but here the private detective is replaced by a squad of professional police investigators; there are no lone sleuths prowling the city streets. According to George N. Dove, all police procedurals have two rudimentary features: 1) they take the narrative form of a clue-puzzle mystery story (the English country house murder mystery common in Agatha Christie novels); and 2) the mystery is solved by a group of tenacious police detectives using normal police procedures (Dove 1982: 47).

Their plots focus almost exclusively on the realistic and often monotonous details of a police investigation as it unfolds from a crime to its solution, and always in an urban setting. These detectives rely on routine and arduous police investigative methods – long stakeouts, conducting countless interviews, cultivating informants, detailed forensic analysis, legwork, tailing a suspect – rather than on the techniques of ratiocination and extraordinary powers of observation employed by classic amateur detectives like Sherlock Holmes or the street wise, violent, gut instinctual approaches of the hard-boiled private eye. They also have to abide by internal rules and regulations, and, most importantly, obey the law when conducting a criminal investigation. And, unlike both the classic detective and private eye who work alone or with just one other partner, the police procedural detective labours with a corps of colleagues who divide up the mundane tasks of routine police work.

Dove goes on to note several narrative conventions of the police procedural fiction formula. Though his study is limited to police mystery novels, I think we can find the same conventions in film adaptations along with some additional ones unique to them. I would like to explore these conventions as they are depicted in the first film to be recognised as representative of the genre, *The Naked City* (1948).

The Naked City is the first film to be shot fully on location in New York City without the use of a studio. Directed by Jules Dassin and shot in a semi-documentary style with noir elements that influenced the fledging French New Wave directors a decade later, *The Naked City* portrayed an investigation into a would-be suicide that turns out to be a murder. It follows veteran homicide detective Lt Pat Muldoon and his junior partner Jimmy Halloran as they work through routine, step-by-step investigative techniques to meticulously piece together the clues to solve the murder. Beginning with the murder itself staged to look like a suicide (which the audience is aware of before the detectives are) the plot shadows Muldoon and Halloran as they interview and re-interview witnesses and suspects, comb through mounds of police records and arrest files, and chase a host of leads, mostly on foot, across the labyrinthine boroughs of New York City.

Halloran, the younger detective played by Don Taylor, typifies all of Dove's conventional attributes of a homicide investigator in a police procedural. First, he is a happily married man who lives in the suburbs. Yet, there is just a slight hint of a troubled family life. In Halloran's case, his trouble is the trivial disagreement between him and his wife about whether a parent should ever whip a child. When he comes home from work after a particularly stressful shift, his wife informs him that she would like him to whip their young son for running to the park unaccompanied and without her permission. He begs off with the excuse that he is too tired before wondering out loud to her about the merits of corporal punishment. He is only saved from the chore by a phone call from Lt Muldoon informing him that he is needed back in the city precinct house immediately.

This brings us to another convention in our formula: the police detective is always overworked and has little time for himself or his family. He is never off duty, because time is always against him when he is on a case. Crimes like murder have to be solved quickly – usually with the first 48 hours – or the case risks going cold.

Another convention is the quotidian nature of the police detective. Halloran is a commonplace man with only ordinary abilities and talents for investigation. He possesses no real extraordinary abilities, intellectually or physically, and relies instead on a combination of a doggedly tough work ethic, dedication to police work, teamwork, self-discipline, and sheer luck to solve a case. Because of these traits, he is seen as an efficient homicide detective. He may be capable of heroic action, but because he is so meticulously by the book in his methods, he can usually solve a case and bring someone to justice without the theatrics of putting himself in too much physical danger.

The most routine method of detection used by Halloran is walking, and the camera strides with him. Early in the investigation, Muldoon recognises from the crime scene that the girl is a victim of homicide when he finds a bottle of sleeping pills under her bed. He sends Halloran out to 'start the legwork' of visiting the pharmacist who filled the prescription, the doctor who wrote it, and finally the dress shop where the victim worked. In the next scene we see Halloran walking briskly down a Manhattan sidewalk and into a chemist as a voice-over narrator explains:

> An investigation for murder is now underway. Will it advance methodically, by trial and error, by asking a thousand questions to get one answer, by brain work and legwork? When it comes to legwork, detective Jimmy Halloran is an expert. In the war he walked halfway across Europe with a rifle in his hand. Up until three months ago he was pounding a beat in the Bronx and now he's playing button up in the city of eight million people.

The persistent dangers and vitality of combat marching have been replaced by the tedious, bureaucratic proceduralism of police legwork. Like the private eye, Halloran walks alone; but in contrast to someone like Marlowe, his walking is stripped of the possibility of introspection encouraged by the rhythms of walking. For the police detective, walking is an act of professional utility and routine procedure, no more, and no less. This matter-of-factness about walking as routine is reinforced as Halloran leaves the chemist. The narrator tells us that to get to the victim's doctor, he will need to walk 'eighteen blocks south, four blocks west'.

In his legwork, Halloran has to negotiate the spaces of New York and map out what Gary Hausladen calls a 'sense of place'. For Hausladen, this term has a very specific meaning in police procedurals that has affinities with the labyrinth. It maps place as a narrative component of the police procedural film beyond the traditional concept of setting as an element of a film's mise-en-scène. It encompasses the cartographical ideas of locale – the setting where social interactions are established and organised – and location – the geographical setting surrounding the place where these interactions are constituted. He summarises the meaning of a sense of place as:

> all of the physical and human characteristics of the place – the physical and human landscapes, the way in which people interact, the formal and informal institutions that structure society . . . places are different and unique and that 'sense of place' is about these differences, the inherently unique character of different locations in the world. (Hausladen 2000: 23)

Derrida names this sense of place *ontopology*, which he defines as an 'axiomatics linking indissociably the ontological value of present-being [on] to its situation, to the stable and presentable determination of a locality, the topos of territory, native soil, city, body in general' (Derrida 2006: 69). The ontopology of the city is different for the detective from what it is for the villains in police procedurals. The villain has the advantage of not only being ontopologically situated in the above-ground topos of the city, but equally at home in its subterranean spaces. He comes to know these subterranean spaces better than anyone and can walk around them unmolested by the police.

The detectives are often completely ignorant of the existence of a world below street level. On rare occasions, the detective squad might be lucky enough to procure a map from a resourceful engineer toiling away in a tiny office tucked away somewhere in the city's Department of Water and Sewers (Christopher 2010: 39). For example, in the 1948 police procedural *He Walked by Night*, the killer of the policeman uses the extensive network of sewers beneath Los Angeles as escape routes from his armed heists, stashing weapons in strategic places to deploy in case the police pursue him into the tunnels. When the police manhunt finally catches up with him, he escapes by disappearing into a sewer well. After scouring a map of the city sewer system, the detectives submerge to give chase on foot, following the noise of the criminal's footfalls echoing off the cavernous walls. The detectives eventually close in, and he leads them on a running gun battle through the labyrinth of sewers before they shoot and kill him beneath a manhole cover. Shot using high contrast black and white film by John Alton, the lighting and cinematography of these sewer scenes influenced Carol Reed a year later when he shot similar ones in Vienna's sewers in the noir classic *The Third Man*.

In both the detective noir and police procedural film, the labyrinthine endoskeleton of the city is a disorderly setting of danger, intrigue, and unpredictability. Yet, the perambulations of the detective remind us that the city also has its predictable rhythms and orderly patterns which converge on the screen for the viewers. Cinema opens up the closed, prison like spaces of the city, allowing us to walk the streets and to 'set off calmly on journeys of adventure among its far-flung debris' from the safety of the screen (Benjamin 2003: 265).

Notes

1. In fact, Baudelaire credits Poe with the invention of the detective. Citing Baudelaire, Benjamin argued that:

   > the original social content of the detective story focused on the obliteration of the individual's traces in the big-city crowd . . . Photography made it possible for the first time to preserve permanent and unmistakable traces of human being. The detective story came into being when this most decisive of all conquests of a person's incognito had been accomplished . . . Poe's famous tale 'The Man of the Crowd' is something like an X-ray of a detective story. It does away with all the drapery that a crime represents. Only the armature remains: the pursuer, the crowd, and an unknown man who manages to walk through London in such a way that he always remains in the middle of the crowd. This unknown man is the *flâneur*. (Benjamin 2006: 74, 79)

   Many scholars have written about how Poe's detective embodies Baudelaire's concept of *flâneurie*. I discuss the *flâneur* in detail in Chapter 6 and will not approach the subject of this chapter through the lens of *flâneurie*.
2. Because the rubber soles of the shoes rendered them noiseless, London police nicknamed the invention 'sneakers'.

CHAPTER 5

Homing

And I remember that some of it wasn't very nice, but most of it was beautiful. But just the same, all I kept saying to everybody was, 'I want to go home!'
                                                    Dorothy – *The Wizard Oz*

Like walking, the concept of 'home' has been the subject of much scholarly debate over the last two decades. Scholars in disciplines such as literary studies, environmental studies, rangeland management, social work, geography, political science, and philosophy have all published articles exploring our everyday understanding of home. Home can mean many things. It can be a fixed place, such as one's native soil or city of birth, a house or other abode, a street where one grew up, a school, a person or even one's own body. It can be an idea, such as family, security, comfort, familiarity or a sense of belonging. Today, it can even be a GPS point on a car's satellite navigation system, a folder on a computer, a tab on a word processing program or a button on a smartphone.

Phenomenologically, the concept of home overlaps with the important philosophical concept of *dwelling*. In this chapter, I want to explore the narrative theme of 'trying to get home' in a handful of films where walking is relevant to achieving this goal by paying particular attention to home as dwelling. My first task will be to situate my theme in the narrower philosophical context by introducing the views of Heidegger and Levinas on the phenomenology of home.

Dwelling

We can situate the locus of Heidegger's meditations on dwelling in Novalis's claim that philosophy is a form of *homesickness*. Philosophers, he asserts, philosophise because they are driven by an 'urge to be a home everywhere'. What does this mean? Heidegger explains:

> To be at home everywhere – what does this mean? Not merely here or there, nor even simply in every place, in all taken together one after the other. Rather, to be at home everywhere means to be at once and all times within the whole. We name this within the whole and its character of wholeness the *world*. (Heidegger 1995: 5)

One way Heidegger characterises *world* is to ascribe it to Being itself as a whole. Ontologically, a human being (dasein) is a 'being-in-the world' who is restless to return to Being as a whole. Ontologically, then, we are both homeless and homesick. Yet, experientially, our existence is characterised topologically by a definite place, since we are first *placed* in our bodies, *situated* on earth and *bound* by our own finitude.

In his lecture 'Building, Dwelling, Thinking', Heidegger explores our human spatial existence in the world through an analysis of dwelling. In the lecture, he asks two questions that have a bearing on the subject of home: 1) What is it to dwell? and; 2) How does building belong to dwelling? He begins to provide answers by tracing the etymology of the German word *bauen*, which means 'to build', to its origins in the older German word *buan*, which means 'to dwell'. To dwell signifies 'to remain or to stay in place'. Since *bauen* originally meant to dwell, dwelling, then, precedes building. But building is an essential part of dwelling, so to build is really the same thing as to dwell. Here Heidegger is talking about both the 'act' of building and an 'actual' building as a place to dwell. So dwelling takes *place* in the very places we build, mainly in our houses.

But to show us just how far the nature of dwelling reaches beyond our buildings, Heidegger walks the German word *bin*, which means 'to be', back to *bauen* and thus further to its etymological home in *buan*. Our manner of being as humans is *buan*, dwelling. So, to be human means to *dwell* on earth as a mortal being. Heidegger's formula looks like this: building=dwelling=being (Heidegger 2001: 143–5).

To dwell is to settle in a home, but to build a home means more than just building a house in which we settle. Home signifies more than just the private, interior places in our houses where we feel settled and comfortable. Home, as dwelling, is our way of being in the world, of setting up a place in our environment and moving about it. Thus, Heidegger conceives of home as a dwelling built by clearing out a space through setting a boundary or limit:

> What the word for space, *Raum, Rum*, designates is said by its ancient meaning. *Raum* means a place cleared or freed for settlement and lodging. A space is something that has been made room for, something that is clear and free, namely within a boundary, Greek *peras*. (Heidegger 2001: 152)

Yet, he reminds us that the Greek's conception of a boundary is not only something that closes or limits that which is outside it, but also opens up and invites in that which it encompasses: 'That is why the concept is that of *horismos*, that is, the horizon, the boundary. Space is in essence that for which room has been made, that which is let into its bounds' (Heidegger 2001: 152). The outside is already inside.

So to dwell at home means more than just building a space for shelter. A dwelling place is a space that has been made room for lodging within a boundary that marks both the limits of an interior space and the beginning of an exterior one. Dwelling, though fundamental to human existence, is nevertheless an aporia that implies staying put while moving around and through one's environment. Like walking and cinema, it is a combination of stasis and mobility, continuities and discontinuities, indivisibility and divisibility. It oscillates between interiority and exteriority, intimacy and withdrawal, and is a form of recollecting the world that presupposes home. This is why Levinas argues against reducing the idea of home to a physical structure situated in the objective world utilised solely as an implement for habitation. It is, rather, the reverse: 'The objective world is situated to my relation to my dwelling' (Levinas and Lingis 1969: 153). House and home are not the same thing. He goes on to argue that a home is:

> set back from the anonymity of the earth, air, the light, the forest, the road, the sea, the river . . . Circulating between visibility and invisibility, one is always bound for the interior of which one's home, one's corner, one's tent, or one's cave is the vestibule. The primordial function of the home does not consist in orienting being by the architecture of the building and in discovering a site, but in breaking the plenum of the element, of opening in it the utopia in which the 'I' recollects itself in dwelling at home with itself. But separation does not isolate me, as though I were simply extracted from these elements. (Levinas and Lingis 1969: 156)

So human beings abide first in the interior, intimate spaces of 'dwelling', ontologically and existentially, before we set out for the exterior, outside world which is constituted by our dwelling. As we have already said, our first dwelling is our body and incarnated consciousness in which we are at home in ourselves. To be embodied means to inhabit our own private vestibule that is open to the outside world but also acts as a protective barrier against its hostilities. Walking is one way we carry this home to others as a form of hospitality. Our house, wherever we build it, is an extension of this hospitable embodiment in the world which serves to both protect us from the elements and to usher them in, when we allow it. Just as we can open our eyes to let the outside world rush in, so too can we open a door or window of our house to welcome in the elements or a neighbour.

Levinas goes on to connect dwelling to manual labour and, like Heidegger, confines the domain of manual labour to the use of hands. But manual labour cannot be confined to the hands alone. Though we perceive the world with our whole body, we are grounded first by our feet. We forget that the foot is also an organ of touch, which should be obvious to us not only when we walk, but also when we are performing labour. When we build something with our hands, we often check our progress by walking around the object, looking at it, touching it. Manual labour is a coordination between touch, cognition, and locomotion. In this sense, our dwellings contain traces of the builder's footwork constituently with their handiwork.

The Wizard of Oz

Whether we are city dwellers, suburban commuters or inhabitants of small rural towns, most of us are familiar with the longing to hurry home from work, from travel or from anywhere else for that matter. The world's literature is full of epic journeys of heroes struggling against all sorts of odds to return home where they dwell. Odysseus is the most famous, but we should also remember Moses, Gilgamesh, Frodo Baggins or even Lassie. But it is Dorothy's perlocutionary utterance 'There's no place like home' while tapping her ruby slippers together in *The Wizard of Oz* that conjures up the most iconic image of home in cinema.

Most of us probably know the plot. The film opens with Dorothy running home after school to her aunt's farm in Kansas. She rushes through the gate in distress to report to her Auntie Em and Uncle Henry that their neighbour Miss Gulch has struck her dog Toto, claiming the dog broke into her garden and chased her cat. Aunt Em and Uncle Henry are too busy trying to count and save their remaining chicks from a broken-down incubator to pay her much attention. Likewise, the farmhands are immersed in their work and have no time to give Dorothy any more than cursory advice. Miss Gulch shows up on her bicycle with the Sheriff's warrant to seize Toto and, we can assume, have him put down. Toto escapes from Miss Gulch's bicycle basket and runs home to Dorothy who then decides to run away from home with Toto. On the road they meet Professor Marvel, a travelling fortune teller who, after multiple guesses, deduces that Dorothy has run away. He uses his fake crystal ball to trick Dorothy into believing that her aunt is seriously ill and Dorothy races back home. Just as she reaches home, a tornado strikes. The others have taken shelter in the storm cellar, unintentionally locking Dorothy out. She seeks refuge in her bedroom, only to be knocked out by a flying window sash blown out by the powerful winds of the tornado as it hits the house. The twister lifts the house, traps it in its vortex, and sends it spinning upwards through the dark sky. When the house lands, Dorothy finds herself in another world, the land of Oz. The remainder of the film takes the form of a typical hero's quest with all its trials and tribulations, as Dorothy must walk along a yellow brick road to the Emerald City to ask the Wizard there to help her get back home to Kansas. Finally, she awakens in her bed in Kansas and the film ends with her repeating the mantra 'There's no place like home.'

In the book, Baum describes the house where Dorothy lives as a one-room dwelling sparsely furnished with a rusty cooking stove, a dish cupboard, a table and few chairs, and two beds: one for her aunt and uncle and one for her. When Dorothy stands at the doorway threshold and looks out, all she can see for miles and miles is a flat, bleak, grey prairie reaching to a horizon broken up only by dried, cracked, and equally grey, ploughed fields. No other houses or trees are visible. Even the exterior of her house is bleak, its paint baked off by the blistering prairie sun leaving only raw, greyed lumber at the mercy of the elements. These monotone images are impressions of ugliness and death, and hardly evoke the comforts of home. Though written in 1900, Baum's description of Kansas is presciently similar to how dust bowl era Kansas would look a generation later. Released in 1939 during the depression, the film's Kansas scenes were shot in sepia tones, reflecting the realistic contemporary drama of dust bowl weary farmers struggling to stay on their drought struck homesteads throughout the 1930s.

Oz, on the other hand, is a land of colour and great beauty. This is how Baum describes Dorothy's first experience of Oz:

> The cyclone had set the house down very gently – for a cyclone – in the midst of a country of marvellous beauty. There were lovely patches of greensward all about, with stately trees bearing rich and luscious fruits. Banks of gorgeous flowers were on every hand, and birds with rare and brilliant plumage sang and fluttered in the trees and bushes. A little way off was a small brook, rushing and sparkling along between green banks, and murmuring in a voice very grateful to a little girl who had lived so long on the dry, grey prairies. (Baum and Children's Classics 1996: 5)

For the film, Oz is shot in Technicolor.[1] Dorothy opens the front door of her house and steps out from her monotone world and into a suffusion of colour. Her dilapidated house stands displaced in stark contrast to the round, brightly painted blue Munchkin houses and their well-groomed lawns and gardens. Unlike Dorothy's bleak and cluttered Kansas farmstead, the Munchkin farms are tidy affairs, surrounded by freshly painted blue fences and fields ripe with grains and vegetables.

There have been several scholarly analyses of the film from a variety of theoretical perspectives, including psychoanalytical, Marxist, feminist, structuralist, and postmodern. All of these, with few exceptions, agree that the central theme of the book and film is *home*. But what is the film's definition of home? We should first note that Dorothy is carried to Oz in the very house in which she lives. But her house is not the same as her home. For Dorothy, home is not so much a place, but a condition of dwelling. When the Scarecrow asks Dorothy to tell him something about her home in Kansas, her immediate response is to tell him how grey it is. The Scarecrow then remarks, 'I cannot understand why you should wish to leave this beautiful country and go back to the dry, gray place you call Kansas.' Dorothy's reply is to first remind him that he is empty headed (because he lacks a brain, he is not an embodied consciousness) and he can never understand the concept of home: 'No matter how dreary and gray our homes are, we people of flesh and blood would rather live there than in any other country, be it ever so beautiful. There is no place like home' (Baum and Children's Classics 1996: 18–19).

Dorothy's driving motivation is to return home to her aunt in Kansas by any means necessary. However, there is but one means available to her: a long and arduous journey down the yellow brick road to the Emerald City to ask the Wizard there to help her find her way home. When she asks Glinda the Good Witch of the North how she will travel down the yellow brick road to Emerald City, her reply is simply 'you must walk' and she then gives her a new pair of shoes.

In the film, Dorothy arrives in colourful Oz wearing a pair of dull, black lace-up shoes worn by any typical Kansas farm girl. But these are soon replaced when Glinda magically transfers a pair of enchanted ruby slippers to her feet, telling her 'to keep tight inside of them'. Integral to the plot and her character, Dorothy's ruby slippers are rivalled only by Chaplin's costume as the most iconic wardrobe pieces in film history. In Baum's book they are silver. For the film, screenwriter Noel Langley changed their colour to ruby for the simple reason that in Technicolor red is more radiant than silver against the surface of the yellow brick road.

Psychoanalytic critics have noted that in Freudian terms, 'slippers' symbolise the vagina and the colour red suggests menstrual blood. Perhaps, but the shoes placed on Dorothy's feet could hardly count as slippers, if by that we mean the type of light footwear designed to be worn indoors that are easy to slip on and off and evoke all the comforts and cosiness of home. Instead of slippers, costume designer Gilbert Adrian used a pair of ordinary pumps with French heels, dyed them red, and then embroidered red sequins to the leather uppers. Freudian analysis aside, this is hardly practical footwear for someone who is about to embark on a long and dangerous journey on foot.

The yellow brick road begins in the centre of town in Munchkinland as the tip of a spiral spinning anticlockwise, like a tornado, before straightening out in the countryside.[2] Dorothy's first few steps in her new shoes on the yellow brick road are circular and anticlockwise. She has difficulty getting started. She must first find her balance, her rhythm. The corkscrew like road mimics her spiralling spirit as she finds her rhythm in dancing and the joy of stepping out onto a new, unfamiliar road. In her short essay 'Street Haunting: A London Adventure' Virginia Woolf describes the joy of stepping out of our familiar surroundings and walking out onto new streets:

> The shell-like covering which our souls have excreted to house themselves, to make for themselves a shape distinct from others, is broken, and there is left of all these wrinkles and roughness a central oyster of perceptiveness, an enormous eye. (Woolf 1974: 21–2)

The spiral road is Dorothy's seashell, more *secreted* than excreted, which she must slowly slough off on her journey. It is also like the labyrinthine canal inside of her ear, part of the vestibular system which plays a crucial role in helping her to maintain her balance while walking. So, as she begins her journey back to Kansas, her home has not been completely broken.

The first person Dorothy meets on the road is a talking Scarecrow suspended on a pole in a cornfield. She is at a fork in the road and does not know which way to go. Crossing his arms, he points her in both directions at once. In the book, he is described as having a head made of a small sack filled with straw ears and eyes and nose painted on. He wears a blue hat, a blue suit of clothes, and blue topped boots, all stuffed with straw. He tells Dorothy how he was made by two Munchkin farmers and the order in which he was created: head, ears, eyes, nose, mouth, body, arms and finally legs. The one thing they forgot to create for him was a brain. After he was made the farmers declared, 'He is a man', hoisted him on a pole, and then walked away. His first inclination was to walk after them, but his feet were too high off the ground. Though he can move his head and his arms, no mention is made of his ability to move his legs or feet.

This 'straw man' is indicative of the general Western bias of privileging the mind over the body, but it specifically calls to mind what Tim Ingold dubs the 'rise, and eventual triumph, of head over heels'. He goes on to say 'it seems that with the onward march of civilisation, the foot has been progressively *withdrawn* from the sphere of the operation of intellect, that it has regressed to the status of a merely mechanical apparatus' (Ingold

2004: 319). Ingold argues that this state of affairs is a direct consequence of our spending much of our lives wearing tightly laced shoes or boots designed to constrict the foot's freedom of movement and dull its sense of touch. This 'mechanisation of footwork' since the Industrial Revolution has played a large part in making the historically constructed binary separation between cognition and locomotion appear to be natural (Ingold 2004: 319, 321).

Most of us probably do not wear gloves on a daily basis, but when we do, we tend to wear those designed to maintain our hands' prehensile abilities. While work gloves need to be pliant, most work boots are required to be hard and stiff. One can use a nurse's workwear as an example. For footwear, they typically wear leather clogs with reinforced toe caps and protective heel counters combined with contoured midsoles and stiff, rocker bottom hard soles. All of these features help prevent foot fatigue during hours of walking and provide lateral stability while standing for long periods. But these features are also designed to blunt the tactility of the foot in the shoe so that the nurse can forget about their feet and put them out of their mind while working. Their gloves, on the other hand, are designed with a totally different purpose in mind. Medical gloves are designed to fit the hand anatomically like a second skin, allowing for the natural movement of the palm, fingers, and thumbs. They must be thin enough not to interfere with touch sensation or digital dexterity when used to grip, but strong enough not to easily puncture.

The Scarecrow's wardrobe is designed to fit his non-peripatetic nature. He is fitted with gloves typical of those worn by farmhands. He is able to point and grasp things such as the brim of his hat or handfuls of straw to stuff back into his shirt. But his boots are tight fitted, like Dorothy's slippers, and are clown-like, with exaggerated upturned toes. His boots are not really made for walking; but neither is he, since he is made from straw with neither bones nor joints.

When Dorothy pulls him from his pole, since he has never touched the ground, he can barely stand and has trouble finding his balance, like a toddler who tries to walk without ever first learning to crawl. He remarks that he has no feelings in his legs or toes, but he does not mind that sort of numbness. What he does mind is not having a brain and being taken by others for a numb-headed fool. And so he is off with Dorothy to see the Wizard to ask him for his brains. Like Dorothy, he has a hard time starting out on the road.

To make things more difficult, the yellow brick road is not well maintained. It is uneven, and full of pot holes. Dorothy, Toto, and the Scarecrow all have difficulty walking on its broken surface:

> After a few hours the road began to be rough, and the walking grew so difficult that the Scarecrow often stumbled over the yellow bricks, which were here very uneven. Sometimes, indeed, they were broken or missing altogether, leaving holes that Toto jumped across and Dorothy walked around. As for the Scarecrow, having no brains, he walked straight ahead, and so stepped into the holes and fell at full length on the hard bricks. It never hurt him, however, and Dorothy would pick him up and set him upon his feet again, while he joined her in laughing merrily at his own mishap. (Baum and Children's Classics 1996: 18)

After walking awhile, they stumble upon a Tin Man standing immobilised next to his house along the road. Unlike the Scarecrow, he used to be a real human being, who made his living as a woodcutter in the forest. He ran afoul of the Wicked Witch who cursed his axe so that every time he swung at a tree, the axe turned back and struck his body, leaving him headless and dismembered. A tinsmith rebuilt him out of metal, piecing him back together until his entire body was made of tin. But, as we know, the tinsmith forgot to place a heart in his hollow chest. But his new body suited the woodcutter just fine until one day, while out chopping wood, it started raining and he was unable to reach the safety of his house before his joints rusted and he froze into a tin statue. When Dorothy chances upon him she applies oil to the metal joints in his arms and legs and finally he regains the ability to move and walk. The Scarecrow's clumsy, limbering gait is elegant compared to the Tin Man's clanking, mechanical strides. Like the Scarecrow, his legs are wobbly, but he recovers enough motility to join Dorothy on her long walk to find the Wizard who he hopes can make him whole again by giving him a heart.

The Scarecrow must *learn* to walk from scratch and the Tin Man *relearn* to walk from memory. The only companion Dorothy rescues on the road who does not have trouble walking is the Cowardly Lion. As a real lion, he is a natural walker. Though a quadruped, he walks on two legs like a human. In *Philosophical Investigations*, Wittgenstein enigmatically quipped, 'If a lion could talk, we could not understand him.' We might rephrase it as, 'If a lion could *walk on two legs*, we could not understand him.' Though we are used to the andromorphic depiction of animals in fairy tales and cartoons as bipedal, there is still something uncanny about it. Most often the depiction is used for humorous effect, as in every Bugs Bunny cartoon. But sometimes it can be a serious depiction of a regressive degradation from animal innocence to the level of human corruption as, for example, when the pigs suddenly stand upright and begin walking on two legs in Orwell's *Animal Farm*. But in the case of Oz's lion, who lacks courage and therefore does not really possess the true nature of a lion, his bipedalism signifies his deep humanity. It is worth quoting the book at length from the scene in which Dorothy and the others first meet him:

> All this time Dorothy and her companions had been walking through the thick woods. The road was still paved with yellow brick, but these were much covered by dried branches and dead leaves from the trees, and the walking was not at all good . . . here came from the forest a terrible roar, and the next moment a great Lion bounded into the road. With one blow of his paw he sent the Scarecrow spinning over and over to the edge of the road, and then he struck at the Tin Woodman with his sharp claws. But, to the Lion's surprise, he could make no impression on the tin, although the Woodman fell over in the road and lay still. Little Toto, now that he had an enemy to face, ran barking toward the Lion, and the great beast had opened his mouth to bite the dog, when Dorothy, fearing Toto would be killed, and heedless of danger, rushed forward and slapped the Lion upon his nose as hard as she could, while she cried out, 'Don't you dare to bite Toto! You ought to be ashamed of yourself, a big beast like you, to bite a poor little dog!' 'I didn't bite him', said the Lion, as he rubbed his nose with his paw where Dorothy had hit it. 'No, but you tried to', she retorted. 'You are nothing but a big coward.' 'I know it', said the Lion, hanging his head in shame. 'I've always known it. But how can I help it?' (Baum and Children's Classics 1996: 30–1)

He goes on to ask Dorothy whether the Scarecrow and Tin Man are both creatures who are stuffed. After hearing her angrily reply that the Scarecrow is indeed stuffed but the Tin Man is made of tin, he asks of Toto, 'Is he made of tin, or stuffed?' Dorothy responds right away with 'Neither', but then stumbles trying to find the next words before finally stuttering, 'He's a – a – a meat dog.' When she questions him about the origin of his cowardice he replies simply 'It's a mystery . . . I suppose I was born that way' (Baum and Children's Classics 1996: 32).

The lion is the least understandable of Dorothy's walking companions in the film, because he is the only natural creature of the three. He is a real animal, naturally mobile, and free to roam the forests of Oz on his own. Like Toto, he is a 'meat' creature, made of real flesh and blood. A mortal creature, he was simply born without the trait of courage which, while unusual for a lion, is not really mysterious; it is simply his individual nature to be cowardly. The Tin Man and Scarecrow are artificial creatures fashioned by their makers to lack a heart and brains, respectively. Walking is an alien activity to them. As a flesh and blood animal, the Cowardly Lion is a natural walker, and Dorothy's closest peripatetic companion.

Dorothy does make it home to Kansas, but not in the way she expected. She is conveyed back to Kansas by walking, often in a roundabout way. Her strong desire for home combined with the magic properties of the ruby slippers finally help her transport back to her dwelling in Kansas all on her own.

Rabbit-Proof Fence

Perhaps there is no greater motivation for returning home than that of a child escaping their abductor. This is what motivates the peripatetic journey of the Aboriginal children in the Australian film *Rabbit-Proof Fence* (2002) directed by Philip Noyce.

The film is based on a true story set against the backdrop of a shameful episode in Australian history. In 1906, the Australian parliament passed the Aboriginal Act which mandated the forcible removal of so called half-caste children (the progenies of a white father and Aboriginal mother) from their Aboriginal families by the government and their placement in government-run boarding schools to train as domestic servants for white families. Multiple justifications were made for enforcing the policy, ranging from saving the tribal Aboriginal population from extinction by helping them to assimilate into white society to protecting young Aboriginal girls from predatory sexual exploitation by white men. The act created a new colonial administrative position with the title of Chief Protector of Aborigines who was appointed the legal guardian of every Aboriginal and half-caste child under the age of eighteen in Australia. He was given the power and authority to remove any half-caste child from their Aboriginal family and place them in a government boarding school. The practice of removing these children, who have since been labelled the 'stolen generations', continued until 1967 when the law was finally overturned. In the Western Territory, many of the children's white fathers had come to the territory to work on what came to be called the 'rabbit-proof fence', and who, when the work was over, abandoned their Aboriginal families. The rabbit-proof fence was designed to keep agricultural pests like the rabbits of the eastern desert regions out of the Western Australian cattle and sheep pastoral grasslands. There are three such fences in Australia, but the first one to be completed in 1907 (called Number One Fence) is the longest, bisecting the continent north to south from the Indian Ocean to the Southern Ocean and running for 1,139 miles.

The Number One Fence cuts through many Aboriginal settlements, including the community of Jigalong, established in 1907 at the western edge of Little Sandy Desert near the fence's northern terminus as a maintenance and supply post for whites working on the fence. In 1931 three half-caste girls – fourteen-year-old Molly Craig, her eight-year-old sister Daisy, and their ten-year-old cousin Gracie – were abducted from their home in

Jigalong by order of the Chief Protector of the Aborigines A. O. Neville and taken south to the Moore River Native Settlement boarding school. Their traumatic abduction, eventual escape from the school and subsequent embarkation on an epic thousand-mile trek on foot through the Australian outback to Jigalong along the fence is the subject of the book *Follow the Rabbit-Proof Fence* by Molly's daughter Doris Pilkington and the 2002 film adaptation *Rabbit-Proof Fence* directed by Philip Noyce.

Set in 1931, the film begins as the three girls are living with their mothers and grandmothers at the Jigalong depot. In Perth, the Chief protector of the Aborigines A. O. Neville (played by Kenneth Branagh) signs the order for the girls' forcible removal and transport to the Moore River Settlement 1,200 miles away to the south so that they can begin their training to enter service. The order is carried out by the local constable who whisks the three girls away from their family's camp, forcing them into a car and then on to a train. When they arrive at the school, they are placed in a dormitory with other half-caste children who have been stolen. The nuns who run the school forbid them to speak their native tongue. When Neville visits the school he examines Molly and decides that, because she has a whiter complexion than the other girls, she will be sent to a more advanced school for white skinned half-castes. The girls witness an Aboriginal tracker named Moodoo return a runaway back the school. The nuns promptly lock the girl in a shed and beat her. Molly convinces Daisy and Gracie that they must run away and the three of them escape during a rainstorm. Neville is informed and sends Moodoo to track them. Walking east, they eventually find the rabbit-proof fence and begin an arduous trek home, heading north along the fence through the hostile outback. Gracie is eventually recaptured, but Molly and Daisy elude their pursuers and, against all odds, make it back to their families in Jigalong.

The film opens with an aerial shot above a desert landscape as a voice-over of Molly says: 'This is a true story of my sister Daisy, my cousin Gracie, and me when we were little.' As she describes how the white man came to build an outpost in Jigalong and her people came to settle near the fence depot, the camera tilts up to the sky then tilts back down to frame a long fence snaking across an empty desert.

For Molly's people, the Jigalong band of the Mardudjara, the fence is a physical manifestation of the racist, hegemonic colonising project of white Europeans. It symbolises the domination of the colonisers over the colonised, white men over black women's sexuality, civilisation over wildness, controlled cultivation over feral invasion and paternalistic protectionism over assimilation. The fence operates as a border, which is the opposite of a boundary indicating a home as a place for dwelling, because it closes space without any room for openness. This deterritorialisation of space makes the dwelling place of Molly's tribe inhospitable and renders the Mardudjara homeless. The act of creating a homeless population of indigenous people through colonisation, Eric Harper argues, is a form violence that can only be produced in:

> places in which the other has no mental or physical space into which they can retreat and move . . . homelessness and violence are linked in multiple ways. Those considered not to be at home are abused and violated . . . they are open to subtle forms of violence from stigmatisation, prejudice, and 'othering' to more overt forms of violence like physical abuse and violence (such as murder and rape). In each of the acts, there is a loss of space to retreat into. When the home – mental, physical, spiritual or material space – is under attack, regardless of the source of violence, be it from within or without the home, there is a demand for submission of space, a giving up of space. Home as a site of retreat, is emptied out by the weight of violence. Homelands, my home, my sanctuary, the place from which I come into the world is swallowed up by the impact of direct and indirect violence through a forced removal, a taking away of the space to express a personal rhythm, different sites of enjoyment and from which to feel safe to enter out into the world. (Harper 2012: 73–4)

Following Franz Fanon, Harper argues that the archetypical name for this act of violence is *torture*. Colonisation is just another name for torture that is rendered as a 'spatial metaphor of occupation', whose aim is to 'totally and absolutely appropriate the body, thought and soul of the colonised, such that the person is reduced to a nameless and homeless state, flesh, property that belongs to the coloniser'. This form of violence can only result in the forced assimilation of the colonised wherein the 'coloniser restricts the spatial possibility within which the colonised body moves and constricts the movement of the coloniser through imposing of habits . . . that leave the imprints of the coloniser on the body, thought and ancestors of the colonised' (Harper 2011: http://fondation-frantzfanon.com/what-if-fanon-read-biko/). The combination of the Number One Fence and the Aboriginal Act together fulfilled these aims against the Mardudjara.

We learn from Molly that the Mardudjara were once a nomadic tribe, criss-crossing the Western Australian desert in their bare feet, dwelling freely for over 40,000 years all over the land on the rabbit side of the fence before it was constructed. Walking is not only the Mardudjara's sole means of travelling, it is also a ritually sacred act. Central to the belief system of the Mardudjara is the idea of a songline or dreaming track. Songlines are invisible pathways made by the totemic ancestor creator-beings who, while walking across the Australian continent in Dreamtime, 'scattered a trail of words and musical notes along the line of [their] footprints . . . singing out the name of everything that crossed their path – birds, animals, plants, rocks, waterholes – and so singing the world into existence' (Chatwin 1987: 2, 13). These songlines – the mythical footprints of the ancestors – are preserved and passed down in songs, rituals, art, and stories, and contain numerous references to features of the landscape. As long as a person knows the song of a particular dreaming track and can sing it in its proper sequence while walking, they can navigate their way over immense distances, even in parts of the country where they have never before been, without getting lost. Interwoven across the entire continent of Australia, these meandering song tracks serve as geographical direction finders and cognitive maps of the landscape.

Part of the Mardudjara's belief in songlines is the idea that all living things had originally been created in secret beneath the earth's crust and were called up to the surface each in its turn by the ancestors walking a songline. To walk a songline is to sing with the landscape and help to keep the world alive by 'singing up the land', through re-enacting the sacred time when the ancestors sung up the country. But also originally secreted are all of the technologies white Europeans brought to Australia, including ones yet to be invented which are 'slumbering below the surface, waiting their turn to be called' (Chatwin 1987: 15). Thus, ironically, the rabbit-proof fence the girls follow can be identified as a songline that serves as a cartographical marker of home.

In the first ground level shot of the fence, the three girls are shown playing alongside it and talking to a white man. Molly asks him 'how far does rabbit fence go to?' The workman replies:

> Rabbit-proof fence? Goes all the way to the sea that way [pointing north] right to the top of Australia. Longest fence in the world. And all the way down to the sea that way [pointing south]. 1,500 miles long. Keeps the rabbits on that side of the fence and keeps the farmland on this side.

The fence has cut off Molly's people from their nomadic traditions and forced them to live on the settled farmland side. It as much contains the Mardudjara inside as it does the rabbits outside and is a material reminder of how the colonisers view Molly's people as a pestilence that needs to be domesticated and controlled. And indeed, this is exactly the purpose of the Moore River Settlement, which resembles and is run more like a concentration camp than a boarding school. All of the girls there are destined like cattle to be farmed out as domestic servants to white farmers. But once the three girls escape and find it, the fence takes on new meaning as a familiar songline and homing beacon to walk along. The fence, once a barrier and a device of incursion – shutting her people off from uninhibited walkabouts, imprisoning them, turning them into settlers – now serves as a symbol of 'love, home, and security' (Pilkington 2002: 109). The fence becomes a symbol of homecoming. Like Dorothy, the girls are motivated to make a long journey on foot by the simple desire to return home to their mother's camp at the Jigalong depot alongside the fence. Their home territory is etched in their 'memory's landscape' and the fence is part of that, a songline they can follow to sing up their home country.

The Way Back

Peter Weir's film *The Way Back* (2011) is a film about a group of prisoners who escape a Soviet gulag in Siberia during World War II and walk 4,000 miles to freedom in British India. It is based on the 1956 memoir *The Long Walk: The True Story of a Trek to Freedom* by Polish soldier Slavomir Rawicz. Though the authenticity of his epic journey as told in the memoir has been partly discredited by historians, Weir uses only the bare bones of Rawicz's story to create the narrative for the film. At the heart of this narrative is a story about walking.

The film opens in 1940 in Russia-occupied Poland with the sentencing of a Polish soldier named Janusz (Jim Sturgess) who has been found guilty of espionage based on the false testimony of his Polish wife who betrayed him to the Soviet Union's secret police organisation the People's Commissariat of Internal Affairs. He is sentenced to twenty years in a Siberian labour camp where the conditions are beyond harrowing. The weather is so frigid and the camp so remote that the gulag needs only a handful of soldiers to guard it. Janusz, who grew up in rural Poland and has learned wilderness survival skills, hatches an escape plan to return home to find his wife and forgive her (he knows she was tortured into falsely informing on him). Under the cover of a blizzard, he and six other prisoners – Mr Smith (Ed Harris), a taciturn American engineer who fled the depression to seek work in the Soviet Union; Valka (Colin Farrell), a tattooed and violent Russian thug; a stage actor named Khabarov; Voss, a priest from Latvia; a Polish artist named Tomasz; his fellow Pole Kazik; and Zoran, a Yugoslav accountant – make their escape from the camp. And so begins their 4,000-mile trek through the frozen wilds of Siberia, across the high plateaus of the Mongolian steppes, the scorching Gobi Desert, through the ruins of the Great Wall of China and into Tibet, and finally over the Himalayas to British India.

Kazik freezes to death the second night of the journey. The remaining five men take care to avoid any occupied settlements, and after several days of trudging through an unbroken sea of frozen forest, they finally emerge from the Siberian wilderness at Lake Baikal where they find themselves joined by Irena (Saoirse Ronan), a fourteen-year-old Polish orphan from Warsaw.

Weir has made an epic film, but does not populate it with heroic characters. There is hardly any backstory about the men's lives or homes before their escape, and what little we do learn has to be coaxed from them by Irena. The manhunt by the Soviet authorities to recapture the prisoners, if there even is one, is never shown. Instead, Weir focuses on the weather and harsh landscape as the only things pursuing the group. They are chased by blinding blizzards, scorching heat, and a colossal sandstorm, to name just a few weather hazards. The real heroic characters are the legs of the escapees that carry them as they fight not only the elements but also fatigue and the limits of their own physical and mental endurance. All of the mobility in the film is peripatetic. There is not a single scene in which the prisoners are offered the chance of another means of conveyance.

Weir's camera dwells at first on the escapees' frostbitten fingers and toes and then, when they reach the scorching sands of the Gobi Desert, focuses on their blistered, pustule ridden feet, legs and faces. In the desert, Weir intercuts long, high angle shots of the group walking against the backdrop of the barren landscape with low angle ground-level shots of individuals walking. The dialogue in these scenes is mostly about walking and how much further they have to go to reach British India. When someone asks, 'How do we get over the Himalayas?' Janusz responds simply, 'We walk.' When a mounted group of Mongolian herders ride up and interrogate them, Mr Smith lies and tells them they are pilgrims walking to Lhasa. When the leader asks them why they have no horses, he says they are too poor to afford horses and so must walk.

Irena, wearing a hat made of interlaced branches that looks like a crown of thorns, her feet swollen with gangrene, becomes too weak to walk and has to be carried by Janusz. She dies in the desert and her comrades bury her.

Tomasz is the last to die. It is night. Tomasz is laying in the sand as his comrades gather around him admiring his sketch of Kazik. Tomasz remarks, 'Poor Kazik, always has trouble with his feet.' Tomasz closes his eyes, and Janusz tells him, 'You are a great artist Tomasz, it's almost like photography, the shadows.'

We learn of his death through a shot of footprints composed by Weir to look like one of Tomasz's charcoal drawings. The shot is an affirmation of Janusz's insight about the photographic realism of the shadows in Tomasz's drawings, but Weir reverses the roles of the two mediums to show how the shadows in photography resemble drawings. Just after Janusz speaks, Weir cuts to a low-angle shot framing four sets of footprints climbing up a sand dune. The shot is composed in low key lighting so that the tracks are only partially illuminated and appear as dark shadows on a flat surface of undulated sand. The camera tilts up and back along the footprints to reveal a cross with Tomasz's knife dangling on a piece of rope tied to it. As the cross fills the frame, the sun rises over the dune and fully illuminates the footprints leading away from Tomasz's grave.

When they are safely in Tibet and have been warned not to attempt to continue to India until spring, the four survivors discuss what they will do now since they have escaped. Janusz says, 'I'll keep going until it's over, keep walking.' Until what is over? Until his wife forgives herself, until Stalinism is finished. The next shot is of him continuing over the mountains. The rest follow (except for Mr Smith who will go to Lhasa as he said before to the Mongolian horseman). When the three reach India, they are asked where they came from. They reply Siberia and the Indian official asks, 'How did you come here?' they reply, 'We walked.'

The film ends with a close-up of Janusz's feet walking through India in double exposure over a montage of newsreel footage showing VE day, the Russian occupation of Poland, the Hungarian uprising, the building of the Berlin Wall, the Prague Spring, the Polish solidarity movement and the collapse of communism in Eastern Europe. Finally, after fifty years, Janusz walks up to the door of his wife's house. As he opens the door, he takes the final step towards reconciliation with her history and home.

Notes

1. For an interesting analysis of how Baum uses colour theory in the story, see *The Annotated Wizard of Oz*, p. 61.
2. Though Dorothy's full name is never mentioned in the film, her maiden name in the books is Gale. There is an obvious association with the tornado that brings her to Oz, but it is not too much of a stretch to associate it with the beginning of her odyssey on the yellow brick road. Just before she takes her first step on the road, Glinda flickers upwards and away as a ball of light and Dorothy remarks, 'My, people come and go so quickly here.'

CHAPTER 6

Aimless Walks

Guy Debord once remarked, 'One day, we will build cities for drift.' Drift is the Anglicised version of the French word *dérive* which Debord laconically defines as a 'technique of rapid passage through varied ambiences' in an urban milieu. A *dérive* is an urban drift, an artful practice of getting lost in a city to pay attention to and bring to the foreground everyday urban practices that go unnoticed in a typical urban commute. The varied ambiences Debord has in mind are the three spatial zones in a city: work, rest, leisure. As a form of aimless wandering, or 'locomotion without a goal', *dérive* cuts through all three of these zones, unmaking our conventional, everyday experiences of the spaces of the city shaped to commodify our customary encounters with the urban environment as a socio-political and economic force. To *dérive* is to trample upon lines of official urban demarcations meant to prohibit or control pedestrian mobility, remapping the contours of a city in pursuit of liberty. Debord offers a more detailed definition of *dérive* as a walk through a city in which:

> one or more persons during a certain period drop their relations, their work and leisure activities, and all their other usual motives for movement and action, and let themselves be drawn by the attractions of the terrain and the encounters they find there. Chance is a less important factor in this activity than one might think: from a *dérive* point of view cities have psychogeographical contours, with constant currents, fixed points and vortexes that strongly discourage entry into or exit from certain zones. (Debord: Theory of the Dérive)

For city dwellers, urban space is far from neutral. Following Lefebvre and de Certeau, we can define urban space as the 'active sphere of everyday life and as a form of discourse'. The drifter is an urban practitioner of *psychogeography*, another term invented by Debord, who defined it as the 'study of the precise laws and specific effects of the geographical environment, consciously organised or not, on the emotions and behaviour of individuals'. Alongside the *dérive*, Debord adds another concept to psychogeographical practice: *détournement*. An English translation of this word might be rendered as deflection or rerouting. For psychogegaphers, it is a way of overturning the normal uses of the built environment and inventing new ways to use it. Modern cities, as Merlin Coverley observes, are hostile to the pedestrian, and walking itself viewed as 'contrary to the spirit of the modern city with its promotion of swift circulation and street level gaze' (Coverley 2006: 12). Thus, walking as a psychogeographer 'requires one to challenge the official representation of the city by cutting across established routes and exploring those marginal and forgotten areas often overlooked by the city's inhabitants' (Coverley 2006: 12).

By combining *dérive* with *détournement*, the psychogeographer aims to practice a phenomenology of the sidewalk, taking note as they walk how streets, buildings, bridges and other features of the urban landscape resonate with their own states of mind and desires through movements that are often counter to the types of mobility for which the environment is designed (Plant 1992: 58). Cities are like books made legible through walking. Phenomenologically, psychogeography is both an intercession and an intervention between geography and psychoanalysis:

> The sudden change of ambience in a street within the space of a few meters; the evident division of a city into zones of distinct psychic atmospheres; the path of least resistance which is automatically followed in aimless strolls (and which has no relation to the physical contour of the ground); the appealing or repelling character of certain places – all this seems to be neglected . . . The production of psychogeographic maps, or even the introduction of alterations such as more or less arbitrarily transposing maps of two different regions, can contribute to clarifying certain wanderings that express not subordination to randomness but complete *insubordination* to habitual influences. (Debord: Introduction to a Critique of Urban Geography)

As an experimental modality of walking, the twentieth-century *dérive* is the contemporary cousin of the nineteenth-century idealised figure of the *flâneur*. There exists today a vast literature on the *flâneur* as a historically important modality of walking. In his famous essay 'The Painter of Modern Life', Baudelaire describes the *flâneur* in a way that somewhat resonates with drifting:

> The crowd is his element, as the air is that of birds and water of fishes. His passion and his profession are to become one flesh with the crowd. For the perfect *flâneur*, for the passionate spectator, it is an immense joy to set up house in the heart of the multitude, amid the ebb and flow of movement, in the midst of the fugitive and the infinite. To be away from home and yet to feel oneself everywhere at home; to see the world, to be at the centre of the world, and yet to remain hidden from the world – impartial natures which the tongue can but clumsily define. The spectator is a prince who everywhere rejoices in his incognito. (Baudelaire 1964: 9)

Baudelaire lived in Paris at the time Hausmann was remodelling the city, demolishing the narrow streets, alleyways and overcrowded tenements in the medieval quarters and rebuilding them to bring 'light and air' into the city. In their place, he built a network of long, broad, straight boulevards, public parks and squares to unify the city's various neighbourhoods and connect the outer suburbs to the city centre, transforming Paris into the modern 'city of light' we know today. The new thoroughfares were flanked on each side by wide, smooth pavements which in turn were lined with modern apartment buildings, hotels, shops and cafés. Baudelaire soon declared Paris the 'capital of the nineteenth century', brimming with foreigners from all over the world, its different districts each offering their own unique variety of attractions and spectacles which were now much more easily accessible on foot. Paris was by then a large-scale, densely populated modern metropolis, where the crowd was made up of the nameless masses, a phalanx of strangers rushing past one another in the urban hustle of work, business and commerce. Anonymity was all but assured, as a multitude of unknown faces passed one another on the pavements. The streets took on a new signification of estrangement (in a positive, exotic way) that led to new possibilities of engagement, where bohemian libertines, unemployed loiterers, idle refugees and well-heeled loafers flitted by one another.

The *flâneur* could only exist in such a city as Paris. The new city seemed purpose built for the urban pastimes of strolling, sauntering, loafing and crowd watching. Its streets bustled with pedestrians who welcomed the riotous assault on their senses from the myriad of noises, smells, sights and the rapid change of tempo every turn onto a new boulevard presented. Throw into this tumultuous mix what Gros calls the mercantilisation of the world, 'where the concept of merchandise extended beyond industrial products, to include art works and people', and you have all the ingredients to attract the *flâneur* to pedestrian friendly Paris (Gros 2015: 177).

A typical *flâneur* is a solitary upper middle-class gentleman whose means of support are invisible and who shows little sympathy for domestic life. He spends most of the day idly promenading down the Parisian boulevards silently observing the urban spectacle of everyday people going about their daily business, aesthetically consuming such things as the latest fashion in dress, crowded stores and arcades, cafés and book stalls. On the surface, his idle strolling incognito appears to be an exalted form of loafing or loitering. His unhurriedness among the humming crowds could be mistaken for a form of apathy, his attentive gazing through shop windows without ever making a purchase a callous subversion of the values of consumption. Though his aloofness seemed to other hurried pedestrians either a pretence or the mark of a feckless and detached dandy, behind his attenuated gait lay a goal beyond that of a mere hapless idler:

> And so away he goes, hurrying, searching. But searching for what? Be very sure that this man, such as I have depicted him – this solitary, gifted with an active imagination, ceaselessly journeying across the great human desert – has an aim loftier than that of a mere *flâneur*, an aim more general, something other than the fugitive pleasure of circumstance. He is looking for that quality which you must allow me to call 'modernity'; for I know of no better word to express the idea I have in mind. He makes it his business to extract from fashion whatever element it may contain of poetry within history, to distil the eternal from the transitory . . . By 'modernity' I mean the ephemeral, the fugitive, the contingent, the half of art whose other half is the eternal and the immutable. (Baudelaire 1964: 12–13)

So, the goal of the *flâneur* is to 'distil the eternal from the transitory'. He finds great joy in pooling with the multitudes in the ebb and flow of their movement and even more pleasure in his refusal to become a part of the crowd. The *flâneur* is the embodiment of modernity itself, one who seizes the transient experience of the moment electrified by the metropolis through the simple act of walking. He is more than simply a pedestrian: he is a heroic pedestrian who maintains his individuality within the crowd while all the others lose theirs. But this seems to be an impossible task unless one is an artist, one whose stock-in-trade is to spark the relay between the 'fugitive and infinite' by recording the wealth of impressions gathered through his ambulatory gaze in words or images (or even in music). This is exactly the condition Baudelaire places on the *flâneur*: he is an artist collecting mental notes on his leisurely walks, who reflects on, records and is in turn reflected in the transient moment as he disappears into the flux of modern life. Susan Sontag viewed early photographers as meeting this condition of being this type of peripatetic artist:

> The photographer is an armed version of the solitary walker reconnoitring, stalking, cruising the urban inferno, the voyeuristic stroller who discovers the city as a landscape of voluptuous extremes. Adept of the joys of watching, connoisseur of empathy, the *flâneur* finds the world picturesque. (Sontag 1989: 55)

Nineteenth-century Parisian poets, writers, musicians and painters (especially the French Impressionists) were also adroit practitioners of *flâneurie*, each searching to fix the fleeting moments of transient experience in the intransigent tones of their respective mediums. To be a *flâneur* in Baudelaire's Paris meant yielding to the logic of the mobilised gaze, with 'little attention paid to the physical act of walking or to the individual interiority that might inflect [their] reputedly detached manner of observation'

(Forgione 2005: 665). So as undirected urban amblers, Baudelaire's *flâneurs* could hardly be described as psychogeographers.

The real progenitors of *dérive* as proto-psychogeographers were the Parisian Surrealists, who in the 1920s revived Baudelaire's concept of the *flâneur* with a new emphasis on the role chance coupled with a penchant for digression might play in the art of straying. They devised peripatetic experiments of meandering through a city with set rules that left open the chance for random encounters, such as opening a map of London and using it as a guide around Paris, picking a particular colour and charting a course in response to seeing it, or following a beautiful, exotic woman through the streets. The Surrealist *flâneur* peeled away the epidermis of the city to reveal spaces hidden 'behind the banal surface of everyday life', such as its carnivalesque flea markets, seedy tenement street cafés and neglected squares, as places to rendezvous with the marvellous or ripe for the chance of an 'amorous encounter spontaneously ignited by a glance charged with meaning' (Melly 1991: 51). André Breton's *Nadja* and Louis Aragon's *Le Paysan de Paris* were two novels that documented some of these early experimental peripatetic wanderings through Paris (both works are often cited as the first psychogeographical novels). Breton and Aragon together invented the deliberately haphazard system of *flâneurie* so typical of surrealist strolling. Walter Benjamin was so enthralled after reading *Le Paysan de Paris* that he conceived of a massive work of cultural criticism examining in detail the street life and culture surrounding the Paris arcades – glass roofed walkways lined with shops – in which the *flâneur* would play a central role. He viewed the arcades as a thrilling amalgamation of exterior and interior spaces, with competing elements of enclosure and transparency. To Benjamin, the arcades was the ideal milieu for *flâneurie*:

> The leisurely quality . . . fits the style of the *flâneur* who goes botanising on the asphalt . . . *Flâneurie* could hardly have assumed the importance it did without the arcades. 'These arcades, a recent invention of industrial luxury', says an illustrated guide to Paris of 1852, 'are glass-roofed, marble-paneled corridors extending through whole blocks of buildings, whose owners have joined together for such enterprises. Lining both sides of these corridors, which get their light from above, are the most elegant shops, so that the *passage* is a city, a world in miniature'. It is in this world that the *flâneur* is at home; he provides the arcade – 'the favourite venue of strollers and smokers, the haunt of all sorts of little *metiers*' – with its chronicler and philosopher . . . The arcades are something between a street and an *interieur*. The street becomes a dwelling place for the *flâneur*; he is as much at home among house facades as a citizen is within his four walls. (Benjamin 2006: 68)

Benjamin relished the sort of spatial ambiguity he saw in the arcades and even argued that the *flâneur* could experience the streets as an interior space.

He began collecting quotations and sketching notes in 1927 and would work on it up until his death by suicide in 1940. Left unfinished at the time of his death, Benjamin's fragmentary opus has since been published in English as *The Arcades Project* and has proven to be one of the most important works in twentieth-century cultural theory. His main means of research was to practise being a *flâneur* himself, walking for long hours around Paris making notes from his observations of everything from prostitution to advertising, shedding light on the daily life of Parisian urbanites. In one important passage, Benjamin gives Baudelaire's *flâneur* a more contemporary, post-industrial revolutionary flair by speaking about the *flâneur* strolling through the arcades as itself a type of commodity:

> The arcade is a street of lascivious commerce only; it is wholly adapted to arousing desires. Because in this street the juices slow to a standstill, the commodity proliferates along the margins and enters into fantastic combinations, like the tissue in tumours. The *flâneur* sabotages the traffic. Moreover, he is no buyer. He is the merchandise. (Benjamin 2002a: 42 – A3a, 7)

In her book *Window Shopping: Cinema and the Postmodern*, Anne Friedberg argues that Benjamin's study of the arcades takes us through a gradual passage from the virtual mobility introduced by pre-cinematic apparatuses such as the panorama or diorama found in the arcades – devices which simply extended the field of visibility and allowed the past to be transported to the present – to the fully developed mobilised virtual gaze realised as an integral feature of the cinematic apparatus. By combining the mobile and the virtual with an imaginary gaze, the cinematic apparatus changed how we perceive both the present and the real, revealing how the past is now 'inexorably bound with images of a constructed past' (Friedberg 1994: 7, 49).

Cinematic *Flâneurie*

The *flâneur* has been a subject of the cinema since the early silent era. In *Theory of Film*, Siegfried Kracauer relates that Eisenstein already observed in the early 1920s how the characters in D. W. Griffith's films often seem to walk straight from the flow of life in the city streets right onto the screen (Kracauer 1960: 72). He goes on to describe the flow of street life in which the *flâneur* exists and the cinema's natural affinities for capturing this flow of life equated with the street:

> The street in the extended sense of the word is not only the arena of fleeting impressions and chance encounters but a place where the flow of life is bound to assert itself. Again one will have to think mainly of the city street with its ever-moving crowds.

> The kaleidoscopic sights mingle with unidentified shapes and fragmentary visual complexes and cancel each other out, thereby preventing the onlooker from following up any of the innumerable suggestions they offer. What appeals to him are not so much sharp-contoured individuals engaged in this or that definable pursuit as loose throngs of sketchy, completely indeterminate figures. Each has a story, yet the story is not given. Instead, an incessant flow casts its spell over the *flâneur* or even creates him. The *flâneur* is intoxicated with life in the street – life eternally dissolving the patterns which it is about to form . . . The medium's [film] affinity for the flow of life would be enough to explain the attraction which the street has ever since exerted on the screen. (Kracauer 1960: 72)

In a later chapter, Kracauer ascribes to the film spectator some of the characteristics of the *flâneur*. Like the *flâneur*, the film spectator is struck by the rapid flux of 'transient real-life phenomena' rushing by on the screen along with the 'fragmentary happenings' indicative of street life which 'stimulate his senses and provide him with the stuff of dreaming' (Kracauer 1960: 170).

Kracauer cites Karl Grune's German silent feature *Die Strasse* (1923) as the first film to deliberately portray the street as the main scene of life, but, as I have already shown in Chapter 2, almost all of Chaplin's Tramp films from 1914 onwards highlight the rapidity of impressions and changing flow of experiences that form individual and social life in the city. The Tramp is perhaps the cinematic *flâneur* par excellence who pushes *flâneurie* right up to threshold of *dérive*. But one of the very first films to feature *flâneurie* as its central narrative is the 1930 avant-garde short *Bezúčelná procházka* (*Aimless Walk*) by Czech film-maker Alexandr Hackenschmied. The film follows a young man as he strolls – aimlessly, as the title suggests – from Prague's city centre to its outskirts, observing the people and the mostly dilapidated buildings he sees along his route. At just under eight minutes long, it belongs to the experimental documentary genre of city symphony films, such as *Manhatta* and *Berlin, Symphony of a City*. Though *Aimless Walk* is a short, narrative feature films soon followed which journeyed into the realms of *flâneurie*. Although the *flâneur* film has never risen to the level of being classified as a genre in its own right, we can nevertheless trace its figure through a handful of feature films that share stylistic, narrative and structural interests in *flâneurie*. For the remainder of this chapter, I want to explore characters and cameras who *dérive* and practice the art of *flâneurie* in two great filmic cities: Paris and Rome.

Paris: *Breathless*

Just over a century after Hausmann's radical renovations of the streets and architecture of Paris, the city underwent another, equally radical, series of major urban planning projects between 1954 and 1974. Though untouched by German or Allied bombing during World War II, a post-war baby boom and unprecedented levels of migration from war-ravaged parts of Europe into the city meant that Paris had to embark on a major redevelopment scheme and building boom which would reconfigure its urban spaces. The plans included demolishing and rebuilding nearly a quarter of the city's built environment.

In his book *Paris Movie Walks*, Michael Schürmann reminds us how much of our knowledge of the look and feel of Paris comes from movie scenes shot on its streets (Schürmann 2009: 9). Almost any film shot on location in Paris is bound to showcase its street life with its outdoor cafés and landmark buildings, parks, squares and famous boulevards such as the Champs-Élysées. Nowhere is this more apparent than in the films of the French New Wave where the 'border between cinema and city is porous' (Tweedie 2013: 53). When it comes to the Parisian films of Jean-Luc Godard, this sounds like an understatement.

As perhaps the most cerebral and celebrated of the New Wave Directors, an entire scholarly industry has sprung up examining the life and work of Jean-Luc Godard. Godard is a film director apart from any other. If the imperative of art is a whispered 'look again', then in Godard's voice it is a shout turned up in volume to a hyperbolic eleven. His first feature film *Breathless* introduced many new innovations in a feature film to make us look again – jump cuts within a scene, documentary like techniques, actors directly addressing the camera staged to resemble eyes on the camera interviews of his subject-characters, a freewheeling approach to dialogue, such as lifting passages whole from literary, philosophical and cinematic works and placing them in the mouths of characters, quite often in the middle of conversation without conventional context – that were to become staples in his subsequent work. It also marked the beginning of his preference for shooting from a 'plan-of-action script' written almost on the fly rather than from a full-fledged screenplay turned into the more traditional 'programme-script' that lays out dialogue and scenes into fixed structure ready to be filmed each day (Marie 2002: 77). According to his own testimony, Godard's discovery of cinema was not through seeing a great film but through reading André Gide's prose-poem *Fruits of the Earth*, a literary work. He might have even pursued a literary career, but as he told Marguerite Duras, 'I hate writing. Not writing in itself, but the moment in which it comes, all of that time.' He went on to remark to her, 'I don't write texts, since they are there.'

Godard's path to film artist did of course cut through his years spent as a film critic, where he learned how to include and master his own subjectivity (Cavell's terms) required to bridge the gap between agreement and argument that is the task of the critic performed for his readers, and also that of the artist in making and presenting a work of art. But writing can be chaste, requiring too much effort at self-intimacy. So he found in the automatism of cinema a perfect apparatus for putting philosophy and literature in dialogue, indeed as spoken dialogue, much as Derrida does in his written texts, taking full advantage of the French language's natural propensity for word play, puns, double meanings and aporias, often without attribution. This is how he preferred to write and shoot *Breathless*.

To show his bona fides as a Hollywood B-grade film noir cinephile, Godard once remarked that to make a film all you need is a 'girl and a gun'. The formula is simple: a man on the run after using a gun to commit murder seeks refuge in the arms of a femme fatale who is destined to betray him. In Godard's case, the man is car thief Michel Poicard who flees to Paris after killing a motorcycle policeman. The femme fatale is Patricia, an American student in Paris.

The film's plot takes place over a twenty-four-hour period, almost all of the action focused on a single day and night in Paris. The main protagonist is car thief Michel, a fast-talking French version of Dean Moriarty who prefers to steal American cars and speeds around the streets of Paris uttering phrases such as, 'Don't use the brakes. Cars are made to go, not to stop!' He idolises Humphrey Bogart's American movie noir gangster persona and postures as a gangster himself, complete with a fedora and an endless chain of cigarettes between his lips, mimicking Bogart's facial tics and hand gestures. Though he pretends to be a tough guy, he has just gunned down a motorcycle policeman in a cowardly way on the outskirts of Paris and is on the run. But instead of laying low in Paris, he seeks out Patricia, an American student who hawks the Paris edition of *New York Herald Tribune* and works as a cub reporter while waiting to enrol in the Sorbonne. The two had a brief affair some months before and now Michel wants her to leave Paris and travel to Rome with him. The rest of the film is about Michel waiting for two things: Patricia's answer about going to Rome; and to cash a cheque given to him by another wannabe thug. And, so he wastes most of his day wandering the streets on foot, killing time. For such a car crazy cool character, it is ironic that he only spends around eight minutes of the entire film driving (Tweedie 2013: 104).

Like most good noir stories, *Breathless* was inspired by the real-life headline-grabbing case of Michel Portail who in 1952 killed a motorcycle policeman after being stopped driving a stolen Ford Mercury. Beyond the news headlines, as Winston Wheeler Dixon notes, the origins of the bare bones scenario of *Breathless* remain almost legendary. By one account, the most probable, Godard adapted the plot from a fifteen-page scenario written by François Truffaut (who is credited in the film). The other apocryphal one is told by Roger Vadim. According to Vadim, Godard showed up unannounced on the set of a film he was directing, thrust a box of matches into his hand and declared, 'I'm a genius.' Scrawled in Godard's handwriting on the box of matches were these few sentences spelling out the scenario for *Breathless*, 'He's a hooligan. Obsessed by heroes of American films. She sells the *New York Herald Tribune*. It's not really love, it's an illusion of love. It ends badly. Well, no. Finally, it ends well. Or it ends badly' (quoted in Dixon 1997: 15).

Godard himself admits:

> *À Bout de Souffle* [*Breathless*] began this way. I had written the first scene (Jean Seberg on the *Champs-Élysées*), and for the rest I had a pile of notes for each scene. I said to myself, this is terrible. I stopped everything. Then I thought: in a single day, if one knows how to go about it, one should be able to complete a dozen takes. Only instead of planning ahead, I shall invent at the last minute. If you know where you are going it ought to be possible. This isn't improvisation but last-minute focusing. (Milne 1972: 172–3)

Part of Godard's improvisational style is to lift dialogue whole from literary or philosophical texts. To cite just one example in *Breathless*, in one scene Michel and Patricia go to the cinema to lay low and watch the American western *Westbound*. The short scene consists of a single close-up of the two lovers kissing, the dialogue from *Westbound* playing in the background, audible not just to us, but presumably also to the characters as diegetic sound. But the words we hear playing in the movie theatre are not from *Westbound*'s soundtrack. Instead, we hear short snippets of two amalgamated poems, one by Apollinaire and the other by Aragon, modified, melded and spoken by Godard and Jean Seberg. Godard alters the words of the poems with absolutely no fidelity to the original poetic texts or, for that matter, to the original dialogue belonging to *Westbound*'s soundtrack.

This is a seminal example of Godard's dexterity for creating novel word-image translations. In later films, entire scenes might consist of nothing more than characters reading aloud to one another, quoting almost randomly from literature, philosophy, history, sociology and other texts. As Godard once told an interviewer, 'Readings are just fantastic! When you get right down to it, the most fantastic thing you could film is people reading.'

Breathless is an ambulatory film in plot and its spontaneous style, born out of necessity due to budget and the time constraints that shooting on location in Paris required. The conditions of production multiplied the technical handicaps cinematographer Raoul Coutard had to work to overcome. Since Godard's budget could not afford studio sets with things like arc lighting, moveable walls, false ceilings or even extras, everything had to be shot guerrilla style on the streets. Coutard used a Cameflex camera and newly invented high speed Ilford HPS film stock. Since he was alternating between shooting in small, tight knit spaces like low-lit hotel rooms or elevators and crowded streets (often without permits and no crowd controls), using synchronised sound recorded on location was impossible. But perhaps the biggest hurdle Coutard had to overcome was how to shoot Belmondo and Seberg walking through the streets of Paris candidly without drawing attention to himself and his camera. The goal was to capture their peripatetic conversations naturally without hindering their movements, while at the same time being able to shoot very quickly. Relying on his experience as a war correspondent and battlefield camera operator in Indochina, Coutard developed a few ingenious solutions to camouflage the camera while remaining light, fluid and mobile to follow the actors' movements.

For indoor tracking shots, Coutard improvised by filming from a wheelchair pushed by Godard to avoid having to lay down dolly tracks. By far the most complicated and eloquent one is a long, circling tracking shot in

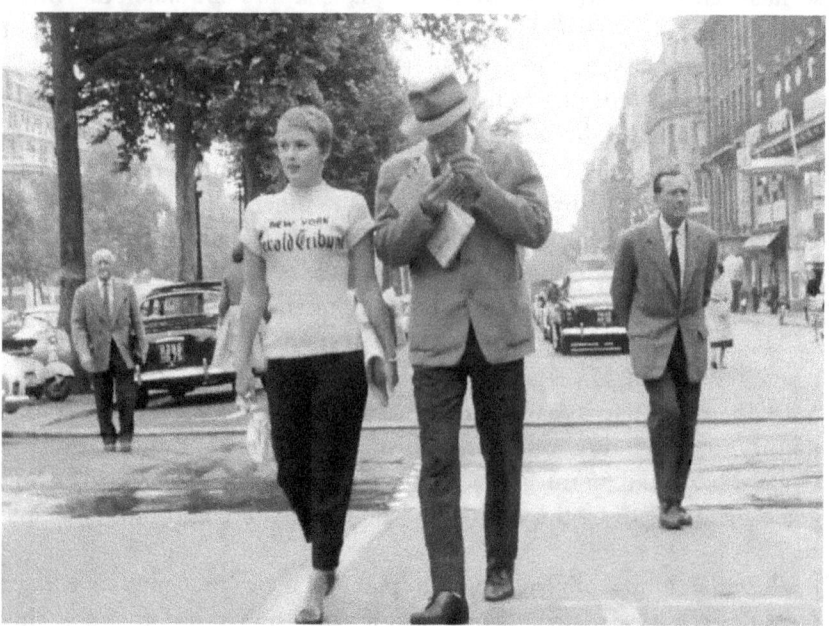

Figure 6.1 Breathless.

the InterAmericana travel agency. The camera picks up Michel as he walks through a set of glass doors into the agency after he has just witnessed a fatal traffic accident. The camera tracks him from the front in a medium shot, turning with him as he stops at the reception desk to ask the whereabouts of his friend Tolmatchoff. The camera circles around him as he turns to walk in the other direction around the desk, partially retracing his previous steps, framing him again frontally in a medium shot until he stops in front of another desk behind which Tolmatchoff is working. After exchanging greetings with Michel, Tolmatchoff walks to his left out of the frame. Then, in a doubling of the first movement, the camera turns again to track Poicard walking back towards the reception desk. Tolmatchoff re-enters the frame from the right and puts his arm around his Michel's shoulder. The camera holds them both in mid-frame as they walk together in conversation advancing towards the camera, then seamlessly changes direction as the two friends cut left across the camera's path to yet another counter where several clerks are working. The camera pauses briefly as Tolmatchoff is handed an envelope from a clerk then moves again in advance of the two as they turn and walk along a corridor, tracking them all the way back to Tolmatchoff's desk where Poiccard makes a phone call. The shot finally ends as Michel turns towards the camera and walks out the same glass doors through which he entered at the beginning of the shot, just as police Inspector Vital and another detective are walking in to look for him.

As I have already mentioned, tracking shots on the streets posed the problem of how not to attract the attention of passers-by. In one of the most famous scenes, Belmondo and Seberg pace up and down in circles along the Champs-Élysées conversing about love while she hawks the *New York Herald Tribune*. The shot is almost three minutes long, following the couple from behind before they turn, the camera pulling them as they walk back to where they started. The angle is low and their bodies are kept in full frame. The boulevard is crowded with passers-by who glance fleetingly at the couple – but never at the camera – as the two actors perform in an 'uncontrollable mass of other bodies, buildings, shops, automobiles, street signs, and movie marquees, the stuff that together constitutes the mise-en-scène of Paris in the 1950s and 1960s' (Tweedie 2013: 87). The cinema-vérité look of the shot was achieved by hiding Coutard in a postal cart under a pile of mail. Once in position, Coutard aimed the camera through a hole cut out in the front of the cart which an assistant surreptitiously pushed as Godard followed close by. This improvised contraption is used again in another scene tracking Patricia and Michel walking in the Opéra district. As the two stroll along the boulevard, they are 'surrounded by the accidents of that particular moment in history: people on the sidewalk, the ephemera of light and weather', as well as witness to a military procession parading up the street (Tweedie 2013: 111).

Michel's ramble through Paris is the criminal version of a dérive. He is someone just killing time and not too worried about getting caught. He strolls around Paris looking in shop windows, going to cafés and most famously stopping in front a movie theatre poster of Humphrey Bogart to mimic his gesture with a cigarette and whisper, 'Bogey.' But Bogey is a man of action, not someone starring in their own existentialist anti-hero, self-made tragedy who idly kills time for the sake of love. Yes, Bogey falls in love fast in his films and drives his cars just as fast, but he is never idle. Michel is numbed to action, his walking and strolling just a way to stave off his boredom and justify his inaction in a world where action is impossible. He is the opposite of Bergman's knight who just wants to perform one significant action to give meaning to his life. Michel is not on a crusade; boredom and waiting are his only modus operandi. His only significant action is to die in a meaningless escape from his false sense of what love is.

Godard's working methods during filming have all the elements of an intellectual dérive. He conceived of *Breathless* as an action film, but not like a Hollywood action movie. Instead, Godard had in mind the spontaneous method of action painting by Jackson Pollock. Pollock created his painting by laying his canvas on the floor, stepping into it, and walking around the canvas dripping paint from brushes or sticks he held in his hand. Describing his method of action painting, he said, 'When I am in my painting, I am not aware of what I am doing. It is only after a sort of get acquainted period that I see what I have been about. I have no fears about making changes, destroying the image, etc., because the painting has a life of its own.' We need only to substitute the word 'film' for 'painting' and Pollock's statement could be mistaken for a pronouncement by Godard on the making of *Breathless*.

Like Pollock, Godard's spontaneous methods meant for him that the 'act and moment of making the film were as much of a part of the work's meaning as its specific content and style' (Brody 2008: 116). Partly out of ignorance of technical matters but also from an unbridled passion for experimentation and innovation, he meandered through an array of film techniques completely indifferent to planning or continuity and remained totally open to chance. During the shoot, he wrote to a friend claiming ecstatically that he 'wasn't thinking of anything'. The shooting schedule was fast and breathtaking. Godard even pushed the high speed film stock to its limitations in low-light conditions by developing it in a special chemical bath to make it even more light sensitive, declaring that, 'even the film stock . . . will be out of breath' (Brody 2008: 119). Godard wrote the 'script' on the fly, retreating alone to a café each morning to write that day's scenes over breakfast while the cast and crew waited. He emerged with sheaves of dialogue that the actors had barely any time to look at, much less memorise before Godard started shooting. Because the film was shot without direct sound, Godard was able to vocally feed the actors' lines to them while the camera was rolling (the dialogue was later dubbed in post-production). This idiosyncratic method of working, along with Godard's vague directions, left the actors frustrated, especially Seberg. Eight years later, on the set of *Two or Three Things I Know About Her* (1967), actress Marina Vlady expressed similar frustrations working with Godard. When Vlady complained to Godard that he never really tells her anything about what he wants from her and then asks him what she is supposed do, he responds by blurting, 'Instead of taking a taxi to the shoot, all you have to do is come on foot. If you really want to act well, that's the best thing to do' (Brody 2008: 288). This could just as well have been the acting direction he gave to Seberg in *Breathless*.

The merging of Godard's aimless, peripatetic directing methods with his impulsive peripatetic character is nowhere more evident than in the iconic last scene of the film where Poicard stumbles down the middle of rue Campagne-Première in Montparnasse after being shot by Vital and falls, dying on a crosswalk at rue Raspail. The long tracking shot, intercut with a few jump shots of Patricia running after Michel, is one of the most famous 'dead man walking' scenes in cinema. According to Belmondo, Godard's only direction to him was to run and not fall down until he gets to the end of the street. Godard exaggerates the length and time the mortally wounded Michel staggers before he collapses in the street, letting his audience feel Michel's breathless exhaustion to the very end. A curious throng of Parisian pedestrians, who really have no idea that they are part of a movie, crowd around Belmondo as he lays prone in the crosswalk mumbling Michel's last words, 'I am really nauseating' (*dégueulasse*). When Patricia asks Vital what Michel said, he lies to her, telling her, 'He said you really are nauseating.' In the last shot, Patricia stares straight at the camera in close-up, and, co-opting Bogey's gesture from Michel, runs her thumb over her lips and asks, 'What does nauseating mean?' And so ends Michel's story.

Paris: *Cléo from 5 to 7*

Is there such a thing as a *flâneuse*? A peripatetic female who is the equivalent of a male *flâneur*? A cursory glance at the literature of modernity would suggest that the *flâneuse* is a non-existent creature; the walkable public spaces created by Hausmann in Paris seem to have belonged exclusively to the male. This has led sociologist Janet Wolff to argue that the (scholarly) literature of modernity is 'impoverished by ignoring the lives of women' in the city and that for a feminist sociology of modernity there 'is no question of inventing the *flâneuse*' (Wolff 1985: 47).

There certainly are precursory models for the *flâneuse* in the canonical images and literature of modernity. In her novel *Mrs. Dalloway*, Virginia Woolf sets Clarissa Dalloway loose on the streets of central London on her morning stroll to buy flowers for a party, recording her walk in such detail that it is possible to retrace Clarissa's steps today. In her short essay 'Street Haunting', Woolf writes about a woman's perambulation through the streets of London on a pedestrian endeavour to buy a pencil, documenting her fleeting impressions of the city along her way.

In Paris, we can point to the writer George Sand. In 1831 she dressed in men's clothing disguised as a male *flâneur* to ramble around the streets of Paris. She writes about the experience in language that conjures up Baudelaire's own writing on *flâneurie*, 'I flew from one end of Paris to another . . . No one paid attention to me, and no one guessed at my disguise . . . No one knew me, no one looked at me, no one found fault with me; I was an atom lost in that immense crowd' (Sand 1991: 893–4). An exhilarating experience of *flâneurie* to be sure, but only made possible through disguise and ruse; the non-existent role of *flâneuse* was not available to her.

We might even find a forebear of the *flâneuse* in Baudelaire's poem 'To a (Female) Passer-by':

> The deafening street roared around me
> Tall, slender, in heavy mourning, majestic in her grandeur
> A woman walked passed me, her sumptuous hands
> Lifting and swinging her hem as she went.
>
> Swift and graceful, with legs like a statue's
> Twitching like a madman, I drank in
> Her eyes, a pallid sky where storms are born
> the sweetness that charms and the pleasure that kills. (Quoted in Elkin 2017: 9)

The speaker of the poem is quite obviously a *flâneur* 'botanising on the asphalt' in the midst of the deafening roar and spectacle of the streets. The poem is addressed to an unnamed woman who startles him both by her beauty and the fact that she is walking the streets alone. Public spaces in nineteenth-century Paris were assumed to be masculine, constructed for and shaped by the male pedestrian gaze (Milburn 2014: 327). As Janet Wolff contends, the only type of woman who dared promenade unescorted in these male gendered spaces were 'prostitutes, widows, lesbians or murder victims but the "respectable" woman could not stroll alone in the city' (quoted in Milburn 2014: 327). Many readers have mistaken the intrepid woman in the poem for a prostitute, since she is walking the streets with neither the requisite female nor male escort that nineteenth-century mores prescribed. But the text of the poem does not support such a reading. The second line makes it clear that she is a widow in mourning, though for whom the speaker either does not know or does not say. (It was typical in nineteenth-century France for a woman in mourning to spend a short period in complete solitude and then afterwards, when appearing in public, to observe mourning etiquette by wearing the attire proper to the various stages of mourning; lengths of times and the type and colour of clothing varied based on who the mourning was for, for example, a spouse, parent, uncle and so on). The speaker first comments on her gait, noting especially the way she uses her 'sumptuous hands' to lift and swing the hem of her skirt as she walks. It is hard to know from this description if she is holding on to her skirt because she is walking hurriedly (almost running) or if she is gaily sauntering down the sidewalk in celebration of her freedom of mobility after her long period of mourning in solitude. Either way, her movements are 'swift and graceful' and the speaker is mesmerised by her statuesque beauty. We get the sense that the speaker wants to stop her in the street and talk to her. But as they make eye contact, the speaker, 'twitching like a madman' is suddenly seized by a sexual anxiety. She moves from being an object of desire to a proto-femme fatale, a dangerous erotic object who possesses a 'sweetness that charms and the pleasure that kills'. She is only a spectacle to be looked at and not overtly encountered. Though she is in no way a *flâneuse*, she does momentarily disarm the speaker's power as a *flâneur* to remain aloof from his desires of possession.

Benjamin claims that Baudelaire's poetry intermingles the images of death and woman together in the image of Paris. These three images combined constitute modernity itself as a dialectical image of ambiguity. Ambiguity is dialectical movement arrested and at a standstill. Benjamin sees this dialectical image of standstill presented in three images associated with modern Paris: the commodity as fetish, the arcades (both a street and an interior), and the prostitute (both seller and sold). The final act of the *flâneur* is to face death, which is the ultimate novelty.

Like *Breathless*, the plot of Agnès Varda's *Cléo from 5 to 7* is deceptively simple. Self-absorbed young pop singer Cléo (Corinne Marchand) has two hours to wait before meeting with her oncologist to find out the results of her biopsy after undergoing tests for stomach cancer. After visiting a tarot card reader who reveals a card with the Astrological sign of Cancer and says she sees death in her near future, an anxious Cléo fills the first hour shopping for a hat and visiting a café with her assistant, spending a few moments with her lover, and rehearsing with her songwriters in her loft apartment. None of these activities or interactions exorcise her fears. On the verge of panic, she spends the second hour wandering around Paris, dropping in on a friend modelling in an art studio and visiting her friend's boyfriend in the projection room of a cinema. She finally finds comfort talking with a young soldier named Antoine she meets walking through Parc Montsouris who is on leave from the Algerian war and anxious about his own mortality. Together, they walk to the hospital to learn her diagnosis where they find her doctor as he is just about to drive through the hospital gates in his convertible. He stops and reveals that she does have cancer but delivers a hopeful prognosis that with chemotherapy she will make a full recovery.

The film is divided into thirteen chapters with subtitles indicating the length of plot time for each one. Despite the title, the plot time of the thirteen chapters adds up to only ninety minutes (not one hundred and twenty). The thirteen chapters also correspond to Cléo's trek around Paris beginning in the 1st arrondissement and ending in the 13th. Furthermore, we can divide the film into two halves. In the first half, Cléo is positioned as a woman masquerading her interior self behind a disguise of a commodified form of femininity. As a commercial pop star, she buys into her own manufactured image as a fetishised commodity to be looked at, but who is not yet capable of being a subject who looks herself. In the second half, Cléo has an epiphany, takes off her mask (figuratively, in the form of tossing off a wig) and sets off alone to walk the street of Paris in search of self-transformation. Along the way, we discover the vibrant and photogenic city of Paris just as she does. As Janice Mouton observes:

> As we see Cléo walking through the city's 'sensory streets', vital and dynamic with their mix of people, newsstands and bookstalls, trees and flowers, bicycles, cars, and buses, dogs and pigeons, shops and cafés, our attention is focused on the city as much as on the woman . . . What makes Cléo's walk so fascinating is the transformation she undergoes, brought about by her interaction with the city during an afternoon of *flâneurie*. (Mouton 2001: 3)

The film's narrative is structured around Cléo's apprehension punctuated by moments of distraction, sensation and self-yearning. Immediately after the opening tarot card scene, it becomes apparent that Cléo's trepidations are not solely about her possible cancer diagnosis, but also a fear that her looks will succumb to death and shatter her deathless image of beauty. This is evident the first time we see her interact with her own self-reflection in a mirror when she says to herself, 'Hold on pretty butterfly. Ugliness is a kind of death. As long as I'm beautiful, I'm more alive than others.' As a young, beautiful pop star Cléo sees in the mirror what others see when they look at her: a commodity and image simply to be gazed at (and heard, but only as a disembodied voice on the radio). She has no true image of herself but is trapped in a self-image created for her by the dispositif of popular culture. When she looks in the mirror, it is not a person that is reflected back but an idealised image of physical beauty.

James Tweedie argues that Cléo's attempt to reconcile her self-projection of a deathless image, one that attracts looks of recognition and attention, with her own emerging self-awareness of her real, physical body prone to disease and death is the intellectual crux of the film. Her journey to reconcile these two images is a peripatetic one:

> The film begins by engineering this clash between the vision of identity as pure appearance and the mortality of the body, between the image viewed as the emblem of a new society of the spectacle and a seemingly archaic conception of cinema as an index of reality. And the stage for these dramatic and philosophical conflicts is the terrain of the city . . . If illness serves as a pretext that launches the film, Cléo then embarks on a journey with only a tangential relationship to the plot and its rigid progress from minute to minute and event to event. At once literal and figural, her walk through Paris is a 'voyage of self-discovery' that could devolve into the kind of cliche suggested in that common idiom; but the film complicates that familiar narrative as it follows Cléo's physical itinerary through the mise-en-scène of contemporary Paris and charts her position within that adamantly concrete space. (Tweedie 2013: 122, 123)

As she leaves the fortune teller, she is already beginning to mourn her loss of beauty. The first time we see her walking down the sidewalk away from her reading, Varda's camera follows her in a medium shot from a distance using a long lens. The street is in a working-class quarter, full of street vendors and small shops. She is wearing a tight fitting polka dotted dress and is the object of everyone's gaze – rather than gazing at the crowd herself – and of her own as she constantly stops to look in the mirrors that proliferate the screen. There is one peripatetic scene in the first half where Varda expertly shoots Cléo as an object through the intricate interplay of multiple mirrors. Cléo and her assistant are having a coffee in a café where Cléo sits with her back to a mirror. She is immobilised by anxiety as she silently eavesdrops on the conversation of a young couple arguing just behind and to the left of her. Varda frames the shot as if it is a split screen with the edge of the mirror behind Cléo's booth composed as the dividing line with Cléo framed on one side and the couple the other contrasting Cléo's anxious stasis with the couple's moving argument. She then cuts to a wide shot of Cléo gazing into a compact mirror fixing her make-up as other customers move freely about the crowded café. Through the window we can see pedestrians strolling past the café. Cléo, sitting in a booth next to the window in virtual stillness, creates another split screen with her own body this time between interior and exterior; she is the only one who is not moving or engaged in conversation. Looking at her reflection in the compact mirror, she does not really see herself as anything other than a commodity and participates in her fetishisation. The multiple mirrors in the café bring the open expanse of the city and streets inside, interweaving exterior and interior spaces into a single, alluring spectacle in which Cléo plays her part (Benjamin 2002a: 537).

When she leaves the café, we see her composed in the same shot as before when she left the psychic walking down the pavement, only now she is walking in the other direction and with her assistant. After they walk across a busy intersection, Varda cuts to a deep focus shot through the window from inside a hat shop as we see the two approach the store window from the street. The foreground of the shot is crowded with women's hats displayed behind the window. We then get a series of shots and reverse shots cutting back and forth between close-ups of the women's faces looking through the window and their subjective points of view of various hats displayed in the window. After lingering on one hat in particular, Varda cuts back to a shot from inside the store as Cléo points to the hat and says, 'I want that one' and walks in. As they enter, we see Cléo's ghostly reflection intermingle with those of pedestrians and the city itself on the other side

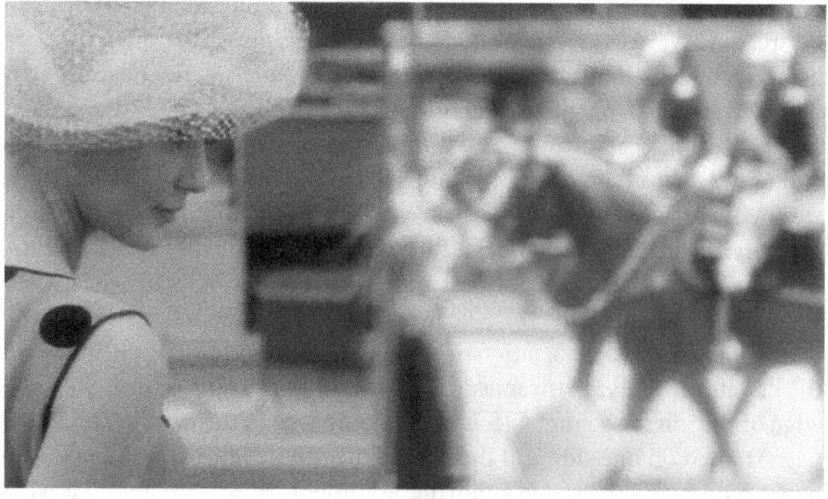

Figure 6.2 Cléo.

of the plate-glass window. What follows is an intricate series of shots of Cléo gazing at herself in the store's multiple mirrors as those same mirrors reflect the images of people and traffic passing by the store on the sidewalk. Her own reflection is always fragmented, her face diced up into close-ups or scattered as shards across multiple mirrors like a cubist painting. Likewise, the mirror surfaces and plate-glass window splinter Cléo's figure into parts, never reflecting her whole body. Cléo creates a fragmented spectacle for herself and everyone else who can see her. In some shots, Cléo shares the interior mirror space with the pedestrians outside, but she does not acknowledge them, either from vanity, distraction or fear – or perhaps a combination of all three. What comes next is the most complex tracking shot of the entire film. The camera now tracks across the store window from outside on the pavement. The camera follows Cléo as she walks through the store trying on hats. Again, we see the reflections in the window of people passing by from behind the camera, spectators as *flâneurs*. But we also catch glimpses of Cléo's reflection as if she too is strolling by the shop window from inside as we watch her from outside. Further, as she walks around trying on hats, she herself becomes part of the window display. She becomes a kind of mobile mannequin in an intricate play of spectacle and consumption where 'fetishism and feminine masquerade converge' (Mouton 2001: 6).

As I have written elsewhere, both mirrors and shop windows share affinities for projecting ambiguous images that exist somewhere between the virtual and the real. Echoing Marcel Duchamp, we can say that the picture of Cléo behind and reflected by the shop window from inside the store creates an image of her as an 'apparition of an appearance' (Duchamp 1970: note 36). Duchamp was writing about the pedestrian gazing through a shop window where immobile objects (such as hats) are on display and interrogating his own image reflected by the glass as if he is already inside with the objects. The desire to possess the displayed objects is enhanced by the image of the spectator's virtual proximity to them as if he has already 'cut the pane' and entered the store to purchase the objects of his desire. Anne Friedberg compares window shopping to cinema spectatorship where objects of desire are framed and placed behind a glass (camera-projectors lenses or a shop window) so that they remain inaccessible to the pedestrian or spectator (Friedberg 1994: 66). Shop windows, like film frames, are organised as enticements to stop and gaze, and even though the commodities displayed become a spectacle in their own right, the goal of the display is for the customer to come in and make a purchase (the equivalent to this in a film is product placement and subsequent merchandising). So, like the cinema screen, the shop window:

becomes a surface upon which the spectators/pedestrians can map out the coordinates of their desire, helping to position themselves in relation to the objects of desire behind the glass. The glass maps out the route through which these objects can easily be possessed but at the same time serves as a detour to desire fulfilment. This chiasmic journey always ends at its starting point: the self as a desiring subject. (Tucker 2010: 33)

The *flâneur* subverts this goal by only momentarily stopping and then idly strolling on to gaze in the next window without ever entering the store. The glass makes his desire transparent, for he is aware of the glass itself as a barrier. His indifference is a stronger barrier, however, because he knows that 'desire is best explored virtually behind glass, not as an engaged voyeur but as an indifferent mobile pedestrian who uses the glass as a transparent and safe substitute for his or her own longing to possess the objects on display' (Tucker 2010: 33).

This is not the case with Cléo. She is a shopper. Varda's tracking shot makes the pedestrian act of window shopping interchangeable with the act of filming it by implicating the film viewer in Cléo's own self-fetishisation as a commodity. It is we who are the *flâneur*, but Varda complicates the ambiguities between the real and virtual images of desire by pulling us into the store, then outside again, then back in again. Each time, glass – in the guise of either a window or mirror – intercedes between us and Cléo and between Cléo and her self-identity. She is part of the pageantry of displayed objects, like the carnivalesque spectacle of the frog swallower and the man piercing his bicep that she witnesses on the street, akin to the marvels of the Paris flea market that so enthralled the Surrealists.

In the second half, Varda sets both Cléo and the camera free to move from fetish to a *flâneuse*, from image to subject. She flings off her wig, shedding her childish image of herself, changes into a black dress (in mourning?) and walks out of her apartment to wander Paris alone. Her solitary strolling around Paris becomes one of self-discovery rather than suppression of herself. She is still being looked at, but now she looks back. Her journey takes her from one to be looked at to one who looks, and in the second half the camera moves from images of exteriority to images that reflect Cléo's interiority. As Lauren Elkin notes, in the second half of the film Varda 'specifically challenges the idea that a woman could not walk the streets the way a man does, anonymously, taking in the spectacle; a woman is the spectacle ... Looking, not simply appearing, signals the beginning of women's freedom in the city' (Elkin 2017: 220). Varda cuts back and forth in a tracking shot from a passing pedestrian's points of view to Cléo's uneasy view of that same passer-by so that we become entwined in the exchange of looks between them as she walks down the pavement. Her tracking shots in the second half have the look and feel of ones we found in Murnau's *Sunrise*. Though the film was shot over a decade before the invention of the Steadicam, Varda's peripatetic tracking shots in the second half of the film give us flashes of the dorsal nature of later Steadicam camera movements. This what Tweedie recognises in these shots:

> The scenes that correspond directly to her point of view also bear traces of their conditions of production, as the pedestrians who cross paths with Cléo stare into the camera with the sometimes knowing and sometimes uncomfortable look of people being filmed. A camera has replaced the body of Cléo in order to gather the footage for this sequence, and the deliberate and empowering act of walking in the city is interchangeable with the process of filming it. (Tweedie 2013: 127)

The first place Cléo stops on her second walk is the Le Dôme café. In this scene, instead of sitting down, she moves through the café as a *flâneuse* observing people. The café is a large and labyrinthine space which serves Cléo's desire for urban anonymity well. The scene begins with a shot through a floor-to-ceiling window inside the café showing Cléo crossing the street and walking towards the café. Varda then cuts to a subjective POV shot of Cléo opening the glass door, entering the café, walking past the bar, where she looks at a man playing pinball, and past several booths before alighting on the jukebox. Then there is a cut to an objective angle behind Cléo and she puts money in the jukebox and plays one of her own songs and puts on dark sunglasses. The camera follows her as she goes through a revolving door to the café's outdoor, glass covered patio (an arcade like space). As the camera follows Cléo through the café, we listen to bits of the conversation between café patrons that Cléo overhears. Then, there is a cut to a tracking shot from in front of her as she walks through the patio looking at the customers on either side followed by a short tracking POV shot of her view walking past patrons on her right. The patrons are sitting with their backs to the glass wall of the café, and as she passes by we catch glimpses of customers inside as well as reflections of passers-by on the pavement outside. The shot ends at a couple sitting at a table just inside the patio and we get a full view of the street with its cars and pedestrians, before cutting back to a frontal shot. Cléo then turns around to retrace her steps and we then see a cut to a POV shot tracking along the faces of the people on the other side of the patio, along with a view of the street. The next two shots track Cléo walking to another part of the café and sitting down alone at a table and ordering a cognac. We then get a sequence of shots that cut back and forth between Cléo looking at people and subjective POVs of the people she sees. In the sequence, she observes ordinary people in conversation going about their lives. There are two women at a table, one with a baby in her arms and the other cradling a toddler; an older couple sitting at a booth beneath prints by Manet and Klee; a young, modern couple in love. In this entire scene, nobody looks at Cléo (or the camera); Cléo is the only one who looks. Though she is surrounded by mirrors, she does not glance at herself once.

Throughout the rest of the film we follow Cléo – mostly on foot, though she does ride on a tram and in a taxi – as she wanders aimlessly around Paris as a *flâneuse*. She goes to an art studio and then to the cinema where she is shown a short silent film featuring Jean-Luc Godard and Anna Karina (shot by Varda). She meets Antoine walking in the park. At the hospital her illness is confirmed but her prognosis is hopeful. The film ends with a backward tracking shot of Cléo and Antoine in medium close-up walking silently towards the camera. The camera walks ahead of them, holding their now calm and serene faces in the frame as bells chime in the background.

Rome: *Umberto D.*

The defeat of fascism in Italy along with the Allied occupation in 1944 ushered in a period of widespread poverty and depredations for the Italian people. In the aftermath of fascism, their country ravaged by war, ordinary citizens face a daily struggle to stay alive. The economy was depressed and rampant unemployment brought many of the working class to the brink of starvation. These conditions led to a new form of Italian cinema that focused on the impoverished conditions of the working class, especially in urban centres, that has since been labelled Italian neo-realism. Susan Hayward identifies five principles that the content and style of Italian neo-realist cinema demands: 1) it should project a slice of everyday life in all of its gritty reality; 2) it should focus on the social reality of widespread unemployment and poverty that plagued post-war Italy; 3) it should feature non-professional actors whose language and dialogue is realistic and natural using authentic regional dialects; 4) films should be shot on location, in the streets, avoiding the use of studios whenever possible; and 5) films should be shot in the style of documentary, using hand-held cameras and natural lighting (Hayward 2000: 202–3). Citing Italian screenwriter Cesare Zavattini, Deleuze further adds that Italian neo-realism is 'an art of encounter – fragmentary, ephemeral, piecemeal, missed encounters' (Deleuze 1995: 1).[1]

For Deleuze, neo-realism represents a rupture in cinematic movement, marking the end of the movement-image and the emerging of what he calls the 'time-image'. Neo-realism embodies a crisis in action, where 'linear actions dissolve into the form of aleatory strolls' and characters' movements are 'dispersive, elliptical, errant or wavering' (Deleuze 1995: 1; Rodowick 1997: 12). The characters walk and act in indeterminate city spaces, inhabited yet deserted, what Deleuze calls 'any-space-whatever' such as 'disused warehouses, waste ground, cities in the course of demolition or reconstruction' (Deleuze 1995: xi). Summarising Deleuze, Gregory Flaxman characterises neo-realism as a form of realism where:

> Situations lose their objective assurance, hence the emergence of pure optical and sonic images . . . that have been delinked from the chronological series of the present, cut off from motor extension, from action . . . for here the film is wedded to a wandering movement in which anything or nothing can happen . . . (Flaxman 2000: 31)

Hayward cites only one film that meets all of the tenets of the exacting demands of Italian neo-realism: Vittorio De Sica's *Bicycle Thieves* (1948) (Hayward 2000: 202–3).[2] While I agree in her assessment about *Bicycle Thieves*, I would add that De Sica's other great neo-realist film *Umberto D.* (1952) belongs alongside it.[3]

Images of walking are abundant in Vittorio De Sica's films. Walking certainly plays a constitutive role in *Bicycle Thieves*, a film about which much has been written. We can also cite Sophia Loren's character's frantic trek with her teenage daughter back to their rural home village in the mountains to escape the Allied bombing of Rome in *Two Women*. The scenes of retreating Italian soldiers slogging through the wintery Russian landscape in the war drama *Sunflower* also come to mind. But for me, *Umberto D.* stands out. There are multiple images of walking in this film, but I want to focus specifically on two instances that are important to its narrative and theme: marching in protest, and dog walking.

Umberto D. focuses on the life of an elderly pensioner named Umberto Domenico Ferrari, played by Carlo Battisti who, after working for thirty years in the Public Works department of Rome has retired and lives on a modest pension. Buts Italy's post-war inflation has reduced his pension to a below subsistence level pittance. He believes that he is owed a twenty percent increase by the city government so that he can pay his debts. The theme of the film focuses on impoverished but proud Umberto's daily struggle to maintain his hope and dignity in life despite all the inhumanity and cruelty surrounding him in society.

The film follows Umberto as he struggles against his penury while trying to hold on to his self-respect. Central to his struggle are the series of obstacles he faces trying to find the fifteen hundred lire in back rent he owes to his callous landlady, who threatens to evict him from the room where he has lived for the past two decades if he does not pay by the end of the month. His only family is his cherished dog Flike and only friend the young pregnant maid who works for his landlady. Forced to sell some of his most prized possessions in order to placate his ruthless landlady he tries to buy more time to raise the funds and stave off homelessness, but his landlady is obstinate and throws him out so that she can make more money by renting the room by the hour to adulterous couples. This causes him to lose sight of the joys in life, including his bond with Flike, and pushes him to the brink of suicide.

Protest March

The film opens with an overhead shot of a wide Roman boulevard bustling with traffic and pedestrians. As the credits begin to fade, a multi-columned group of protesters comes into view marching up the middle of the street. The camera pans slightly downwards as the marchers fill most of the frame. We then see a low angle medium shot from beneath an overpass of a series of picket signs parading past proclaiming, 'raise our pensions . . . we worked our whole lives . . . justice for pensioners'. The film then cuts to a series of medium shots of a group of elderly men holding signs and shouting, 'We want an increase!' They march up to the front of city hall situated in a plaza where they are halted by the police. Through a series of close-ups, we see the men in unison protest that they want to see the government minister. The pensioners are dispersed by police who use jeeps to herd them like sheep out of the city square, funnelling them into narrow side streets. Umberto takes refuge with his dog Flike and several other protesters underneath an archway covering an arcade-like street, where they hide behind columns and cower in apartment door vestibules. Once the police are out of sight, they argue about whether or not the organisers of the protest should have secured a permit. They finally leave the covered street and scatter in different directions through the square, disappearing into side streets that appear as pedestrian corollaries of a ruined past and an uncertain future. Umberto, with Flike on a leash, walks with another pensioner discussing the perils of being elderly and poor, living only on a fixed pension. Umberto unsuccessfully tries to sell his watch to his friend before they part ways.

Protests are usually, with few exceptions, urban affairs. Cities are ideal spaces for protest marches because their populations exist readymade as what Benjamin refers to as a 'collective'. He writes that:

> Streets are the dwelling place of the collective. The collective is an eternally restless, eternally moving being that – between building walls – lives, experiences, recognises,

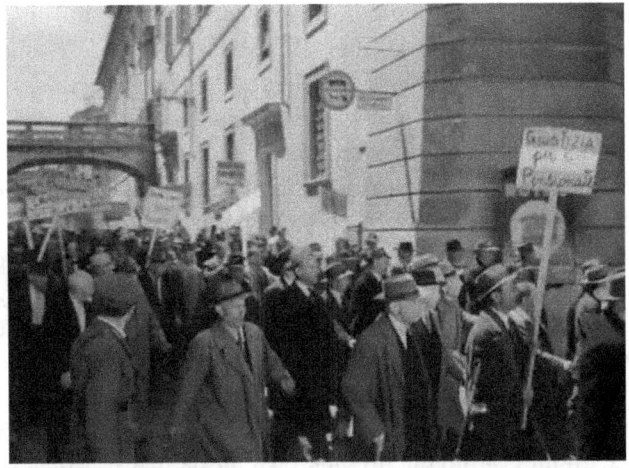

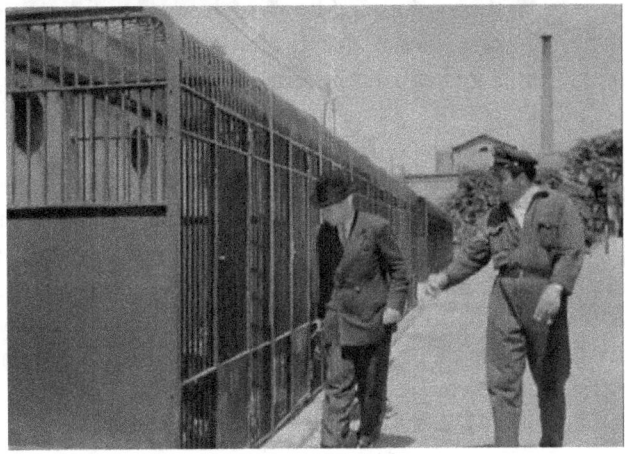

Figures 6.3 and 6.4 Umberto D.

and invents as much as individuals do within the protection of their own four walls. For this collective, glossy enamelled shop signs are a wall decoration as good as, if not better than, an oil painting in the drawing room of a bourgeois; walls with their 'Post No Bills' are its writing desk, newspaper stands its libraries, mailboxes its bronze busts, benches its bedroom furniture, and the café terrace is the balcony from which it looks down on its household . . . and the gateway which leads from the row of courtyards out into the open is the long corridor that daunts the bourgeois, being for the courtyards the entry to the chambers of the city. (Benjamin 2002a: 423)

The collective is the presentation of a city's unconscious, buried in its depths like a dream, until it manifests itself bodily in action through public protests. For Benjamin, this latent collective consciousness, which can only be made manifest through the streets and spaces of the city, quite literally forms a *mass dream* (Miller 1996: 104). Like a dream (and the arcades), the collective has no real outside. For the collective, streets and urban spaces function as interiors where they can gather en masse to voice their common private concerns in public. The entire city space – with its riotous mix of movement, progressions and sensations – is open to the collective's political dreaming.

In protest, the *flâneur* is no longer a solitary spectator but a collective force who transforms the city into a public loudspeaker, remaking it into a 'place whose centre did not belong to businesses or to cars, but to pedestrians moving down the street in this most bodily form of free speech' (Solnit 2001: 227). Walking as protest is a form of public speech, where individuals with shared circumstances and political convictions march as one voice without ever giving up their own individuality – the exact opposite of military marching where soldiers' 'lockstep signifies that they have become interchangeable units under absolute authority' (Solnit 2001: 217). Masses on the march are in turn transformed collectively by the city, becoming a new, unified type of *flâneur*, the slowness of their march mirroring the individual *flâneur*'s rejection of speed (Gros 2015: 198).

Paris has always been the model city for the *flâneur* and for revolutions, insurrections and protest marches, but we can find historical parallels in other old European cities such as London, and most certainly in Rome.[4] Paris, London and Rome, with their central squares, public monuments, and endless walls and building facades ripe for plastering signs and slogans, are all pedestrian cities that seem ideally built for marches and protest. As historian Eric Hobsbawm argued, the perfect city for riot or insurrection should:

> be densely populated and not to large in area. Essentially it should still be possible to traverse it on foot . . . In the ideal insurrectionary city the authorities – the rich, the aristocracy, the government or local administration – will therefore be intermingled with central concentration of the poor as possible. (quoted in Solnit 2001: 219)

Rome's streets are older than those of Paris, gritted by history of empire and emblems of civilisation, not the least of which are the roads the Romans built all over the Western world. Its cobblestone streets conjure up images of Roman legions marching through the city, sometimes in triumph and at other times in revolt. In recent history, Italian fascist mobs marched along its streets, heeling to the jack-booted steps of Mussolini and his armed squad of goons.

Benjamin argued that the origins of fascism are found in an attempt to 'organise the newly created proletarian masses without affecting the property structure which the masses strive to eliminate' (Benjamin et al. 1968: 241). The response of fascism to massification is to withdraw the proletariat's right to change their property relations while giving them a 'chance to express themselves' while preserving property in its capitalistic form. In this way, fascism denies the masses power exercised through material rewards and substitutes power with emotional rewards. The logical result of this violation of the masses is the aestheticisation of politics which can only lead to one thing: war.[5] By the time De Sica made Umberto D., war had meant the substitution of Italian fascist soldiers marching through Roman streets by an army of Nazi German goose stepping down its boulevards. When it was all over, it was Allied armies doing the marching until it was finally time for the collective citizens of Rome to take back their streets during a new time of social, political and economic upheaval.

We are very familiar with films about university student protest, but it is rare that we get to see images of elderly pensioners as an unruly mob parading in the streets voicing their collective grievances and demands. In fact, Umberto D. is one of only a handful of feature films to include scenes of a senior citizen street protest. Unfortunately, the Roman police treat Umberto and his fellow senior citizens as if they are participating in a children's march and do not take them seriously as a threat. His mistreatment by society will continue throughout the film.

Dog Walking

Roger Grenier writes that a 'pet is a protection against life's insults, a defence against the world . . . a way of being both less alone and more alone' (Grenier 2000: 23). Perhaps this is most true of man's most loyal pet companion, the dog. Like humans, dogs are natural wanderers but evolution has trained them to dwell in our company, sharing in the sedentariness of our modern life. Baudelaire called dogs the 'friendly, lively muse of the cities' (Grenier 2000: 13). One advantage they have over other pets such as cats or turtles is that they enjoy a good walk in the city with their human companions. In *The Walk: Notes on a Romantic Image*, Jeffrey C. Robinson reflects on why dogs are such good walking partners:

> The dog is the perfect compromise between the severity of solitude and the clutter of companionship, put positively the freedom of one and the comfort of the other. Without inhibiting one's thoughts, it comforts the walker in his solitude by mirroring his activities, and like the image in a mirror, the dog requires the human walker for its own continued motions. A person and his dog compose an idyll of walking. (Robinson 2006: 88)

When walking beside their human companion, it is often the faster four-legged dog that voluntarily heels to the slower speed of bipedalism, but not always.[6] Sometimes the dog forces their human partner to slow down, tugging at the sight of a squirrel or a familiar person, or pausing to smell an odour imperceptible to all but themselves (stepping out on to the pavement with a dog on a leash and letting it lead you by its nose is perhaps the ultimate form of dérive). As Ingold argues, when humans and dogs walk together:

> The social relations of walking crosscut the divide between human and animal, between the pace of two feet and four . . . tautness in the leash is an index of conflicting agencies as first one and then the other, digging in the heels or leaning backwards to maintain stability, is induced to step forward in order to remain upright. The balance of power, in this case, can swing like a see-saw, as first the human then the animal gains the upper hand. Each, alternatively, 'walks' the other. (Vergunst and Ingold 2008: 12)

This peripatetic relationship between a dog and human is one of mutual trust, affection, harmony and respect, which is an extension of their domestic interactions. Umberto is kindred with his dog, and Flike brings out a joy and tenderness in Umberto that is missing in his social relations with other people. He hardly ever leaves his room to walk the streets without taking Flike with him.

Umberto is someone who, as he tells another pensioner, has 'no one, no son or brother, to help me out'. His only true source of love, happiness, security and belonging is Flike, who he describes as 'a mutt with intelligent eyes, white with brown spots [and] impossible to hate'. Walking a dog in the city is a social activity, and has been shown to foster new encounters between people on the street, helping lonely and forgotten senior citizens such as Umberto to maintain their current social networks and cultivate new ones. But while Umberto and Flike occasionally run into some of his old colleagues and acquaintances on their walks, they are all too wrapped up in their own troubles and recoil like strangers at Umberto's overtures of continued friendship. Other than Flike, his only other source of comfort is the adolescent maid Maria, and that friendship is strained when she accidentally lets Flike run away while Umberto is laid up in the hospital for a few days convalescing with a fever.

Immediately upon his release from hospital, Umberto hails a taxi, hurrying to the city pound to look for Flike. In one of the most harrowing scenes of the film, Umberto frantically searches almost every inch of the pound for Flike before he is gassed along with the unclaimed strays. The tension builds as he witnesses dog after dog being lifted out of the dog catcher's truck with hooked staffs and thrown into cages to be wheeled into the gas chamber. Standing in the doorway of the killing floor, he watches in horror as a cage full of these dogs, their tails wagging in ignorance of their fate, is pushed into the chamber and the door shut. After he turns away in despair and disgust, the camera tracks him as he slowly walks along a row of cages, looking perilously into each one hoping to find Flike. Just as he is about to give up, he glimpses Flike being pulled out of a truck, and runs over, unhooks him from the staff and embraces him. Then, he puts him gently on the ground, attaches his leash to his collar, and together they walk away as if escaping a concentration camp.

The above scene shows that Umberto, fearing his own possible fate at a homeless shelter of being cast off in a way similar to Flike's near liquidation at the pound, has found some hope in their shared welfare. When he is finally defeated by his landlady and forced out of his apartment, he still has no intention of going to live in a crowded and inhumane shelter with Flike. Still thinking of Flike's welfare, he walks him to a tenement where a dishevelled looking couple board dogs, hoping to find Flike a stable home. After seeing the conditions there, he has a change of mind and takes Flike and walks away.

In one of the last scenes, Umberto tries to give Flike away to a little girl who is playing in the park. She is excited to take him, but her Nanny relents, saying that a dog is too much trouble to care for and her parents will not want him. Despondent, Umberto tries to abandon Flike in the park, but cannot see it through. He picks him up and stands next to the tracks as a

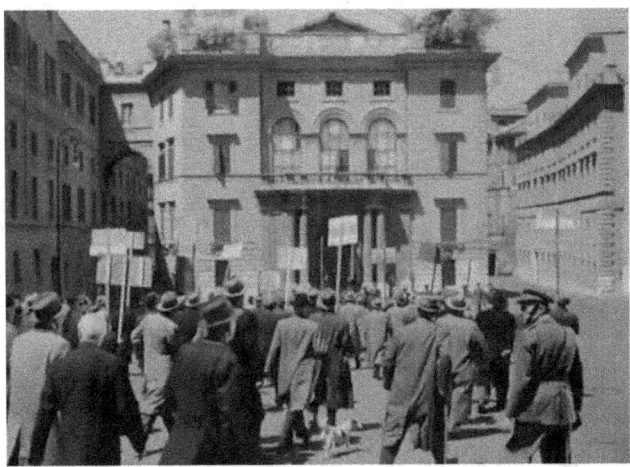

Figure 6.5 Umberto D.

train speeds towards them in a joint suicide attempt. Just before he can step onto the tracks, Flike yelps and wriggles out of his grip and runs back to the park. Umberto follows him and coaxes him into retrieving a pine cone he throws as playful children run alongside. The last shot of the film shows Umberto and Flike walking off together into the background, continuing their game of fetch out of the frame and into an uncertain future.

Notes

1. Bazin praised these films as *reconstituted reportage* or fact-images.
2. Like *Breathless*, the plot of *Bicycle Thieves* is peripatetic. Antonio Ricci is an impoverished and unemployed working-class Italian living in depressed post-World War II Rome. He is finally offered work, delivering and hanging up movie posters around the city. The job requires a bicycle, so his wife Maria sells the family's bed linen to redeem Antonio's bicycle from a pawnshop so that he can start his new job. However, on his first day at work, his prized bicycle is stolen and Antonio desperately scours the crowded streets of Rome on foot with his son Bruno in search of the thief to retrieve his bike and save his job. The film follows the father and son and they confront one obstacle after another along the bustling streets. He finally finds and confronts the thief, but since he did not catch him red handed and there are no other witnesses, the police tell Antonio that his accusation is not enough proof and he leaves empty-handed. Near the end of the film, in desperation Antonio attempts to steal a bicycle parked near a packed football stadium but is caught by a mob who tussles him towards a police station and humiliates him in front of his son. Before he can be arrested, the owner declines to press charges. The film ends with Antonio and Bruno walking through a crowd hand in hand, each reduced to tears. Though the film does involve a good bit of walking, Antonio's peripatetic search is done with a definite purpose; it is not an aimless walk, and thus did not merit analysis in this chapter.
3. Bazin agrees, writing that:

    . . . the perfection of *Ladri di Biciclette* [*Bicycle Thieves*] was only a beginning, though it was regarded as a culmination. It took *Umberto D* to make us understand what it was in the realism of *Ladri di Biciclette* that was still a concession to classical dramaturgy. Consequently what is so unsettling about *Umberto D* is primarily the way it rejects any relationship to traditional film spectacle. (Bazin 1971: 80)

4. In *The Arcades Project*, Benjamin penned this note:

    Paris created the type of the *flâneur*. What is remarkable is that it was not Rome. And the reason? Does not dreaming itself take the high road in Rome? And isn't that city too full of temples, enclosed squares, national shrines, to be able to enter tout entière with every cobblestone, every shop sign, every step, and every gateway-into the passer-by's dream? (Benjamin 2002a: 417 – M1, 4)

One could make the same argument about Rome creating a type of pedestrian protester. For instance, the women of Rome took to the streets in 195 BCE to protest the Senate's failure to repeal *Lex Opia* after the end of the Second Punic Wars. *Lex Opia* was a series of austerity laws passed during wartime aimed solely at females that curbed a woman's right to purchase and publicly flaunt expenditures on adornment and finery, such as multi-coloured clothing or riding in a carriage within one mile of city. The Senate repealed all other wartime measures, but left *Lex Opia* on the law books during peacetime. Women poured into the streets from the suburbs and rural areas and marched into the centre of Rome, blocking streets as they moved before gathering in the Forum to make speeches arguing for the repeal of the emergency measure. Despite attempts by the conservative Roman patriarchal establishment to quash the women's march, the women as a collective were triumphant and the law was repealed.

5. Communism, fascism's opposite, results in the politicisation of art.
6. It is curious that among all of Marey's chronophotographic studies of the anatomical movement of four-legged animals, such as those of cats (he showed that they do indeed always land on their feet), horses and even a goat, only a handful are of dogs. Even more curious is that not one of these scrutinises how the gaits of a dog and human walking together interact (that task would fall to Giacomo Balla in his 1912 painting *Dynamism of a Dog on a Leash*). Also, in 1887 Eadweard Muybridge shot a series of chronophotographic stills of a dog running from two different angles, one from the side and the other from the front.

Conclusion: Running Out of Frames

If this work seems incomplete, that is because an entire series of books on the topic of walking in cinema would probably not exhaust the subject. As I have argued, film-making and walking have been inextricably linked together since the birth of cinema. By way of conclusion, I want to map out some territory for future research on the subject that this work has not covered by citing a few case studies.

Hiking Films

In his 1861 treatise *Walking*, Thoreau proclaimed the true essence of walking lies in the art of *sauntering*:

> I have met with but one or two persons in the course of my life who understood the art of Walking, that is, of taking walks, – who had a genius, so to speak, for *sauntering*, which word is beautifully derived 'from idle people who roved about the country, in the Middle Ages, and asked charity, under pretence of going *à la Sainte Terre*,' to the Holy Land, till the children exclaimed, 'There goes a Sainte-Terrer,' a Saunterer, a Holy-Lander. (Thoreau 2010: 35)

If we can master the art of sauntering, then 'every walk is a sort out of crusade'. Since Thoreau regards man as 'an inhabitant, or part and parcel of Nature, rather than a member of society', he extols hiking long distances in the wilderness as a spiritual exercise and the highest form of sauntering. He claimed he could never preserve his own spiritual health unless he spent at least four hours a day 'sauntering through the woods and over the hills and fields'. Hiking in nature, the walker reaffirms that, 'Wildness is the preservation of the World.'

Over the past two decades, there have been a slew of feature films about long distance wilderness treks. Below are short case studies of three of these. All share roughly the same theme of broken characters who set out on a long distance hike as a form of healing or self-discovery.[1]

Southbounders (2005, dir. by Ben Wagner)

This low-budget Indy feature follows a young woman named Olivia as she attempts to walk the entire 2,170 miles of the Appalachian Trail from Maine to Georgia. The title is a hiking term that refers to someone who walks the Appalachian Trail from north to south, the opposite direction of most hikers who embark on the southern portion of the trail. Olivia, a college student studying to be a physical trainer, decides to take a break from her studies to rethink her life's direction. Soon after embarking alone on her six-month journey, she crosses paths with other colourful hikers, including a young poet named Rollins with whom she develops a romantic relationship. The film is shot with a digital camera, giving it a documentary feel. The camera stays close to Olivia and Rollins, focusing on their romance as it buds through long, arduous days of walking. The director uses lots of hand-held mobile shots that follow the hikers, focusing on the physical and mental hardships they must endure daily as they walk long distances from one wilderness shelter to the next. But unlike the characters in *The Way Back* whose lives depended on how far they could walk each day, the challenges of multi-day walking faced by Olivia and her companions are self-willed. They are not escaping the wilderness back to society but escaping into the wild from society.

Wild (2014, dir. by Jean-Marc Vallée)

Wild is a film based on the memoir by Cheryl Strayed about her decision in 1995 to walk the Pacific Crest Trail as a journey of healing following a string of setbacks in her life, including drug addiction, a divorce, an abortion and the death of her mother. Despite having no previous hiking experience Strayed, played by Reese Witherspoon, leaves her home in Minneapolis to walk 1,100 miles of the Pacific Coast Trail from the Mojave Desert in California to Southern Oregon. The film follows the woefully ill-prepared Strayed as she struggles with her equipment, the weather and her own lack of walking fitness. During her walk, she reflects back on the catastrophic events in her life that culminated in her undertaking this journey through a series of flashbacks.

A Walk in the Woods (2015, dir. by Ken Kwapis)

Another film about hiking the Appalachian Trail, this one featuring two old friends who reconnect on the trek northbound from Georgia to Maine. The film is based on the 1998 memoir of the same title by travel writer Bill Bryson, played by Robert Redford.

After attending a funeral in New Hampshire where he lives, sixty-something Bryson decides spontaneously to walk the Appalachian Trail alone. His wife and son object to the dangers of such a strenuous a trek for a man his age (his son tells him it takes five months, five million steps and that only ten percent of twenty-year-olds finish it), but relent when his old friend Stephen Katz (Nick Nolte) offers to come along as his hiking companion. Like Strayed in *Wild*, neither of them are physically fit enough for long distance hiking and they soon suffer multiple setbacks. But once they fall into the day-to-day rhythm of walking, they begin to take pleasure in each other's company and other hikers they meet on their journey. However, after walking for three months, they are discouraged to learn from looking at a map that they have covered only half of the length of the trail. Later on their trek, after ignoring a sign on a section of the trail posted 'for experienced hikers', they both trip and fall down a rocky cliff onto a ledge. Unable to climb their way back up to the trail, they are forced to spend the night. After they are rescued in the morning by other hikers, they call it quits and go home.

Pilgrimage Films

Setting off on foot from home and leaving the routines of everyday life behind, the pilgrim is someone who seeks a religious experience mediated through walking as a liminal state between home and their sacred destination, between the profane world and the hallowed one. (Whalen 2011: xii). This liminal status might be marked by specific clothing or a badge, such as a shell, worn by the pilgrim, signalling to others the religious nature of their peripatetic journey. A pilgrim, as Frédéric Gros reminds us, is 'never at home where he walks: he is a stranger, a foreigner' (Gros 2015: 107).

From the middle ages right up until today, pilgrimage has been a concrete, micro-cosmic representation of the human condition and our journey from birth to death (Gros 2015: 110). Though the motivations for the modern pilgrim vary – whether it be penance, thanksgiving or devotion – one thing they all have in common is a need to reconnect with some part of themselves that has been lost or forgotten. Below are short case studies of two films whose narratives are centred on pilgrimage.

The Way (2010, dir. by Emilio Estevez)

Of the three great Christian pilgrimages – Jerusalem, Rome and Santiago de Compostela – only Santiago de Compostela still draws throngs of

CONCLUSION 133

walkers today. There is an entire network of ancient pilgrim routes traversing Europe, collectively known as the Camino de Santiago, that converge together on the tomb of St James in the city in north-west Spain that bears his name. But the most popular route by far is the Camino Francés which runs 780 km in a single, well marked path from the Basque town of Saint-Jean-Pied-du-Port in France to Santiago. A well maintained infrastructure of hostels and cafés with specially priced accommodation and meals for walkers has been developed along the route, and every year over 150,000 pilgrims complete some portion or all of the journey.

There are numerous documentaries about the Camino Francés, but only one feature film is set along its route: *The Way*, starring Martin Sheen and written and directed by his son, Emilio Estevez. Martin Sheen plays Tom, an ophthalmologist who lives a comfortable, upper middle class life in Southern California. His son Daniel (Emilio Estevez) decides to quit graduate school to travel the world, starting with walking the Camino. Tom is opposed to his son's plans and they argue on the way to the airport. A few days later Tom is on the golf course when receives a phone call from a French gendarme informing him that his son has died in a freak snowstorm in the French Pyrenees on the first leg of the Camino. Tom flies to France to identify Daniel and retrieve his remains. After learning from the police chief about the spiritual significance of the Camino (he tells Tom that has walked to Santiago seven times), Tom makes an impulsive decision to take up and finish his son's pilgrimage as a way of processing his grief. Wearing Daniel's hiking boots and backpack, Tom walks the entire Camino, scattering handfuls of his ashes at various important shrines along the way.

Tom starts out on his trek alone, but he is eventually joined by three other fellow pilgrims who become his regular walking companions. The first one he meets is Joost (Yorick van Wageningen), a cheerful, overweight Dutchman who is walking the Camino to lose weight for his brother's wedding. Joost and Tom are next joined by Sarah (Deborah Kara Unger), a crass, judgemental chain-smoking Canadian, with a rude and stand-offish demeanour that offends Tom. Though she says she is on pilgrimage to quit smoking, we learn that she is carrying a deep personal tragedy. The last to join the group is Jack (James Nesbitt), an Irish travel writer suffering from writer's block who says he is on the Camino to merely write a travel guide but refuses to enter any churches along the way.

Estevez shot the film sequentially as the cast and crew travelled the Camino. The star of the film is the Camino itself. Estevez focuses on the rituals of walking as pilgrimage, exploring the ancient protocols and codes to which modern pilgrims still adhere, such as the ritual of having the credential or pilgrim's passport stamped along the way to verify the pilgrim's route in order to receive the official Compostela issued by the Cathedral of St James at the end of the pilgrimage journey.

In interviews, Estevez has called the film a retelling of *The Wizard of Oz*. The Camino is the yellow brick road, Santiago the Emerald City, and the Church is the Wizard. Tom is Dorothy, blown to Spain by the emotional tornado of Daniel's death. Jack, who we first meet pacing back and forth behind bales of hay, represents the Scarecrow, Sarah the Tin Man, and Joost the Cowardly Lion.

The Burmese Harp (1956, dir. by Kon Ichikawa)

The story focuses on a group of Japanese soldiers known as the 'Singing Company' who are awaiting repatriation to Japan from Burma in the aftermath of the Japanese surrender. The soldiers have maintained a sense of humanity and morale throughout the war by singing songs from various countries accompanied by homemade instruments. The heart of the group is Corporal Mizushima, a spiritual young man who plays a Burmese harp and arranges pieces for the men to sing. One day, he is summoned by the Americans to a mountain redoubt to persuade a company of Japanese holdouts to surrender and go home. After he does not return to his own company, his comrades worry about what has become of him. Meanwhile, Mizushima disguises himself as a Buddhist monk, embarking on a pilgrimage across Burma to find and bury the bodies of Japanese soldiers left on the battlefield. Traipsing across the Burmese plains, dense jungles and river flats, Mizushima stoically tends to the forgotten war dead in a personal pilgrimage to understand and transcend the causes of war and of human suffering. As we follow Mizushima's pilgrimage, the camera focuses on his feet as he is transformed from a marching soldier to an itinerant monk.

Running Films

There is a plethora of films about runners and the sport of running. However, there are a handful of films where running is constitutive of the plot and not the focus of the narrative. Below, I sketch out two that might deserve further exploration.

Run Lola Run (1999, dir. by Tom Tykwer)

Run Lola Run has a simple premise: a girl named Lola has twenty minutes to rescue her boyfriend from a mobster.

CONCLUSION

The film opens as Lola answers a phone call from her boyfriend Manni, a low-level courier working for a violent crime boss, who calls her in an obvious panic from a payphone on a Berlin street. He had just concluded a routine pickup/drop off, and all that was left to complete the job was to wait for Lola to pick him up and drive him to the rendezvous site with his boss where he would then hand over 100,000 DM to him. The deadline for handing over the cash was noon, but when Lola's moped is stolen, she arrives too late and Manni has already headed for the subway. But in a stroke of bad luck and mental distraction, Manni accidentally leaves the bag of money in the subway car and it is immediately swiped away by a homeless vagrant. By the time Manni calls Lola, his boss is on his way to pick up the money and Manni has only twenty minutes to replace the money or he will be killed. Lola tells him to wait at the phone booth, that she will find the money for him and be there, somehow, in twenty minutes. Manni is not fully convinced and hedges his bets on Lola by persuading himself that the quickest way to get the money, should she stand him up again, is through an armed robbery of the supermarket across the street.

Lola rushes out of her apartment, down the stairs and into the street, attempting to get to Manni. Along the way, she hopes to convince her father, who is in charge of a large bank, to give her the 100,000 DM before the time runs out. The film then focuses on Lola running against the clock and, through a barrage of images and music, unpacks a narrative about the interplay of chance and destiny and the fine line between the two.

Instead of showing us only one outcome of Lola's mission, Tykwer presents three different alternate realities and possibilities for Manni and Lola's fate; one story is told through three different plots. Each alternate scenario is marked by seemingly trivial variations in Lola's path towards Manni, and Tykwer uses these to show how the destinies of various people are altered by their contact with Lola. In further experimentation with the presentation of narrative structure, Tykwer shoots each of the three versions in the 'real time' of the twenty-minute plot time, and gives them all totally distinct outcomes.

Style in *Run Lola Run* is so highly accentuated that one cannot help but notice the material aspects of the film. One of the most unique and innovative devices is the use of flash-forward as an emblem of running ahead of time. As Lola races against the clock down the streets of Berlin, she slams into various token passers-by: a snarling, middle-aged woman pushing a baby carriage; a man pedalling a stolen bicycle; and a sultry female bank employee making copies on a Xerox machine. As Lola rushes past these characters, Tykwer flashes forward through a series of still photographic images into distinct futures for each character that are altered after each of their brushes with Lola. With each altered scenario, the destiny of each person is again changed after running into Lola.

The narrative function of this device is to reiterate the 'what-if?' theme of destiny which redounds throughout the film. It is meant to show how Lola's frantic dash through Berlin affects the destinies of people with whom she comes into contact during her struggle to reach Manni before his twenty-minute deadline runs out. Just as running might be viewed as an excessive form of walking, the flash-forwards are intermedially excessive: they literally run by the viewer like a music video. There is no time for the viewer to contemplate the images in the photographs, some of which are obscure and invite speculation. For example, during the first flash-forward into the bicycle thief's future, we see him getting beaten by thugs who steal his bike, being treated in a hospital, eating lunch with a nurse, then getting married. All of this takes place in less than eight seconds. Even as Tykwer cuts back to Lola racing over a bridge, we are left contemplating the arbitrariness of this alternative narrative.

Gallipoli (1981, dir. by Peter Weir)

Gallipoli, one of the most highly rated Australian films to date, is an anti-war film about Australia's disastrous campaign on the Gallipoli peninsula during the early days of World War I. The story follows two exceptionally fast short-distance sprinters from Western Australia – rancher Archy (Mark Lee) and jack of all trades Frank (Mel Gibson) – who enlist together in the Australian army in 1915 after meeting at a race. After training in Egypt, the two mates are sent to Gallipoli, where they join the Allied forces struggling to break through the Turkish defences. The situation in Gallipoli is grim. In an effort to divert Turkish attention away from a British landing force on a nearby beach, the Australians are ordered on a futile mission to go over the top of the trenches in three waves and attack the Turkish entrenchment manned by machine gunners. After the first two waves are cut down, Frank persuades his commander to let him run to headquarters to ask the general to call off the third wave, the one of which Archy will be part. The general reconsiders the attack, but Frank, despite running his hardest back to the trenches, is too late with the news and Archy and his comrades go over the top to their deaths, cut down by machine gun fire. The final shot is a freeze frame of Archy being hit by bullets across his chest, falling backwards with his head tilted back, as if breaking the tape at the finish of race.

The first third of Gallipoli focuses on running and reads like a typical sports film. But the film soon progresses into a story about two friends, both short distance runners who specialise in the 100-metre event, whose equally short foresight leads them into the abysmal horrors of trench warfare. Running embodies the nature of both Archy and Frank as well as the nation of Australia that is running headlong into a war on the other side of the world, only because it is subject to British rule. Running is more than a subject of the film; it is its ontological theme, intrinsically connected to the tragic excess of death in war.

Apocalyptic Walking

Another area I have left unexplored is the surfeit of films set in a dystopian post-apocalyptic world in which walking is foregrounded. This would include most of the recent and popular zombie apocalypse films. The apocalyptic world of zombie films is more often than not post-technological where walking is the sole means of transport (and an essential characteristic of a zombie). Walking is also an essential element in more realistic post-apocalyptic narratives such as John Hillcoat's *The Road* (2009) based on the book with the same title by Cormac McCarthy. All in all, the many films produced over the last two decades in this genre would warrant an entire book exploring images of walking.

Note

1. There are a handful of films that might be said to fit this thematic mould, but have a much more tragic bent to their narratives. Titles include, among others, *Gerry* (2014), Gus Van Zandt's film about two young male friends, both named Gerry, who go for a hike in the desert without food, water, shelter or a compass to look for some mysterious object. Failing to find it, they decide to walk back to their car and get hopelessly lost; *A Lonely Place to Die* (2011), a thriller about hikers in the Scottish highlands who stumble upon and rescue a kidnapped woman and must elude her captors; and *The Loneliest Planet* (2011), a story about an engaged couple's backpacking trip in the Caucus Mountains that takes a tragic turn.

Bibliography

Agamben Giorgio (1993), *Infancy and History: On the Destruction of Experience*, trans. Liz Heron, London: Verso Books
Agamben, Giorgio (2000), *Means Without End: Notes on Politics*, Minneapolis: University of Minnesota Press.
Agamben, Giorgio (2007), *Profanations*, trans. Jeff Fort, New York: Zone Books.
Agamben, Giorgio (2011), 'Nymphs', in Jacques Khalip and Robert Mitchell (eds), *Releasing the Image: From Literature to New Media*, Stanford: Stanford University Press, pp. 60–82.
Albéra, François (2010), 'The case for the epistemology of montage: the Marey moment', in François Albéra and Maria Tortajada (eds), *Cinema Beyond Film: Media Epistemology in the Modern Era*, Amsterdam: Amsterdam University Press, pp. 59–78.
Altman, Rick (1984), 'A semantic/syntactic approach to film genre', *Cinema Journal* 23, no. 3, pp. 6–18.
Amato, Joseph (2004), *On Foot: A History of Walking*, New York: NYU Press.
Andrew, Dudley (1976), *The Major Film Theories: An Introduction*, Oxford: Oxford University Press.
Andrew, Dudley (1984), *Film in the Aura of Art*, Princeton: Princeton University Press.
Antunes, Luis (2012), 'The vestibular in film: orientation and balance in Gus Van Sant's cinema of walking', *Essays in Philosophy* 13, no. 2, article 10, pp. 522–49.
Aragon, Louis (1998), *Le Paysan De Paris*, Paris: Gallimard.
Aristotle (2013), *Delphi Complete Works of Aristotle (Illustrated)*, Hastings: Delphi Classics.
Artaud, Antonin (1998), *Antonin Artaud: Selected Writings*, ed. Susan Sontag, reprint edition, Berkeley: University of California Press.
Badiou, Alain (2007), *Being and Event*, trans. Oliver Feltham, London: Continuum.
Bataille, Georges (1985), *Visions of Excess: Selected Writings, 1927–1939*, ed. Allan Stoekl, Minneapolis: University of Minnesota Press.
Baudelaire, Charles (1964), *The Painter of Modern Life: And Other Essays*, London: Phaidon.

Baum, L. Frank (2015), *Oz: The Complete Collection*, illustrated edition, Rochester, NY: Maplewood Books.
Baum, L. Frank and Children's Classics (1996), *The Wonderful Wizard of Oz*, Mineola: Dover Publications.
Baum, L. Frank and Martin Gardner (2000), *The Annotated Wizard of Oz: The Wonderful Wizard of Oz*, New York: W. W. Norton & Company.
Bazin, André (1968), *What Is Cinema? Vol. I*, trans. Hugh Gray, 4th edition, Berkeley: University of California Press.
Bazin, André (1971), *What Is Cinema? Vol. II*, trans. Hugh Gray, Berkeley: University of California Press.
Bazin, André and François Truffaut (1992), *Orson Welles: A Critical View*, reprint edition, San Jose: Acrobat Books.
Bean, Jennifer M. (2011), 'Charlie Chaplin: the object life of mass culture', in Jennifer M. Bean (ed.), *Flickers of Desire: Movie Stars of the 1910s*, New Brunswick, NJ: Rutgers University Press, pp. 242–63.
Benedetti, Robert (2000), *The Actor at Work*, 8th edition, Boston: Pearson.
Benjamin, Walter (1979), *One-Way Street and Other Writings*, trans. K. Shorter and E. Jephcott, London: Verso Books.
Benjamin, Walter (1997), *Charles Baudelaire: A Lyric Poet in the Era of High Capitalism*, London: Verso Books.
Benjamin, Walter (2002a), *The Arcades Project*, trans. Howard Eiland and Kevin McLaughlin, Cambridge, MA: Harvard University Press.
Benjamin, Walter (2002b), *Selected Writings: Vol. 3: 1935–1938*, eds Howard Eiland and Michael W. Jennings, trans. Edmund Jephcott and Howard Eiland et al., Cambridge, MA: Harvard University Press.
Benjamin, Walter (2003), *Selected Writings: Vol. 4: 1938–1940*, eds Howard Eiland and Michael W. Jennings, Cambridge, MA: Harvard University Press.
Benjamin, Walter (2006), *The Writer of Modern Life: Essays on Charles Baudelaire*, Cambridge, MA: Harvard University Press.
Benjamin, Walter, Hannah Arendt and Harry Zohn (1968), *Illuminations: Essays and Reflections*, New York: Harcourt, Brace & World.
Blanchot, Maurice (1989), *The Space of Literature*, trans. Ann Smock, Lincoln: University of Nebraska Press.
Blanchot, Maurice (1993), *The Infinite Conversation*, Minneapolis: University of Minnesota Press.
Bordwell, David and Kristin Thompson (2004), *Film Art: An Introduction*, New York: McGraw-Hill.
Braun, Marta (2009), 'BIU Santé - La Science Du Mouvement et l'image Du Temps: 473 Plaques Photographiques d'Étienne-Jules Marey', http://www.biusante.parisdescartes.fr/marey (last accessed 20 January 2018).
Breton, André (1994), *Nadja*, trans. Richard Howard, New York: Grove Press.
Brody, Richard (2008), *Everything Is Cinema: The Working Life of Jean-Luc Godard*, New York: Henry Holt and Company.

Brunette, Peter and David Wills (2014), *Screen/Play: Derrida and Film Theory*, Princeton: Princeton University Press.
Buck-Morss, Susan (1992), 'Aesthetics and anaesthetics: Walter Benjamin's artwork essay reconsidered', *October* 62, pp. 3–41.
Cahoone, Lawrence E. (ed.) (2003), *From Modernism to Postmodernism: An Anthology*, London: Wiley-Blackwell.
Cain, Deborah (2004), 'A fence too far?', *Third Text* 18, no. 4 (July), pp. 297–303.
Campany, David (2008), *Photography and Cinema*, London: Reaktion Books.
Careri, Francesco (2002), *Walkscapes*, Barcelona: Editorial Gustavo Gili SL.
Carr, Jeremy. 'Béla Tarr'. *Senses of Cinema* (blog), 22 June 2017. http://sensesofcinema.com/2017/great-directors/bela-tarr/ (last accessed 3 December 2018).
Casey, Edward (2013), *The Fate of Place: A Philosophical History*, Berkeley: University of California Press.
Cavell, Stanley (1979), *The World Viewed: Reflections on the Ontology of Film*, enlarged edition, Cambridge, MA: Harvard University Press.
Certeau, Michel de (2011), *The Practice of Everyday Life*, trans. Steven F. Rendall, 3rd edition, Berkeley: University of California Press.
Chandler, Raymond (1944), 'The simple art of murder', *Atlantic Monthly*, vol. 174, no. 6 (December), pp. 53–9.
Chandler, Raymond (1992), *Farewell, My Lovely*, reprint edition, New York: Vintage Crime/Black Lizard.
Chandler, Raymond (1998), *The Big Sleep*, reprint edition, New York: Vintage Crime/Black Lizard.
Chaplin, Charlie (2005), *Charlie Chaplin's Own Story*, Scotts Valley, CA: CreateSpace Independent Publishing Platform.
Charney, Leo (1998), *Empty Moments: Cinema, Modernity, and Drift*, Durham, NC: Duke University Press Books.
Chatwin, Bruce (1987), *The Songlines*, New York: Viking.
Christopher, Nicholas (2010), *Somewhere in the Night*, New York: Simon and Schuster.
'Cinemetrics – Movie', http://www.cinemetrics.lv/movie.php?movie_ID=801 (last accessed 18 December 2017).
Colvin, J. Brandon (2017), 'The other side of frontality: dorsality in European art cinema', *New Review of Film and Television Studies* 15, no. 2 (3 April), pp. 191–210.
Coverley, Merlin (2006), *Psychogeography*, Harpender: Pocket Essentials.
Coverley, Merlin (2012), *The Art of Wandering: The Writer as Walker*, Harpenden: Oldcastle Books.
Cronin, Paul (2014), *Werner Herzog: A Guide for the Perplexed: Conversations with Paul Cronin*, Kindle edition, New York: Faber & Faber.
Cutler, Randy Lee (2014), 'On speculative walking: from the peripatetic to the peristaltic', *C Magazine*, Issue 21: Walking, (Spring), feature article.

Daly, Fergus and Maximilian Le Cain (2001), 'Waiting for the prince: an interview with Béla Tarr', *Senses of Cinema* (blog), 13 February, http://sensesofcinema.com/2001/feature-articles/tarr-2 (last accessed 7 March 2019).

Davies, W. H. (2015), *The Autobiography of a Super-Tramp*, New York: Waxkeep Publishing.

Debord, Guy (1959), 'Situationist International Online', https://www.cddc.vt.edu/sionline/si/theory.html (last accessed 19 February 2019).

Dekkers, Wim (2011), 'Dwelling, house and home: towards a home-led perspective on dementia care', *Medicine, Health Care, and Philosophy* 14, no. 3 (August), pp. 291–300.

Deleuze, Gilles (1986), *Cinema 1: The Movement-Image*, trans. Hugh Tomlinson and Barbara Hammerjam, Minneapolis: University of Minnesota Press.

Deleuze, Gilles (1995), *Cinema 2: The Time-Image*, trans. Hugh Tomlinson and Barbara Hammerjam, Minneapolis: University of Minnesota Press.

Derrida, Jacques and Paule Thévenin (1998), *The Secret Art of Antonin Artaud*, trans. Mary Ann Caws, Cambridge, MA; London: The MIT Press.

Derrida, Jacques (2006), *Specters of Marx: The State of the Debt, The Work of Mourning & the New International*, New York: Routledge Classics.

Dixon, Wheeler Winston (1997), *The Films of Jean-Luc Godard*, Albany: SUNY Press.

Dove, George N. (1982), *The Police Procedural*, Bowling Green, OH: Popular Press.

D'Souza, Aruna and Tom McDonough (2006), *The Invisible Flâneuse?: Gender, Public Space, and Visual Culture in Nineteenth-Century Paris*, Manchester: Manchester University Press.

Duchamp, Marcel (1970), *Notes and Projects for the Large Glass*, trans. A. Schwarz, London: Thames and Hudson.

Eisenstein, Sergei (1969a), *Film Form: Essays in Film Theory*, trans. Jay Leyda, New York: Harcourt Brace Jovanovich.

Eisenstein, Sergei (1969b), *The Film Sense*, trans. Jay Leyda, revised edition, New York: Harcourt Brace Jovanovich.

Eisner, Lotte H. (1973), *F. W. Murnau*, Berkeley: University of California Press.

Elkin, Lauren (2017), *Flâneuse: Women Walk the City in Paris, New York, Tokyo, Venice, and London*, New York: Farrar, Straus and Giroux.

Emberley, Julia (2008), 'Epistemic encounters: indigenous cosmopolitan hospitality, Marxist anthropology, deconstruction, and Doris Pilkington's rabbit-proof fence', *English Studies in Canada* 34, no. 4, pp. 147–70.

Epstein, Jean and Stuart Liebman (1977), 'Magnification and other writings', *October* 3, pp. 9–25.

Espedal, Tomas (2010), *Tramp: Or the Art of Living a Poetic Life*, Kolkata: Seagull Books.

Esquevin, Christian (2015), 'The wizard of Oz: costuming a classic', *Silver Screen Modes* (blog), 26 April, http://silverscreenmodes.com/the-wizard-of-oz-costuming-a-classic (last accessed 10 December 2018).

Ezra, Elizabeth (2010), 'Cléo's masks: regimes of objectification in the French New Wave', *Yale French Studies*, no. 118/119, pp. 177–90.

Farish, Matthew (2005), 'Cities in shade: urban geography and the uses of Noir', *Environment and Planning D: Society and Space* 23, no. 1 (1 February), pp. 95–118.

Ferrara, Serena (2001), *Steadicam: Techniques and Aesthetics*, Oxford: Focal Press.

Flaxman, Gregory (ed.) (2000), *The Brain Is the Screen: Deleuze and the Philosophy of Cinema*, Minneapolis: University of Minnesota Press.

Forgione, Nancy (2005), 'Everyday life in motion: the art of walking in late-nineteenth-century Paris', *The Art Bulletin* 87, no. 4, pp. 664–87.

Freud, Sigmund (1994), *The Interpretation of Dreams*, New York: Modern Library

Freud, Sigmund and Josef Breuer (2004), *Studies in Hysteria*, London: Penguin Books, Ltd.

Friedberg, Anne (1994), *Window Shopping: Cinema and the Postmodern*, reprint edition, Berkeley: University of California Press.

Frymer, Benjamin, Matthew Carlin and John Broughton (eds) (2011), *Cultural Studies, Education, and Youth: Beyond Schools*, Plymouth, UK: Lexington Books.

Garcia, Maria (2016), 'Rebel citizens and filmmakers'. *Cineaste* 41, no. 2 (Spring): 24, https://ezproxy.chadronstatelibrary.com/login?url=http://search.ebscohost.com/login.aspx?direct=true&db=ulh&AN=113408877&site=eds-live&scope=site (last accessed 12 September 2018).

Geuens, Jean-Pierre (1993), 'Visuality and power: the work of the Steadicam', *Film Quarterly* 47, no. 2 (Winter), p. 8.

Gide, André (2002), *Fruits of the Earth*, New York: Vintage.

Godard, Jean-Luc and Annette Michelson (1986), *Godard on Godard*, ed. Tom Milne, revised edition, New York: Da Capo Press.

Golec, Michael J. (2010), 'Motionmindedness: the transposition of movement from factory to home in Chaplin's modern times', *Home Cultures* 7, no. 3 (November), pp. 287–312.

Gordon, Rae Beth (2001), 'From Charcot to Charlot: unconscious imitation and spectatorship in French cabaret and early cinema', *Critical Inquiry* 27, no. 3, pp. 515–49.

Grenier, Roger (2000), *The Difficulty of Being a Dog*, Chicago: University of Chicago Press.

Gros, Frédéric (2015), *A Philosophy of Walking*, trans. John Howe, reprint edition, London; New York: Verso Books.

Gunning, Tom (2006), 'The birth of film out of the spirit of modernity', in Ted Perry (ed.), *Masterpieces of Modernist Cinema*, Bloomington: Indiana University Press, pp. 13–40.

Gustafsson, Henrik and Asbjorn Gronstad (eds) (2015), *Cinema and Agamben: Ethics, Biopolitics and the Moving Image*, London; New York: Bloomsbury Academic.

Hansen, Miriam Bratu, (1999) 'Benjamin and cinema: not a one-way street', *Critical Inquiry* 25, no. 2, 'Angelus Novus': Perspectives on Walter Benjamin, (Winter), pp. 306–43.

Hansen, Miriam Bratu (2012), *Cinema and Experience: Siegfried Kracauer, Walter Benjamin, and Theodor W. Adorno*, Berkeley: University of California Press.

Harmetz, Aljean (2013), *The Making of the Wizard of Oz*, Chicago: Chicago Review Press.

Harper, Eric (2011), 'What if Fanon read Biko?' Conference paper, *Foundation Frantz Fanon*, 20 September, http://fondation-frantzfanon.com/what-if-fanon-read-biko (last accessed 12 November 2017).

Harper, Eric (2012), 'Homelessness and Violence: Freud, Fanon and Foucault and the Shadow of the Afrikan Sex Worker', Thesis, University of the Western Cape http://etd.uwc.ac.za/xmlui/handle/11394/4034 (last accessed 12 November 2017).

Hausladen, Gary J. (2000), *Places for Dead Bodies*, Austin: University of Texas Press.

Hayward, Susan (2000), *Cinema Studies: The Key Concepts*, London: Routeledge.

Hazlitt, William (1845), *Table-Talk: Original Essays on Men and Manners*, vol. II, 3rd edition, London: C. Templeman.

Heidegger, Martin (1976), *What Is Called Thinking?* New York: HarperCollins.

Heidegger, Martin (1995), *The Fundamental Concepts of Metaphysics: World, Finitude, Solitude*, Bloomington: Indiana University Press.

Heidegger, Martin (2001), *Poetry, Language, Thought*, New York: HarperCollins.

Herodotus, John Gardner Wilkinson, Henry Creswicke Rawlinson and George Rawlinson (eds) (1859), *The History of Herodotus: A New English Version*, New York: D. Appleton.

Herzog, Werner (2002), *Herzog on Herzog*, New York: Farrar, Straus and Giroux.

Herzog, Werner (2014), *Of Walking in Ice: Munich-Paris, 23 November–14 December 1974*, Kindle edition, Minneapolis: University of Minnesota Press.

Howells, Richard (2006), 'Louis Le Prince: the body of evidence', *Screen* 47, no. 2 (20 June), pp. 179–200.

Husserl, Edmund (1981), 'The World of the Living Present and the Constitution of the Surrounding World External to the Organism', in Peter McCormick and Frederick A. Elliston (eds), *Husserl: Shorter Works*, Notre Dame, IN: University of Notre Dame Press, pp. 238–50.

Hynes, Eric (2016), 'Center of gravity', *Film Comment*, November/December 2016 Issue, (11 December), feature article.

Ingold, Tim (2004), 'Culture on the ground: the world perceived through the feet', *Journal of Material Culture* 9, no. 3 (1 November), pp. 315–40.

Ingold, Tim (2008), 'Against space: place, movement, knowledge', in Peter Wynn Kirby (ed.), *Boundless Worlds: An Anthropological Approach to Movement*, New York: Berghahn Books, pp. 29–44.

Kamin, Dan (2008), *The Comedy of Charlie Chaplin: Artistry in Motion*, Lanham: Scarecrow Press.

Kerouac, Jack (2007), *Jack Kerouac: Road Novels 1957–1960: On the Road / The Dharma Bums / The Subterraneans / Tristessa / Lonesome Traveler / Journal Selections*, ed. Douglas Brinkley, Boston: Library of America.

Khalip, Jacques and Robert Mitchell (eds) (2011), *Releasing the Image: From Literature to New Media*, Stanford: Stanford University Press.
Kirby, Peter Wynn (ed.) (2008), *Boundless Worlds: An Anthropological Approach to Movement*, New York: Berghahn Books.
Kofman, Eleonore and Elizabeth Lebas (eds) (1996), *Writings on Cities by Henri Lefebvre*, Oxford: Wiley-Blackwell.
Kovács, András Bálint (2013), *The Cinema of Béla Tarr: The Circle Closes*, London; New York: Wallflower Press.
Kracauer, Siegfried (1960), *Theory of Film: The Redemption of Physical Reality*, Oxford: Oxford University Press.
Levinas, Emmanuel and Alphonso Lingis (1969), *Totality and Infinity: An Essay on Exteriority*, Pittsburgh: Duquesne University Press.
Lewis, Alfred Henry (2012), *Confessions of a Detective*, London: Forgotten Books.
London, Jack (2012), *War of the Classes*, Jersey City: Start Publishing.
Long, Richard and Denise Hooker (2005), *Walking the Line*, London: Thames and Hudson.
McCormick, Peter and Frederick A. Elliston (eds) (1981), *Husserl: Shorter Works*, Notre Dame, ID: University of Notre Dame Press.
MacFarlane, Robert (2012), *The Old Ways: A Journey on Foot*, New York: Viking.
McParland, Robert P (2014), *Film and Literary Modernism*, Newcastle upon Tyne: Cambridge Scholars Publishing.
McQuirk, Charles J. (1915), 'Chaplinitis', *Motion Picture Magazine (Aug 1915–Jan 1916)*, Brooklyn: The Motion Picture Publishing, pp. 85–9.
Marchant, Steven (2009), 'Nothing counts: shot and event in Werckmeister harmonies', *New Cinemas* 7, no. 2, pp. 137–54.
Marey, Étienne-Jules (1972), *Movement*, The Literature of Cinema, Series II, New York: Arno Press.
Marie, Michel (2002), *The French New Wave: An Artistic School*, trans. Richard Neupert, Malden: Wiley-Blackwell.
Mayer, Geoff and Brian McDonnell (2007), *Encyclopedia of Film Noir*, Westport, CT: Greenwood.
Medved, Vladimir (2000), *Measurement of Human Locomotion*, Boca Raton, FL: CRC Press.
Melly, George (1991), *Paris and the Surrealists*, London: Thames and Hudson.
Merleau-Ponty, Maurice (1962), *Phenomenology of Perception*, trans. Colin Smith, London: Routledge.
Milburn, Richard (2014), 'Underground, overground, wandering free: Flânerie reimagined in print, on screen and on record', in Richard Wrigley (ed.), *The Flâneur Abroad: Historical and International Perspectives*, Newcastle upon Tyne: Cambridge Scholars Publishing.
Miller, Tyrus (1996), 'From city-dreams to the dreaming collective: Walter Benjamin's political dream interpretation', *Philosophy and Social Criticism* 22, no. 6, pp. 87–111.
Milne, Tom (ed.) (1972), *Godard on Godard*, New York: Da Capo Press.

Minshull, Duncan (ed.) (2000), *The Vintage Book of Walking: A Glorious, Funny and Indispensable Collection*, London: Random House.

Mouton, Janice (2001), 'From feminine masquerade to Flâneuse: Agnès Varda's Cléo in the city', *Cinema Journal* 40, no. 2, pp. 3–16.

Mulvey, Laura (2006), *Death 24x a Second: Stillness and the Moving Image*, reprint edition, London: Reaktion Books.

Murray, Ros (2013), '"The epidermis of reality": Artaud, the material body and Dreyer's *The Passion of Joan of Arc*', *Film-Philosophy* 17, no. 1 (20 December), pp. 445–61.

Nietzsche, Friedrich (1968), *The Will to Power*, ed. Walter Kaufmann, trans. R. J. Hollingdale, New York: Vintage.

Nicholson, Geoff (2008), *The Lost Art of Walking: The History, Science, Philosophy, and Literature of Pedestrianism*, New York: Riverhead Books.

O'Brien, James (2013a), 'Six methods of detection in Sherlock Holmes', *OUP* (blog), 9 September, https://blog.oup.com/2013/09/six-methods-forensic-detection-sherlock-holmes (last accessed 18 February 2018).

O'Brien, James (2013b), *The Scientific Sherlock Holmes: Cracking the Case with Science and Forensics*, New York: Oxford University Press.

Oppenheimer, John (2003), 'Tour de Force Russian Ark glides through 300 years in a single, uncut Steadicam shot', *American Cinematographer* 84, pp. 84–95.

Osborne, Peter (ed.) (2005), *Walter Benjamin: Modernity*, London; New York: Routledge.

Perry, Ted (ed.) (2006), *Masterpieces of Modernist Cinema*, Bloomington: Indiana University Press.

Petkovic, Vladan (2011), 'Béla Tarr • Director: simple and pure', *Cineuropa*, http://cineuropa.org/it.aspx?t=interview&l=en&did=198131&bid=1 (last accessed 3 June 2017).

Photinos, Christine (2008), 'The tramp in American literature, 1873–1939', *Reconsidering Comparative Literary Studies* 5, no. 1, pp. 1–8.

Pile, Steve (2013), *The Body and the City: Psychoanalysis, Space and Subjectivity*, London; New York: Routledge.

Pilkington, Doris (2002), *Follow the Rabbit-Proof Fence*, New York: Miramax Books.

Plant, Sadie (1992), *The Most Radical Gesture: The Situationist International in a Postmodern Age*, London; New York: Routledge.

Pordzik, Ralph (ed.) (2009), *Futurescapes: Space in Utopian and Science Fiction Discourses*, Amsterdam: Rodopi.

Rawicz, Slavomir (2010), *Long Walk: The True Story Of A Trek To Freedom*, Guilford, CT: Lyons Press.

Rawlence, Christopher (1990), *The Missing Reel: The Untold Story of the Lost Inventor of Moving Pictures*, New York: Atheneum.

Regnault, Félix and Albert-Charlemagne-Oscar de Raoul (1898), *Comment on marche: des divers modes de progression, de la supériorité du mode en flexion*, Paris: H. Charles-Lavauzelle.

Richter, Gerhard (2002), *Benjamin's Ghosts: Interventions in Contemporary Literary and Cultural Theory*, Stanford: Stanford University Press.
Robinson, Jeffrey Cane (2006), *The Walk: Notes on a Romantic Image*, Champaign, IL: Dalkey Archive Press.
Rodowick, David Norman (1997), *Gilles Deleuze's Time Machine*, Durham, NC: Duke University Press.
Rony, Fatimah Tobing (1996), *The Third Eye: Race, Cinema, and Ethnographic Spectacle*, Durham, NC: Duke University Press.
Rosen, Philip (ed.) (1986), *Narrative, Apparatus, Ideology: A Film Theory Reader*, New York: Columbia University Press.
Sallis, John (ed.) (1989), *Deconstruction and Philosophy: The Texts of Jacques Derrida*, Chicago: University of Chicago Press.
Salt, Barry (1992), *Film Style and Technology: History and Analysis*, Mumbai: Starword.
Sand, George (1991), *Story of My Life: The Autobiography of George Sand*, Albany: SUNY Press.
Schrader, Paul (1996), 'Notes on Film Noir (1972)', in Alain Silver and James Ursini (eds), *Film Noir Reader*, New York: Proscenium, pp. 53–63.
Schrader, Paul (2014), 'Game changers: the birth of narrative', *Film Comment*, July/August Issue (7 August), feature article.
Schrader, Paul (2015), 'Game changers: camera movement', *Film Comment*, March/April Issue (11 March), feature article.
Schrift, Alan (2014), *Nietzsche and the Question of Interpretation*, London; New York: Routledge.
Schlosser, Eric (2000), 'Interview with Béla Tarr: about *Werckmeister Harmonies* (Cannes 2000, Director's Fortnight)', *Bright Lights Film Journal*, (1 October), http://brightlightsfilm.com/interview-bela-tarr-werckmeister-harmonies-cannes-2000-directors-fortnight (last accessed 6 July 2018).
Schürmann, Michael (2009), *Paris Movie Walks: Ten Guided Tours Through the City of Lights! Camera! Action!* Branford, CT: The Intrepid Traveler.
Seal, Bobby (2013), 'Baudelaire, Benjamin and the birth of the Flâneur', *Psychogeographic Review* (blog), 14 November, feature article, http://psychogeographicreview.com/baudelaire-benjamin-and-the-birth-of-the-flaneur (last accessed 4 August 2017).
Silver, Alain and James Ursini (eds) (1996), *Film Noir Reader*. New York: Proscenium.
Sklar, Robert (2002), *A World History of Film*, New York: Harry N. Abrams.
Sobchack, Vivian (2000), 'The scene of the screen: envisioning cinematic and electronic "presence"' in Robert Stam and Toby Miller (eds), *Film and Theory: An Anthology*, Malden, MA: Blackwell Publishing, pp. 67–84.
Solnit, Rebecca (2001), *Wanderlust: A History of Walking*, New York: Penguin Books.
Sontag, Susan (1989), *Susan Sontag on Photography*, New York: The Noonday Press.

Stam, Robert and Toby Miller (eds) (2000), *Film and Theory: An Anthology*, Malden, MA: Blackwell Publishing.
Stone, Rob (2013), *The Cinema of Richard Linklater: Walk, Don't Run*, New York: Columbia University Press.
Thoreau, Henry D. (2010), *Walking*, Ocean Shores, WA: Watchmaker Publishing.
Tsivian, Yuri (2006), 'Man with a movie camera – lines of resistance: Dziga Vertov and the twenties', in Ted Perry (ed.), *Masterpieces of Modernist Cinema*, Bloomington: Indiana University Press, pp. 85–110.
Tucker, Thomas Deane (2010), *Derridada: Duchamp as Readymade Deconstruction*, Lanham, MD: Lexington Books.
Tweedie, James (2013), *The Age of New Waves: Art Cinema and the Staging of Globalization*, New York: Oxford University Press.
Vergunst, Jo Lee and Tim Ingold (eds) (2008), *Ways of Walking: Ethnography and Practice on Foot*, Aldershot; Burlington, VT: Routledge.
Vertov, Dziga and Annette Michelson (1984), *Kino-Eye: The Writings of Dziga Vertov*, Berkeley: University of California Press.
Virilio, Paul (2001), *Virilio Live: Selected Interviews*, ed. John Armitage, London: Sage Publications.
Wall-Romana, Christophe (2015), *Cinepoetry: Imaginary Cinemas in French Poetry*, Oxford: Oxford University Press.
Wark, McKenzie (2011), *The Beach Beneath the Street: The Everyday Life and Glorious Times of the Situationist International*, London: Verso Books.
Warshow, Robert (2002), *The Immediate Experience: Movies, Comics, Theatre, and Other Aspects of Popular Culture*, Cambridge, MA: Harvard University Press.
Whalen, Brett Edward (2011), *Pilgrimage in the Middle Ages: A Reader*, Toronto: University of Toronto Press.
Wild, Jennifer (2015), *The Parisian Avant-Garde in the Age of Cinema, 1900–1923*, Oakland: University of California Press.
Wills, David (2008), *Dorsality: Thinking Back through Technology and Politics*, Minneapolis: University of Minnesota Press.
Wolff, Janet (1985), 'The invisible Flâneuse: women and the literature of modernity', *Theory, Culture and Society* 2, no. 3, pp. 37–46.
Woolf, Virginia (1974), *The Death of the Moth and Other Essays*, New York: Harcourt Brace Jovanovich.
Woolf, Virginia (2002), *Mrs. Dalloway*, New York: Harcourt, Inc.
Woolf, Virginia (2013), *Street Haunting: A London Adventure*, New York: Symonds Press.
Zone, Ray (2002), 'Mr. Steadicam: Steadicam inventor Garrett Brown receives the ASC Presidents Award', *American Cinematographer* 83, no. 2 (February), pp. 74–6.

Filmography

A Lonely Place to Die, dir. Julian Gilbey. UK: prod. Michael Loveday, 2011.
A Walk in the Woods, dir. Ken Kwapis. USA: prod. Robert Redford, 2015.
Aimless Walk, dir. Alexandr Hackenschmied. Czechoslovakia, 1930.
Almanac of Fall, dir. Béla Tarr. Hungary, 1984.
Arrival of a Train, dir. Louis Lumière. France, 1896.
Before Midnight, dir. Richard Linklater. USA: prod. Richard Linklater, 2013.
Before Sunrise, dir. Richard Linklater. USA: prod. Anne Walker-McBay, 1995.
Before Sunset, dir. Richard Linklater. USA: prod. Anne Walker-McBay, 2004.
Berlin, Symphony of a City, dir. Walther Ruttman. Germany, 1927.
Bicycle Thieves, dir. Vittorio De Sica. Italy: prod. Vittorio De Sica, 1948.
Boogie Nights, dir. Paul Thomas Anderson. USA: prod. Paul Thomas Anderson, 1997.
Bound for Glory, dir. Hal Ashby. USA: prod. Robert F. Blumofe, 1976.
Breathless, dir. Jean-Luc Godard. France, prod. Georges de Beauregard, 1960.
Cabiria, dir. Giovanni Pastrone. Italy, 1914.
Cave of Forgotten Dreams, dir. Werner Herzog. USA: prod. Werner Herzog, 2010.
Cléo from 5 to 7, dir. Agnès Varda. France: prod. Georges de Beauregard, 1962.
Coup de tourchon, dir. Bertrand Tavernier. France: prod. Henri Lassa, 1981.
D.O.A., dir. Rudolph Maté. USA: prod. Leo C. Popkin, 1949.
Die Strasse, dir. Karl Grune. Germany, 1923.
Double Indemnity, dir. Billy Wilder. USA: prod. Joseph Sistrom, 1944.
Dunkirk, dir. Christopher Nolan. UK: prod. Christopher Nolan, 2017.
Elephant, dir. Gus Van Zandt. USA: prod. Dany Wolf, 2003.
Elevator to the Gallows, dir. Louis Malle. France: prod. Jean Thuillie, 1958.
Farewell, My Lovely, dir. Dick Richards. USA: prod. Jerry Bruckheimer, 1975.
Full Metal Jacket, dir. Stanley Kubrick. UK: prod. Stanley Kubrick, 1987.
Gallipoli, dir. by Peter Weir. Australia: prod. Patricia Lovell, 1981.
Gates of Heaven, dir. Errol Morris, USA, prod. Errol Morris, 1978.
Gerry, dir. Gus Van Zandt. USA: prod. Gus Van Zandt, 2002.
Goodfellas, dir. Martin Scorsese. USA: prod. Irwin Winkler, 1990.
He Walked by Night, dir. Alfred Werker. USA: Bryan Foy, 1948.
Johnny Eager, dir. Mervyn Leroy. USA: prod. Mervyn Leroy, 1941.

Last Days, dir. Gus Van Zandt. USA: prod Dany Wolf, 2005.
Lyon, Place Bellacour, dir. Louis Lumière. France, 1895.
Man with a Movie Camera, dir. Dziga Vertov. USSR, 1929.
Manhatta, dir. Paul Strand. USA, 1921.
Marathon Man, dir. John Schlesinger. USA: prod. Sidney Beckerman, 1976.
Modern Times, dir. Charles Chaplin. USA: prod. Charlie Chaplin, 1936.
Mr. Holmes, dir. Bill Condon. UK: prod. Iain Canning, 2015.
Murder, My Sweet, dir. Edward Dmytryk. USA: prod. Adrian Scott, 1944.
Paranoid Park, dir. Gus Van Zandt. USA: prod Neil Kopp, 2007.
Rabbit-Proof Fence, dir. Philip Noyce. Australia: prod. Philip Noyce, 2002.
Rocky, dir. John G. Alvidson. USA: prod. Robert Chartoff, 1976.
Roundhay Garden Scene, dir. Louis Aimé Augustin Le Prince. UK, 1888.
Run Lola Run, dir. Tom Tykwer. Germany: prod. Stefan Arndt, 1998.
Russian Ark, dir. Aleksandr Sokurov. Russia: prod. Andrey Deryabin, 2002.
Satantango, dir. Béla Tarr. Hungary: prod. György Fehér, 1994.
Sherlock Holmes Baffled, dir. Arthur Marvin. USA, 1900.
Slacker, dir. Richard Linklater. USA: prod. Richard Linklater, 1990.
Southbounders, dir. Ben Wagner. USA: prod. Ben Wagner, 2005.
Stolen Kisses, dir. François Truffaut. France: prod. François Truffaut, 1968.
Sunflower, dir. Vittorio De Sica. Italy: prod. Carlo Ponti, 1970.
Sunrise, dir. F.W. Murnau. USA: prod. William Fox, 1927.
The Big Sleep, dir. Howard Hawkes. USA: prod. Jack L. Warner, 1946.
The Big Sleep, dir. Michael Winner. UK: prod. Jerry Bick, 1978.
The Burmese Harp, dir. Kon Ichikawa. Japan: prod. Masayuki Takagi, 1956.
The Falcon Takes Over, dir. Irving Reese. USA: prod. Howard Benedict, 1942.
The Gold Rush, dir. Charles Chaplin. USA: prod. Charles Chaplin, 1925.
The Loneliest Planet, dir. Julia Loktev. USA: prod. Helge Albers, 2011.
The Naked City, dir. Jules Dassin. USA: prod. Mark Hellinger, 1948.
The Passer-by, dir. Oskar Apfel. USA, 1912.
The Pawnshop, dir. Charles Chaplin. USA: prod. Henry P. Caulfield, 1916.
The Rink, dir. Charles Chaplin. USA: prod. Henry P. Caulfield, 1916.
The Road, dir. John Hillcoat. USA: prod. Paula Mae Schwartz, 2009.
The Searchers, dir. John Ford. USA: prod. Merian C. Cooper, 1956.
The Sheltering Sky, dir. Bernardo Bertolucci. UK: prod. William Aldrich, 1990.
The Shining, dir. Stanley Kubrick. USA: prod. Stanley Kubrick, 1980.
The Third Man, dir. Carol Reed. UK: prod. Carol Reed, 1949.
The Tramp, dir. Charles Chaplin. USA: prod. Jess Robbins, 1915.
The Turin Horse, dir. Béla Tarr. Hungary: prod. Martin Hagemann, 2011.
The Way, dir. Emilio Estevez. USA: prod. David Alexaninan, 2010.
The Way Back, dir. Peter Weir. USA: prod. Peter Weir, 2010.
The Wizard of Oz, dir. Victor Fleming. USA: prod. Mervyn Leroy, 1939.
They Might Be Giants, dir. Anthony Harvey. USA: prod. John Foreman, 1971.
Traffic Crossing Leeds Bridge, dir. Louis Aimé Augustin Le Prince. UK, 1888.

Two or Three Things I Know About Her, dir. Jean-Luc Godard. France: prod. Raoul Lévy, 1967.
Two Women, dir. Vittorio De Sica. Italy: prod. Carlo Ponti, 1960.
Umberto D., dir. Vittorio De Sica. Italy: prod. Vittorio De Sica, 1952.
Wild, dir. by Jean-Marc Vallée. USA: prod. Reese Witherspoon, 2014.
Werckmeister Harmonies, dir. Béla Tarr. Hungary: prod. Ralph E. Cotta, 2000.
Werner Herzog Eats His Shoe, dir. Les Blank. USA: prod. Les Blank, 1980.
Westbound, dir. Budd Boetticher. USA: prod. Henry Blanke, 1959.
Workers Leaving the Lumière Factory, dir. Louis Lumière. France, 1895.

Index

References to images are in *italics*; references to notes are indicated by n

Aboriginal Australians, 91–5
Adrian, Gilbert, 86
Africans, 16–17
Agamben, Giorgio, 9, 16, 22, 29n1
Albéra, François, 16
Almanac of Fall (1984), 54
Altman, Rick, 68
Alton, John, 80
American Civil War, 18
Andrews, Dudley, 49
animals, 14, 16, 89; *see also* dogs
Apfel, Oscar, 45
apocalyptic world, 137
Aragon, Louis, 102
Arcades Project, The (Benjamin), 103, 128n4
Aristotle, 5, 13
Arrival of a Train (1896), 21
Ashby, Hal, 51
Australia, 91–5, 136–7

Badiou, Alain, 57
Bataille, Georges
  'The Big Toe', 6–7
Baudelaire, Charles, 9, 11, 80n1, 125
  and *flâneurs*, 99–100, 101–2, 103
  'To a (Female) Passer-by', 112–13
Baudry, Jean-Louis, 27–8
Bazin, André, 9, 39, 128n3
Before trilogy (1995–2013), 53
Benjamin, Walter, 11, 27, 34–5, 122–5
  and *flâneurs*, 102–3, 113, 128n4
  and innervation, 37–8
Bentham, Jeremy, 5
Bergson, Henri, 21, 22

Berlin, Symphony of a City (1927), 104
Bezúčelná procházka (*Aimless Walk*) (1930), 104
Bible, the, 4
Bicycle Thieves (1948), 121, 128n2
Big Sleep, The (Chandler), 74–5
Blanchot, Maurice, 22, 56
Blank, Les, 3
Bogart, Humphrey, 110
Boogie Nights (1997), 53
Bordwell, David, 44–5
Borelli, Giovanni, 13
Bound for Glory (1976), 11, 51
Breathless (1960), 105, 106–11
Bresson, Robert, 12n4
Breton, André, 102
Breuer, Joseph
  Studies in Hysteria, 35
Brown, Garrett, 11, 50, 51
Bryson, Bill, 132
Burmese Harp, The (1956), 134

Cabiria (1914), 46
camera, 11
  and *Breathless*, 107–10
  and film noir, 71–2
  and motion, 44–5
  and Vertov, 25–8
  see also dolly shots; photography; Steadicam
camera-stylo (camera pen), 46
Camino Francés, 133–4
Careri, Francesco, 4, 11n2
Cavell, Stanley, 40, 57
Certeau, Michel de, 98
  'Walking in the City', 33–4

Chandler, Raymond, 11, 73, 74–6
Chaplin, Charlie, 3, 11, 12n7, 30–1, 32, 34–5
   and *Modern Times*, 40–2
   and movement, 37–9
characters, 68–9
Chatwin, Bruce, 11n2
Christopher, Nicholas, 69, 70
chronophotography, 14–18
cinematic movement, 21–3
cinematography, 18
cities, 33–4, 65–6, 98–9
   and detective noir, 73, 74–5
   and film noir, 69, 70–1
   and police procedurals, 79–80
   see also Paris; Rome
Cléo from 5 to 7 (1962), 113–20
Comte, Charles, 17
Condon, Bill, 64
Coup de tourchon (1981), 53
Coutard, Raoul, 107–9
Coverley, Merlin, 4, 5
Cronin, Paul
   Werner Herzog, A Guide for the Perplexed: Conversations with Paul Cronin, 2
Cubism, 23

Daguerre, Jacques, 18
Daguerre, Louise, 8–9
Dassin, Jules, 77
Davies, W. H., 31
De Sica, Vittorio, 121, 125
Debord, Guy, 98–9
Deleuze, Gilles, 21, 22, 55–6, 59–60, 120–1
dérive (drift), 98–9
Derrida, Jacques, 6, 79
   The Secret of Antonin Artaud, 39–40
detective noir, 11, 72–6
détournement (rerouting), 99
Dixon, Winston Wheeler, 106–7
Dmytryk, Edward, 76
D.O.A. (1949), 71–2
dogs, 125–8, 129n6
dolly shots, 11, 45–7, 48–9
dorsality, 47–50, 51–2, 61–2
Dos Passos, John, 31–2
Dove, George N., 76–7
Duchamp, Marcel, 117
Dunkirk (2017), 53
Dupin, C. August, 64, 65
dwelling, 81–4

Edison, Thomas, 20
Eisenstein, Sergei, 23–5, 103
Eisner, Lotte, 1, 51
Elevator to the Gallows (1958), 72
Elkin, Lauren, 118
Epstein, Jean, 37, 38
Estevez, Emilio, 133, 134
evental site, 57
everyday, 56–7

Falcon Takes Over, The (1942), 76
Farewell, My Lovely (1975), 76
Farewell, My Lovely (Chandler), 75–6
fascism, 120, 124–5
femme fatale, 68–9
Fielding, Henry, 65
film noir, 67–72; *see also* detective noir
flâneurs, 9, 11, 99–104, 124
flâneuses, 111–13
flash-forwards, 135–6
Flaxman, Gregory, 121
foot, the, 6–7, 9, 87–8
   and prints, 66, 96–7
France, 16–17; *see also* Paris
Freud, Sigmund, 35–7
Friedberg, Ann, 9
   Window Shopping: Cinema and the Postmodern, 103
Full Metal Jacket (1987), 53

Gallipoli (1981), 136–7
Gates of Heaven (1978), 3
Gay, John
   Trivia: Or, the Art of Walking the Streets of London, 65
Gerry (2014), 137n1
Gide, André
   Fruits of the Earth, 105
Godard, Jean-Luc, 105–8, 110–11
Gold Rush, The (1925), 3, 38
Goodfellas (1990), 53
Griffith, D. W., 103
Gros, Frédéric, 132
   A Philosophy of Walking, 7–8
Grune, Karl, 104
gumshoes, 64–7; *see also* detective noir
Gunning, Tom, 21

Hackenschmied, Alexandr, 104
Hammer, Mike, 66
hand-held cameras, 45
hands, 12n4, 84, 88
Hansen, Mariam, 37

Harper, Eric, 93
Hastings, Frank, 66
Hawkes, Howard, 75
Hayward, Susan, 120
Hazlitt, William
  'On Going a Journey', 12n3
He Walked by Night (1948), 79–80
Hegel, Georg Wilhelm Friedrich, 5
Heidegger, Martin, 5–6, 81–3
Herzog, Werner, 1–3
  Cave of Forgotten Dreams (2010), 12n5
hiking, 130–2, 137n1
Hillcoat, John, 137
Hobbes, Thomas, 5
Hobshawn, Eric, 124
Holmes, Sherlock, 64–5, 66
home, 11, 81–4
  and *Rabbit-Proof Fence*, 92–3, 95
  and *The Wizard of Oz*, 86, 90–1
Howells, Richard, 19
Husserl, Edmund
  'The World of the Living Present and the Constitution of the Surrounding World External to the Organism', 7
Hynes, Eric, 52

Ingold, Tim, 4–5, 87–8, 126
innervation, 35–8
Italy *see* Rome

Japan, 24
Johnny Eager (1941), 70–1

Kamin, Dan, 38
Kant, Immanuel, 5
Kawin, Bruce, 50
Kierkegaard, Søren, 5
kinoglaz (film-eye), 26–7
kinopravda (film-truth), 25–6
Kovács, András Bálint, 54
Kracauer, Siegfried
  Theory of Film, 103–4
Kubrick, Stanley, 51

labyrinths, 69–71, 79–80
language, 4–5
Le Prince, Louis Aimé Augustin, 10, 18–21
Lefebvre, Henri, 33, 98
Levinas, Emmanuel, 83–4
lighting, 68, 69, 71
Linklater, Richard, 53
Loneliest Planet, The (2011), 137n1
Lonely Place to Die, A (2011), 137n1

Long Walk: The True Story of a Trek to Freedom, The (Rawicz), 95
Lumière brothers, 18, 20, 21
Lyon, Place Bellacour (1895), 21

McBain, Ed, 66
MacDonald, Helen, 1
McDonnell, Brian, 70
Maigret, 66
Malick, Terence, 51
Malle, Louis, 72
Man with the Movie Camera (1927), 27
Manhatta (1921), 104
manual labour, 84
Marathon Man (1976), 53
Marey, Étienne-Jules, 10, 14–17, 22, 129n6
Marlowe, Philip, 66, 74–6
Maté, Rudolf, 71
Medved, Vladimir, 14
Michelson, Annette, 26
mirrors, 115–17
mobile framing, 44–5, 49–50
Modern Times (1936), 40–2
Monitor and Merrimack Engagement (Le Prince), 18
montage, 23–5
Morris, Errol, 3
motion, 14–16, 19, 44–5
movement, 21–3, 37–9, 55–6
Mr. Holmes (2015), 64
Mrs. Dalloway (Woolf), 112
Mulvey, Laura, 10
Murder, My Sweet (1944), 76
Murnau, F. W., 46–7, 48–9, 51–2, 58–9
Muybridge, Eadweard, 10, 14, 15, 22, 129n6

Nadja (Breton), 102
Naked City, The (1948), 77–9
narrative, 69
neo-realism, 120–1
New Wave, 105
Nicholson, Geoff, 5
nomadism, 11n2

O'Brien, James, 66

Paris, 9, 66, 100–3, 104–5, 107–10, 124
  and *Cléo from 5 to 7*, 113–17, 118–20
  and women, 112–13
Passer-by, The (1912), 45–6
pavements, 65–6
Pawnshop, The (1916), 38

Paysan de Paris, Le (Aragon), 102
Photinos, Christine, 31
photography, 8–10, 14–15, 18–21, 22–3
pilgrimage, 132–4
Poe, Edgar Allen, 64, 80n1
Poilpot, Theodore, 18
point of view (POV), 46–7, 48–9, 54–5, 119–20
police procedurals, 11, 76–80
Pollock, Jackson, 110
Portail, Michel, 106
projectility, 40
protests, 122–5
psychogeography, 98–9

Rabbit-Proof Fence (2002), 91–5
Reed, Carol, 80
Regnault, Félix, 16–17
Rink, The (1916), 38
Road, The (2009), 137
roaming, 11n2
Robinson, Jeffrey C.
  The Walk: Notes on a Romantic Image, 125
Rocky (1976), 53
Rodowick, D. N., 22
Rome, 120–2, 124–5
Rony, Fatimah Tobing, 17
Roundhay Garden Scene (1888), 10, 19–20
Rousseau, Jean-Jacques, 5
Run Lola Run (1999), 134–6
running, 134–7
Russian Ark (2002), 53

Sand, George, 112
Santiago de Compostela, 132–4
Satantango (1994), 57–60
Schrader, Paul
  'Notes of Film Noir', 67, 68, 69
Schürmann, Michael
  Paris Movie Walks, 105
Scorsese, Martin, 51
Scott, George C., 64–5
setting, 69
Sheltering Sky, The (1990), 53
Sherlock Holmes Baffled (1900), 64
Shining, The (1980), 53
shoes, 32, 39, 65–6
  and *The Wizard of Oz*, 86–7, 88
shop windows, 115–18
Simenon, Georges, 66
Slacker (1990), 53
Sobchack, Vivian, 22–3

Sokurov, Andrei, 53
Solnit, Rebecca
  Wanderlust: A History of Walking, 5
songlines, 93–4
Southbounders (2005), 131
Spade, Sam, 66
spectatorship, 23–5, 104
Steadicam, 11, 45, 50–5, 57–62
Strasse, Die (1923), 104
Strayed, Cheryl, 131
subjectility, 39–42
Sunrise (1927), 46–7, 48–9, 51–2, 58–9
Surrealists, 102

Tarkovsky, André, 51
Tarr, Béla, 11, 51, 53–5, 57–62
They Might Be Giants (1971), 64–5
Third Man, The (1949), 80
Thompson, Kristin, 44–5
Thoreau, Henry
  Walking, 130
Tourette, Gilles de, 29n1
Traffic Crossing Leeds Bridge (1888), 20
'Tramp, The', 11, 30–1, 32, 34–5, 38–9, 40–2
Tramp, The (1915), 30–1, 32
tramps, 31–3, 43n1
Truffaut, François, 107
Tsivian, Yuri, 27
Turin Horse, The (2011), 60, 61–2
Tweedie, James, 115, 119
Two or Three Things I Know About Her (1967), 111
Two Women (1960), 121
Tykwer, Tom, 135

Umberto D. (1952), 121–2, *123*, 125, 126–8

Vadim, Roger, 107
Van Zandt, Gus, 62n1, 137n1
Varda, Agnès, 113, 115, 118–19
Vertov, Dziga, 25–8
vestibular, 62n1
Virilio, Paul, 41
Vlady, Marina, 111

Walk in the Woods, A (2015), 131–2
walking, 3–8, 13–14
  and apocalyptic, 137
  and art, 8–10
  and *Breathless*, 108, 109–10
  and Chaplin, 32, 34–5, 41
  and cities, 33–4, 65–6, 98–9

and *Cléo from 5 to 7*, 115–17, 118–20
and De Sica, 121
and detective noir, 73–6
and dogs, 125–6
and film noir, 70–2
and Herzog, 1–3
and long-distance, 130–2, 137n1
and Marey, 16–17
and pilgrimage, 132–4
and police procedurals, 78–80
and *Rabbit-Proof Fence*, 92–4
and *The Way Back*, 96–7
and *The Wizard of Oz*, 86–7, 88–91
see also flâneurs
Warshow, Robert, 32
Waters, Alice, 3
Way, The (2010), 132–4
Way Back, The (2011), 95–7, 131
wayfaring, 4–5

Weber, Wilhelm and Eduard
   Mechanics of Walking in Humans, 13–14
Weir, Peter, 95, 96–7
Werckmeister Harmonies (2000), 60–1
Werner Herzog Eats His Shoe (1979), 3
Wexler, Haskell, 11, 51
Whitley, John, 18
Wild (2014), 131, 132
Wills, David, 47–8
Winner, Michael, 75
Wizard of Oz, The (1939), 84–91
Wolff, Janet, 112–13
Woolf, Virginia
   Mrs. Dalloway, 112
   'Street Haunting: A London Adventure', 87
Workers Leaving the Lumière Factory (1895), 21
writing, 5

Zavattini, Cesare, 120

EU representative:
Easy Access System Europe
Mustamäe tee 50, 10621 Tallinn, Estonia
Gpsr.requests@easproject.com

www.ingramcontent.com/pod-product-compliance
Lightning Source LLC
Chambersburg PA
CBHW071848230426
43671CB00012B/2111